To Rowie and May—Ursa Major and Minor

the wisdom of

BIRCH
OAK and
YEW

© Sue Ball

About the Author

Penny Billington is a Druid author, celebrant, and speaker in the Order of Bards, Ovates and Druids. She has edited their magazine, *Touchstone*, for over ten years and regularly facilitates workshops and rituals. Her first book for Llewellyn, *The Path of Druidry*, continues to be widely appreciated, and she has also written three Druid Detective novels. She lives in Somerset, England. Visit her online at www.pennybillington.co.uk.

To Write the Author

If you wish to contact the author or would like more information about this book, please write to the author in care of Llewellyn Worldwide, and we will forward your request. Both the author and the publisher appreciate hearing from you and learning of your enjoyment of this book and how it has helped you. Llewellyn Worldwide cannot guarantee that every letter written to the author can be answered, but all will be forwarded. Please write to:

Penny Billington
℅ Llewellyn Worldwide
2143 Wooddale Drive
Woodbury, MN 55125-2989

Please enclose a self-addressed stamped envelope for reply,
or $1.00 to cover costs. If outside the USA, enclose
an international postal reply coupon.

Many of Llewellyn's authors have websites with additional information and resources. For more information, please visit www.llewellyn.com.

Connect to the Magic of Trees
for Guidance & Transformation

the wisdom of
BIRCh
OAK and
yew

PENNY BILLINGTON

Llewellyn Publications
Woodbury, Minnesota

FIRST EDITION
Ninth Printing, 2024

Book design: Bob Gaul
Cover design: Ellen Lawson
Cover art: iStockphoto.com/9028456/©RiverNorthPhotography, *Plants and Flowers:*
　　　1761 Illustrations for Artists and Designers © Dover Publications
Editing: Lunaea Weatherstone
Interior art: Illustrations on pages 11, 12, 29, 30, 131, 132, 223, 224, 230, 296
　　　by Meraylah Allwood
　　　Illustrations on pages 47, 61, 115, 267 by Llewellyn Art Department

Llewellyn Publications is a registered trademark of Llewellyn Worldwide Ltd.

Library of Congress Cataloging-in-Publication Data
Billington, Penny.
　The wisdom of birch, oak, and yew: connect to the magic of trees for
guidance and transformation/Penny Billington.—First Edition.
　　　pages cm
　Includes bibliographical references and index.
　ISBN 978-0-7387-4090-4 (alk. paper)
　1. Trees—Miscellanea. 2. Druids and druidism. I. Title.
　BF1623.P5B55 2015
　133'.258216—dc23
　　　　　　　　　　　2014048946

Llewellyn Publications
A Division of Llewellyn Worldwide Ltd.
2143 Wooddale Drive
Woodbury, MN 55125-2989
www.llewellyn.com

Printed in the United States of America

CONTENTS

The Oak Tree: Inhabiting Our Space

The Yew Tree: Surrendering to Life

FOREWORD

Do you long to live a magical life?

Are you drawn to the wonders of the natural world, which feed your spirit?

Do your attempts to change your life for the better fizzle out, in spite of your good intentions?

Then here's a quotation you might consider very carefully:

"No problem can be solved from the same level of consciousness that created it."

If that statement makes sense to you, then why not take a voyage of discovery with this book? Because that's where we start: with the conviction that changing our level of consciousness will help us avoid repeating previous mistakes. The exercises given will make you more aware of your proper place through reference to the natural world; you will gain a better perspective. And here is the basic instruction:

Be as a tree.

It might take a leap of faith to read that and go further, or just to take it seriously, but all will be explained. For now, just answer the following questions:

How often have you lost your equilibrium regularly even though you meditate? Felt mildly depressed despite using positive thinking techniques? Responded angrily to every little irritation of life?

It seems that, despite good intentions, we are doomed to repeat our mistakes unless we can develop a different way of looking at things. This new viewpoint will not lift you *above* your usual state—as humans, it is our nature to be earthy and grounded—but hopefully will allow you to take a mental shift *sideways* ... maybe away from the sidewalk and into the forest.

Maybe into the sanctuary of the trees.

INTRODUCTION

The book you're holding is a series of explorations along a magical path of interaction with significant trees, and conclusions about some of the benefits these can bring. In a fragmented society, many of us are searching for a root-connection to life, which will nourish and sustain us, and who better to guide us than the solidly grounded trees?

So, is this a book primarily about magic, about self-development, or about trees?

Well, it's about all those. The aim is a satisfying, enriching exploration of finding your place: your place in the world, in your locality, in your home or office, in your own skin. Ultimately, we all want to feel that we are where we truly belong, and to recognise and celebrate the unique gifts we each have to offer. All the techniques in this book are to help with this process, and the presentation is a nature-based spiritual approach.

The Specifics of What We Will Cover

Magic and the possibility of it is a constant fascination for many of us. When we try to engage with magic, consciously interacting with the patterns of the universe in which we live, we are accepting the world's invitation to be co-creators of our lives. For those of us who have this impulse, magic is the "ingredient x" without which life is just existence. So there is much gentle, experiential, transformational magic within these pages.

Nature-based spirituality is the nourishing current from which this book flows, with as much explanation as is needed to explain how it can benefit us all. You might not want to immerse yourself in exploring this area deeply. That's fine. You'll find within many hints if you *are* interested, and plenty of practical content if you just want to explore the benefits of simple connections to the natural world.

And trees? If you've picked up this book, you have a love of trees—and are open to the idea that we can learn from them in the most magical way.

At some deep level, behind and beyond thought, we recognise our connection to the rhythms of the natural world. We feel that nature has gifts to succour our emotional and spiritual being. But you may never have thought that you can use that feeling to actually affect your life for the better. I think that you can.

We will actively engage with the spirit of three trees significant in history, folklore, and myth, relating them to the stages of our lives, the rhythm of our days, and our daily activities, and at the end of each chapter is a section with practical exercises of all kinds appropriate to the gifts of the trees.

Trees are wise witnesses to our short lives; they nurture our world in the most fundamental way, maintaining our atmosphere; and in our localities, their benefits are legion—social, environmental, communal. They are the backdrop to the first stories we hear in infancy: the deep, dangerous forest, the mysterious fairy tree hiding buried treasure. From the first they have engaged our spirit of wonder, the visceral response of delicious terror, wonder, and delight.

We are about to embark on the adventure of remembering and using those feelings. The power of the imagination is transformative, and connecting to the archetypal nature of trees can bring major benefits to our lives. Bear in mind that trees live far longer than us, are more stable, more resilient, and much larger. By identifying with them, we can start to develop a longer and broader perspective, and connecting to the trees can give us a hint of the larger patterns of life. Instead of being trapped in our little minds, with our problems going round in our heads, we can realise that physical life, immediate circumstance, is not all that there is; and that our understanding the connection of all things is the key to a happy, fulfilled life. Because, let's face it, our lives, privileged as they are, are not perfect. We suspect that, the way we are living, they never will be. Let us remember that quotation, *"No problem can be solved from the same level of consciousness that created it."*

This book is for you if:

- You love trees.

- You believe you can co-create your life.

- You may have tried, but positive techniques didn't seem to help you.

- You yearn for "real" life in the forest, but never seem to get there.

- You want to meditate but somehow just can't find the time.

- You don't respond well to a disciplined routine.

Let us start a journey of exploration to try to change that level of small-minded consciousness. We'll do this through connection to, and identification with, the trees: to their physical, mythic, and folkloric attributes. They have so many lessons for us. Let's widen and deepen our understanding of our lives in a way that will alter our thinking from that level of consciousness that keeps us perpetuating the same mistakes.

Let's go to the forest, drop all our preconceived ideas, and start again.

Here is an example of the recurring pattern of our lives. We start with the best of intentions, but then unexpected events upturn our routines. We are torn—knowing that a disciplined approach makes for success, but, conversely, that extreme focus comes at a cost to other areas of our lives. So we are gentler on ourselves, but then that approach becomes sloth, we seem to be achieving nothing, get disheartened, and we're back to square one … until the next burst of energy for change. And so it goes on …

If this happens to you, work with trees can have a remarkably steadying effect. It's not desirable to transform yourself into a rigorous same time, same place each day exerciser. That sounds more like an approach for a machine than an organic life form like a tree or a human. But tackling this new way of thinking regularly can result, as it has for others, in the remembrance of tree "feelings," which results in you approaching your challenges in a way that supports you in actual real-life situations. We do not have an abundance of solitude and time for contemplation in our lives; the modern world is fast, and we need techniques to fit in, to access instantly, to change our reactions, and to key us into a magical understanding when we're at our most stressed. Can you imagine that having the default question to any situation "How does my tree-self feel?" could transform your responses?

Magical Living

The open secret about magic—why it might work, or why it might not—is that it is experiential, not based on belief. The more you engage with it, the deeper your experience of the world of the imagination, the more likely you are to find that you feel you are experiencing magic in your everyday life.

There is a section on magic and evocation coming, and this is the key to using the book, but here are a couple of vital points. My magic is not manipulative; it does not ask the universe to bend to my will, and it does not compel just so that I can get my whims gratified.

On the other hand, unlike many magical writers, I do not see anything wrong in using magic for one's own benefit. If it involves tuning into natural currents, if it doesn't rely on anyone pushing another person "down" in order to be "up," then how can it be unethical? It is not unfair to utilise a talent for scholarship, music, or accountancy to better ourselves; we use all our other talents to our advantage in this world, and developing a skill at this work is just one more resource we will have.

Magic is about flowing with the rhythm of our lives, rather than fighting the tide of events. It's about fully utilising the talents we have, and stretching ourselves to develop qualities and abilities that are presently latent.

The magic of this book is that of the natural world, and the natural course of our lives. Much of our frustration might be caused by the fact that we humans have developed a society that ultimately doesn't benefit or nurture us. So, whilst holding our place in the world and fulfilling ourselves there, we will start to use techniques, stratagems, spells, or whatever to connect us and key us in to the great source of regeneration: the natural world. And our helpers, mentors, and guides will be the trees.

When we develop a more nuanced view of the mysterious workings of the world, it makes us wonder whether "supernatural" is actually just "natural," but in a way we don't yet quite understand. But enough speculation, for this is a book of action.

How to Use This Book

You are not holding a rulebook, but a guide to provoke your thoughts, talents, ingenuity, and creativity.

Every chapter includes a study session with practical suggestions, and I recommend that you work through the book as it is written, taking time to absorb each section through your personal study before going on. The different strands of the work all complement and support each other, so don't neglect visiting trees, meditating, journaling, daydreaming, and visualising if you want the work to be effective—and there are plenty of craft suggestions to help you ground your work in practical ways.

Avoid the urge to race—that's the cerebral, info-grabbing attitude we've grown up with, "living in our heads." What is lacking in life is the balance of the more contemplative, gentle approach that is advocated here. Changing the way we relate to the world is not accomplished in a week or a month, but the first exercises should help alter your outlook sufficiently to keep you enjoying the winding forest path of discovery. Keep in mind always that any spiritual path is not a race to one particular goal but is best considered as a sustainable way of making our journey through life a joy and delight rather than a struggle.

How long you spend on each chapter will depend upon your prior experience and knowledge of both the techniques and the natural world. You must be the judge of what is right for you. You'll see that the course always defers to your intuitive wisdom in these matters, but guidelines are helpful, so here are my suggestions.

To be fair to yourself and your chance of success, *you must allow time* to internalise the new ideas thoroughly. Learning and changing is an organic process, not a mechanical one, so expect and recognise times both of energetic work and of consolidation, when you will be less active. If you feel indolent or as if you're not getting anywhere during these times, keep your notebook to hand and refer to it regularly. Watch wildlife programmes; go for walks with no intent but enjoyment. The trick is to keep the work in mind so that when the current material is absorbed, the urge to resume active studying and progressing to the next stage will arise naturally.

As a working premise, consider that each chapter and study session together could take a month. Nine months is of significance to us humans, after all. Keep in the back of your mind that during this time, regardless of your gender, age, health, or strength, you are gestating the new you: the ultimate act of creativity. And if the "new you" chooses a longer gestation time, which is quite probable, be gentle and nurture its growth and development. This is a journey to enjoy.

Practical Considerations

The first is of physical health and strength. Challenge yourself to devise ingenious alternatives if your health debars you from following any suggestions. There are a thousand ways to gain understanding and experience, so do not think that you are missing out by any substitutions you make. The only limitation is that of the imagination, which repays development and practice in quite a magical way.

The second consideration is: Do the trees in this book grow near you? What if your region does not abound in the trees you want to study?

There are two points to be made about this. Firstly, these trees do grow *in some form* worldwide. Variants of birch spring up everywhere; there are over twenty species of oak in America and Canada, and three native species of yew, growing from shrubs to large trees, depending on the region.

Secondly, if this is to be a living journey of real worth, then you will tailor it to fit your individual needs—and that applies to noticing and developing a relationship with the trees that are waiting to speak to you outside your front door and in your local park or forest. Far from developing a template and then imposing it on the natural world around us, we will be slowing down and responding to the actual qualities of the trees and the land we are living on. The trees that will ultimately prove most significant to you might not be those in this book, but the work with birch, oak, and yew will have shown you the way to craft a personal spiritual tree connection that enriches your life.

Students worldwide have studied in precisely the way you are about to, and have looked at their local variants of the trees I describe in astonishment, hardly recognising my descriptions of the European species. They have been both creative and ingenious in obtaining or finding ways to view specimens of trees that aren't local to them, and in substituting trees that they feel intuitively have the same messages and resonance as those in the book. Their conclusions are that we can do this work where we are, with what we have to hand.

Here are a few preliminary suggestions from America, New Zealand, and Australia on how to rise to the challenges: Get a friend to send you a twig of the actual European variety, for comparison (check the customs legalities here!). Look on tree websites for your state and visit a specimen tree in a park. Find the nearest arboretum. Suffuse yourself in the ambience of the tree through the Internet, picture books, and posters, until a strong mental image of the tree can be maintained. Watch nature programmes and look beyond the foreground to concentrate on the forest surroundings. Use holidays and travelling as opportunities to visit special trees; like others before you, you will be thrilled to spot newly familiar tree species as you travel.

Performing the imaginative exercises having used photos rather than a living example of the tree can prove surprisingly profound, especially in giving a sense of the history and perspective of a long-lived tree. And it can prepare you for when you do meet a local variety; there can be a sense of immediate recognition because of the inner work you've already done.

Many tree-students with expert knowledge and experienced wood workers regard the different species as having an affinity of kindred spirits but with subtle differences. Think of an apple; so many varieties, each with their own habits of growth and fruiting, but we immediately recognise the essential "appleness" of each of them. Like other students, you will learn to notice the commonalities between varieties of species, and that the terrain in which the tree grows naturally affects it, just as your environment affects you.

You will find suggestions for alternatives and substitutions in the chapters that follow.

How Was the Course Devised?

I have taught all aspects of this course to students, and here have drawn the component parts together to make up a coherent course. This book combines my years of work as an adult education tutor in the positive living field for the Workers Educational Authority, UK; the initial training I received from OBOD (the Order of Bards, Ovates and Druids); and the workshops and training I have subsequently facilitated for OBOD and other groups. I had an "Aha!" moment when I realised just what a breakthrough it could be to combine the two, to allow a view of life wider than from the human perspective. My thanks are due to the core group who worked specifically on exercises in this book, to all past students, and to my OBOD colleagues in different countries who have given such knowledgeable and helpful feedback on all things tree-related.

People and Trees

When you consider our similarities, it doesn't seem too great a leap to refer to trees as "cousins." Like us,

- They stand upright on the earth, head in the sky, feet in/on the earth.

- They have a trunk, a crown, and extremities.

- They have a natural lifecycle that involves gestation, growth, maturity, and death.

- They respire, excrete, reproduce; they metabolise, they grow, they are responsive, and they can evolve in response to their environment.

It is just a wonderful synchronicity that the way they do these things is so immeasurably good for the planet. Upon trees depends our earth's atmosphere; they modify this constantly through breathing or respiring, as we do, and losing water through transpiration—rather similar to us sweating. Taking it down to local level, trees in urban situations benefit the environment, acting positively on air quality, temperature, and immediate atmosphere, reducing air/noise pollution, encouraging wildlife diversity... there are more benefits, if you'd like to add to the list!

Most of our needs are met with trees almost all over the world—they can supply house, hearth, heat, and health, and their fruits assuage our hunger. And, like humans, they have their own personalities—a point which we will consider later. We can learn from them, although not through the kind of conversations that we have with fellow humans.

To see what they might teach us, let's look at the special qualities they all share.

The Essential Nature of Trees

They are conduits of life force.

They are not judgemental.

They are long-lived witnesses.

They are authentic; they present themselves just as they are.

They are of service.

They are nurturing/sustaining.

They are prodigiously generous with their gifts.

They are distinctive.

They are a bridge between the worlds.

Now, just imagine if we had all of those gifts to give to ourselves, to our loved ones, our communities, and our world! And, surprise: read the list again, and you will realise that all these qualities are within us. Some are relative, of course—longevity, for example. But today our species has a longer life expectancy than at any other time in history.

So what stops us from disseminating those qualities within us that we share with the trees?

The answer is simple: our perceptions. We see ourselves as stressed and overworked, and feel we must put on a mask, a persona, in order to face the outside world, so that we will fit in, even if we know that we're in the wrong place or job. We have the urge to be altruistic—if only we had a little more time and money. We have blockages causing ailments and illnesses, and we have no leisure to think of being in control, having time or an abundance of energy, except as a sense of futile longing.

This book might help to rectify those points of view.

The Three Trees

The trees you will be thinking of, dreaming of, developing a relationship with, imagining yourself as part of, are three noble species with important associations. They are all rich in lore, legend, and ancient usage, and their significance will be revealed through the book, but a simple look at them might give you some clues.

The trees are:

Birch Tree

Oak Tree

Yew Tree

Do you know these trees in the wild? Do you have one or all in your local park? Start looking around to find them. But, for now, look at their silhouettes. What do you notice?

Birch is tall, slim, elegant. It looks fragile, and as if it's reaching upwards.

Oak is sturdy with branches set at right angles to the trunk. It looks hugely strong.

Yew is massive, crouched, making caves with its branches. It looks immensely old.

Are there any with similar silhouettes growing near you?

So, in human terms, we could say that the trees have an adolescent, mature, and elderly shape, respectively. Already we are starting to make associations. By association of ideas, they might therefore relate to dawn, full day, and evening, or the spring, summer, and autumn, or beginning of projects, the full flush of work, and the completion ... and so on.

Many other connections will sink into your internal web of associations during your practice of the exercises. And it's important that you know these are not pulled out of thin air or from the imagination: all these ideas derive either from observing the trees' actual appearance and habits or from their folkloric associations. The trees themselves give us hundreds of indications of how we can relate to them—a statement that will become clearer as you read the chapters on how to access their magical lessons.

Magic and Evocation

This section is important to our understanding of magical practice, so let's start with the terminology. Evocation and invocation are often confused; we're concerned with the former, so let's quickly dispose of the latter.

For our present purposes, we will not use *invocation*, which is *calling for assistance; summoning of a deity or asking for supernatural aid.* We will use *evocation*, rather than invocation, to ensure that these exercises will not interfere with the integrity of your own spiritual path or religion, if you have one.

Evocation is the key to this work. So what is it and how does it work? What we will be doing when evoking is *summoning or calling up a response from within ourselves, by use of the emotions, in order to create through our imagination.*

In our everyday lives, we remember incidents, read books, hear music, all of which may evoke very profound emotional states. Who doesn't love watching a weepie? Reading a poignant book that evokes an emotional response in us? Who has cried or felt "choked up" on hearing music? Wiped away a tear at our child's nativity play? Sometimes the depth and quality of response evoked can be a real source of surprise to our conscious mind.

And after these experiences, how do we feel? Often peaceful, as if some healing process or catharsis has taken place.

The important thing is that whatever gets summoned comes from *within* us. Specifically, to come at life from a completely different mind-set, we will be calling forth our inner tree. The exercises involve evoking specific responses in order to change our view of our lives for the better. And I hope that when you've read the preliminary tree section, you'll realise just what close kin we are.

Magic only works to the degree that we can stimulate our imaginative and emotional being—and the more regularly we try, the better we get at it. So from the beginning we must realise that these exercises are not based in the intellect. We are aiming for a visceral reaction, at a gut level. The "grrrr" of anger and the amazed "ahhhh" of sudden wonder are two examples of this feeling, which we feel as an emotional charge through our whole being. Make both these sounds now and see how you feel—even thinking about emotions that induce those sounds might be sufficient to evoke a response within. That's the level of the subconscious, the level of the magical impulses that seep up into our lives, the waves of reaction to our deep-rooted understanding of how life works. It's that deep understanding which prompts our instinctual actions, which in turn create our destinies, in spite of how our rational minds are trying to make us behave. We can access all that via the imagination.

Think of a film now—a rom-com—where the heroine is set on a very sensible life course, but suddenly acts on an irresistible and life-changing whim. That's the message of the magic of subconscious yearnings and urgings. (Which film is now in your mind, I wonder? Mine was *Sleepless in Seattle*.)

I am not concerned here with the scientific proof that imaginative exercises have an effect in the real world, though studies with top athletes provide solid evidence, and visualisation exercises are used widely to aid pain relief. I just know that such things can work, because that's been my experience.

The nineteenth-century British magician John Brodie-Innes is credited with saying, "Whether gods or demons really exist is beside the point; the important thing is that the universe behaves as if they do."

Now, we are not invoking deities, but we can cultivate that same attitude to our magical work. Through trial and error, and evidence-based experiment, we will answer the important question, "Does it work in practice?" We will find out if altering our inner perceptions can cause changes to our relationship to the world, and if that change might be mirrored by our outer circumstances. I, and many others, find that it does.

It is important to feed the imagination, so that evoking particular states becomes easier for us. We need to find pictures and images, music and environments that allow our imagination to flower, and these will be images from nature.

Try an Evocation Exercise Now

Remember, you are only evoking what is *within you*: no worries about any other influences. Just affirm that you are safe and secure within yourself as you relax, and enjoy!

Sit comfortably. Put aside your everyday worries for five minutes. Read the next instructions and then gently shut your eyes and follow them.

You are going to allow a feeling of love naturally to well up within yourself, from the depths of your being: this is evocation. We're not evoking any sensation of physical love, but the deep security of being loved and supported by the whole universe.

First calm your mind by counting ten slow breaths in and out. Then imagine the words "love, love, love" lazily and gently floating through you with the rhythm of your slow breathing and the pulse of your blood. You have nothing to worry about, because everything's

working out just fine. Experience a relaxation of spirit with every
breath; nothing is forced, everything is flowing as it should. Enjoy
for a few minutes… Then, when you are ready, open your eyes.

How did it go? Did ten slow breaths take longer than you anticipated? Did you find it difficult to access the all-important *feeling* from a cold start? Did you *really try*? If so, please don't; the secret is to relax. It's true, as self-help books say: trying too hard makes it very difficult for you to succeed.

On a scale of one to ten, how successful did you *feel* it was? A preoccupation with success and failure is really counterproductive, but that seems to be how we're wired. We'll always be interested in how well we're doing, so don't try to ignore that natural instinct, just be aware and hold it lightly.

Your feeling is the only feedback you're going to get. So evaluate, then stop bothering about it. Did you sense/see words, and if so, where were the words based? Did you see the word "love" written on the screen of your mind? Was there a colour? Did you get a feeling of love? If so, where was that feeling located in your body? As you hadn't been prompted, it won't be surprising if your answer to most of these questions is "No!"

Asking you to do this exercise without preparation was deliberately to make it difficult, like cranking a car engine from cold. From now on, it will only get easier. It's really fairer to the imagination to warm it up first, and we do that by always starting in the same way. Rather as cleaning our teeth gets the mind and body ready for bed each night, so we programme ourselves before an inner experience. We give the imagination lots to feed it—ideas of colour, sound, scent, and sensation to give life and substance to what we do. So if you're not a visual person, don't worry. In your imagination, you can hear, feel, sense, and smell as well as see. And the most important of these senses is *feeling*.

Think now: what colour is a wave of pure love? What does it smell like? What does it feel like? What does it sound like? These questions will be different for every individual. And if you don't know the answers? Never mind.

Just acting "as if" you know and producing an answer for the moment gives you a starting point. It is always exciting when the imagination truly takes over from the thinking part of the brain, so that your rather predictable colour of love suddenly morphs into a rainbow of rhythmic pulsing lights—an image you couldn't have anticipated that you would evoke. When this happens, go with the flow; immerse yourself in experience and enjoy it. You produced this. You are in charge; you have the power to pull the plug on your experience at any time just by opening your eyes, so relax in that knowledge and get the most you can—hopefully a wonderfully relaxing, nurturing, and energising experience.

So now let's do it again, but this time feeding your imagination with pictures to evoke all the senses. By doing the first short exercise, you have primed your mind ...

With each breath, put your attention into your belly, and imagine a cauldron glowing with life and love, feeding your system ... It is a mysterious, misty, magical light ... What colour is it? ... It is an eternal source of loving energy within you, and mist rising from it is suffusing your body.

Feel it spreading, and the pulse of your blood thrumming gently to the words "love, love, love." Give yourself up to the total relaxation of these few moments; with each breath in, imagine the words "sublime love" slowly rising from the depths of your being as you imagine them being written on the screen of your inner sight, all of it melding with a sense of loving security spreading within you ... Send love around your body, and with each breath out, send gratitude. See, feel, or imagine your out breath as mist mingling with the atmosphere, itself suffused with loving energy from the whole natural world and the cosmos, so that there is a cycle of breath breathing you, allowing universal love to permeate your being and connect you to the world of nature.

And when you're ready, open your eyes.

Hopefully that was a nice experience, whose benefits need no justification. What you have done is first evoke a specific feeling or quality *from within*, and then use that feeling to connect you to its equivalent in the world *outside* your body. Evoking loving energy is a prime way of attracting it to ourselves.

This type of exercise is essential to accessing a magical mind-set. But can it truly develop into what we would call "doing magic?" Well, I think it does have magical effects—and the proof is surely in our results. Let's look at a few definitions of magic.

Definitions of Magic

Definition one: Your dictionary will say that magic is something like "an extraordinary power or influence seemingly from a supernatural source" and this is what we see in many films, where a pointed wand results in impossible changes in the natural surroundings. But we know that doesn't happen in real life and that the world is not there for us to manipulate. To work with, to get in tune with, yes; to manipulate, never. Work with the trees shows us our place in the universe. Gaining a wider perspective inspires us to examine the implications of trying to change the world in order to get that job, that man, that house.

Definition number two, widely attributed to Dion Fortune, the foremost woman occultist of the twentieth century, is accepted by many modern occultists: "Magic is the art of changing consciousness at will." If this seems a little tame to you, I agree. In my fantasies, I too point my wand and change my world instantly. But if we also intuitively understand there is a correlation between "within and without, as above so below," then changing consciousness is profoundly magical, leading to actual changes in our lives.

Let's go deeper into the interpretations of magic with definition number three, from another great British occultist of the twentieth century, William G. Gray, who says it is "Man's most determined effort to establish an actual working relationship through himself between his Inner and

Outer states of being. By magic, Man shows that he is not prepared simply to be a pawn in the Great Game … magic is concerned with Doing."[1]

This seems to touch the heart of the matter: we are constantly trying to reconcile our inner and outer worlds to reach a state of authenticity or congruence, and "Doing," working to this aim, is a magical path.

Definition number four, from Starhawk, by its very language evokes a magical feeling within us: "Magic, the art of sensing, and shaping the subtle, unseen forces that flow through the world, of awakening deeper levels of consciousness beyond the rational."[2] Let me turn this around to devise a last definition: "Magic is the art of awakening or accessing the deeper levels of consciousness beyond the rational, to get in tune with and react to the subtle unseen forces that flow through the world, to cause changes to evolve in life."

And if you think back, that's just what you were doing when you evoked love within yourself.

The important thing about our current reality is that we are driven by our consciousness, our limited perceptions; immediate feelings that often lead to knee-jerk reactions. Minute by minute, we tend to react to the surface currents of the sea of life, creating a reality that is not what we want. Meanwhile our true, hidden sense of ourselves is sending signals to try to get us to live our lives according to the dictates of the deeper currents within us. No wonder life is often about frustration and confusion.

We will try to tune into the deeper currents, to engage harmoniously so we will be supported by the flow of life. This means accepting, alongside all our wonderful opportunities, bad luck, sadness, and occasional tragedy: it's all part of the human condition. But it also means that we can co-create the best life for ourselves, with an attitude that supports us through the bad times.

---

1 William G. Gray, *Magical Ritual Methods* (New York: Helios Press, 1969).
2 Starhawk, *The Spiral Dance: A Rebirth of the Ancient Religion of the Great Goddess* (New York: HarperCollins, 1989).

You may have heard this definition of insanity: doing the same thing over and over again and expecting different results. We're going to try something new.

So, although you might have tried the techniques in this book before, this time you will be thinking outside the box, the box that is the human consciousness and perspective. Let's take a different approach to nonmanipulative magical exercises. Let's gently exercise our imaginative muscles.

Guidelines for Study

The "lessons from the tree" study sessions after each chapter are an induction into a different way of looking at the world. The suggestions and exercises are designed to be gentle and have only beneficial effects. They are intended for anyone who feels they only have one way of dealing with everyday challenges, and who wants to develop a wider perspective on life.

If you are very sensitive and can confuse levels of reality in your everyday life, if you have a medical condition that affects your balance and judgement, or if you are currently at a time of upset and trauma in your life, then the exercises might not be suitable, and you are advised not to follow them.

There are repetitions in the exercises of the early chapters, for two reasons. Firstly, repetition aids the memory and over time will help to establish a pattern of getting into a relaxed state quickly and easily. Secondly, they help avoid annoying instructions to turn back to other pages, interrupting the work as you get settled. As you develop your own template for relaxation, the later instructions become shorter and more general.

The quick, imaginative exercises throughout the chapters are to give you a flavour of changing your mind-set between "reading" and "doing" and to help you balance inner and outer work. They are placed as tasters for you to enjoy, with most of the practical exercises in the study sessions at the end of every chapter. This is a book that actively encourages the reader to stop reading at any point that feels appropriate and take a few moments for reverie.

Tackling the Exercises: Common Sense Tips

Do try to dedicate some time for this work, and keep referring to the book to remind you of the coherence of what you're doing.

Get yourself a decent book to write in: you're going to change your attitude to life, and that is certainly worth a new notebook! It needn't be expensive or flashy, but it should be pleasing to you. You might also like a box in which you can keep any wood pieces, craft implements, coloured pens—the things that you might need regularly—so they are always to hand. Find a discreet place to keep them and get them out regularly for your "playtimes," because you must view this as fun and enriching for it to work. What a pity that we have such baggage attached to the word "work." Perhaps we should reframe these exercises as spiritual refreshment and fun!

Four Parts to the Work

You will notice that there are four different types of suggestions set out, falling roughly into these categories:

- Practical/art/craft

- Enjoying/observing nature

- Writing/reviewing

- Inner work/meditation/affirmations

For balance, all are important. Our work is always about developing a wider perspective, and evoking positive and magical feelings to energise us into a state of change. If you are severely restricted, if you can't get out into nature unless you are taken, then use your ingenuity to adapt the suggestions. Ask friends and relatives to drive you out; use your television time to watch nature DVDs—turn down the commentary and enjoy a music soundtrack to help you to evoke the feelings of freedom and connection you may otherwise find difficult. One can even buy a DVD of bonfires burning, and this might become relevant when you do the work of the oak later in the course.

Devising a Schedule

The first job is to decide what schedule will fit into your life as it is at present, so sketch out a few possibilities now. Here's a sample for you from a student's diary:

GETTING OUT INTO NATURE

First week:
Find local birches!

Monday:
Make this a no-TV day!

After work:
Go straight through the house without stopping
    and do half an hour's gardening.
Long visualisation weekly, every Monday.

Every day:
Quick tree movement and greeting the day.
Check my tree diary for progress straight after evening meal.
Positive affirmations and tree thoughts whilst cleaning
    teeth/preparing food.
Put self to sleep with night-time birch thoughts—
    try the cradle visualisation for one week? Vary at need?

Every weekend:
2-hour walk in nature? Sun am?

Wednesday eve:
Listen to radio instead of TV,
    so can do tree craft things at the same time.

Thursday:
Check if I'm on course and doing this. Allow 1 hour
catch-up time if needed or additional visualisations.

You'll have gathered from this that Mondays and Wednesdays are the least attractive TV days for this student, and that she likes the positive psychological effect of getting the week off to a good start by achieving on a Monday. Before we go further, look back at her schedule; she has excellent intentions, but do you think they are realistic?

Time Management and Expectations

Organise your diary with *realistic* aims at the front to give you a permanent check on how you're doing; don't set yourself up for failure by setting the bar too high. The seed of the birch is miniscule, its growth might seem infinitesimal to us, yet with speed photography we see how inevitably and beautifully it grows from shoot to sapling and into a tree to inspire us. You are setting seeds—tiny changes to your life which allow expansion and growth into a new way of living.

Little and often is the way.

That student's plan does seem like a pretty full-on schedule for someone just starting out. On the other hand, she might find writing out an optimum schedule really helpful. Perhaps she'll put a tick by an exercise every day that she achieves it, and then revise the plan? And she will have made the plan with reference to her circumstances. Do you think she has four children and a full-time job? I doubt it. Tailor your work and your schedule to suit *you*. If you don't like getting up, and are frantically organising children, then don't plan to make yourself get up earlier to achieve—that plan will probably be doomed to failure.

Perhaps positive affirmations whilst you clean your teeth are all you can reasonably manage at the moment? That's fine; just do something regularly, however little. Remember, you can always add on to the work. If you get to the end of two weeks and decide you've been too kind to yourself and what you're doing is not enough, then just revise your plan. Keep reviewing, keep on track. And never try to make time by doing *anything* else whilst you're driving!

In order to make progress, the rule with learning anything—an instrument, a language, a new way of living—is to do something every day. Decide what that something will be and stick to it. Keep in mind always: we want to engage the physical, mental, emotional levels, and through them evoke a sense of the spiritual that we can key into, a life we are stepping into that is enriched by that awareness.

"Know thyself" was inscribed on the temple of Apollo at Delphi more than two thousand years ago, and it is still essential advice for us. Are you physically a sloth, emotionally stifled, or mentally lazy? Oh, go on, surely not all three! Decide which aspect of the work you're most likely to fall down on, then devise a stratagem to keep you on track.

Here are some examples:

If going out into nature will be your weakness, you might volunteer to help with your son's/daughter's scout hikes; set up a regular walk with a friend; walk the last few blocks to work, and talk to the trees along the road; go to the park at lunchtime or meet a friend there once a week. The people who'll be with you don't have to know why you're doing this: no one should question your trying to take more exercise.

See how inventive you can be in devising ways of making your weak areas more attractive with fun activity. Don't like writing? Sit down when your children do their homework; they'll be thrilled that you have to do yours as well. You get the picture? Or record your experiences in some other way.

Make your plans well now, so that when you do fall down on your exercises—and a bad day or days will come—you have a stratagem in place. If you really distrust yourself, you could even have a skeleton "must do"—a minimalist list to keep you on track whilst you're really too stressed to contemplate long visualisations. Maybe just an affirmation performed three times a day (you can set your phone alarm for this) or just greeting the day whilst you're in the shower and evoking anticipation within yourself? So be it. You can add on as life gets easier or as the simple work you're doing inspires you to. You are crafting your life, every day, with every action.

So, getting out into nature, writing or otherwise recording—all these are grounding, by which we mean helping to bring your ideas into reality by doing something real in the apparent world. The second part of your work is inner: honing your imagination and attuning your mind to the wider-than-human world of nature through a mixture of affirmations and inner imaginative journeys. We call these journeys visualisations, although often people do not get visual images but simply fully evoke *the feeling* of the experience with the inner senses. When you tell yourself the story of your visualisation—and you will soon be crafting these to suit every occasion—it will help if you remember these guidelines.

GUIDELINES FOR THE INNER WORK

- Always start the same way. This, like any other routine, makes the work easier each time; the brain likes a routine.

- Always end the same way. Breathing deeply and following the same routine of allowing the outer world to come to the forefront of your attention help you to reassert yourself in the real world quickly and easily.

- To help you connect back with the real world, have a drink, eat something, and say out loud that you have returned fully. Do not be tempted to hold on to your inner images; let them fade, knowing that you can return to your inner place whenever you wish.

- State your name and aim to yourself before starting. If you don't have a clear goal, how will you know if you are succeeding? It doesn't have to be grand: just relaxing is an aim.

- Tell yourself the story in your mind to start your visualisation, and, to engage easily, put it in the present: "I am walking under the trees ..." not "I was walking ..."

- Use all your senses to make the scenes real: how do they look, smell (the smell of the forest is bewitching!), feel, sound? Capture raindrops from the leaves and imagine the taste.

- Remember, it is the quality and intensity of the feeling this storytelling induces that is the measure of its success, not whether you see pretty pictures!

- If you don't feel comfortable with any inner experience, then just stop it. State out loud that the visualisation is ended, allow the image to fade, and then follow the instructions for coming back completely. If you want to change your mood in a hurry, switch on the television or radio, have something to eat, and concentrate on something outside of yourself.

- Be gentle with yourself; best results often occur when you lose your high expectations of what "should" happen.

- Practice little and often, so that you look forward to each short break as refreshing and inspiring.

Affirmations

There is evidence that negative or positive thought can cause chemical changes in the body, that affirming statements encourage us in good behaviours, that they make us more open to change and less defensive. All these points make affirmations worthwhile in our journey of gentle change for the better, effecting mood changes that can help us achieve our goals. The spoken word is immensely powerful. We attach a huge importance to it, which is why the person who can lie to another's face is rare. We may all fudge the truth on occasion, or suggest a falsehood, but we try to do it in a way that we can justify, however uncomfortably. We have to believe, or pretend to believe, what comes out of our mouths: it is part of our belief in ourselves.

So we will use affirmations to articulate out into the world those feelings that we will evoke within. These exercises are not for others to hear, they are between us and the universe, us and the forest, us and the unseen reality that underpins our lives. The affirmations that follow are to induce positive moods, new ways of thinking, and to connect to our imaginal view of the essence of the tree-ness.

Using affirmations should effectively widen, broaden, and deepen our human perspective. Keying into the mood of our tree-cousins, we will remind ourselves that we are more than our physical body, and that when the physical, mental, and emotional work together, change can occur.

Rather than learning affirmations by rote, you should go from the suggestions in the chapters to crafting them to suit your own needs. So here are the guidelines to performing affirmations with the best chance of success.

AFFIRMATION TIPS

- Affirmations should always be positive. Never reference the negative or what you're trying to avoid. Example: "I anticipate joy," not "I lose my miserable mood."

- They should be simple.

- They should be stated in the present.

- Speak them out loud regularly, with many repetitions.

- Be inventive and have fun. Sing your affirmation to the tune of your favourite song; sing and dance.

- Breathe in the truth of them; allow it to well up from inside you.

In the beginning, you might set your clock alarm for suitable times to practice affirmations. Or connect them to everyday repetitive acts: washing, doing the dishes, bed making, ironing, gardening. Try saying them looking at yourself in a mirror and see if you get a stronger impression, or if it makes you feel uncomfortable—and always do what feels right to you.

It's more of a challenge when you are out of your own home for a lot of the day, so review to see where repeating affirmations might be possible: walking from the garage or parking lot or in the moments when you are by yourself during the day. And, as with any other inner work, *never* whilst driving.

The rule for all aspects of the work is the same: be gentle, be firm, and *enjoy* yourself.

The Birch Tree
Forging the Way

Birch Qualities:

They are conduits of life force.
They are not judgemental.
They are long-lived witnesses to events.

Bright

Inspirer

Regenerating

Clarifying

Healing

1

Birch and the Magic of Anticipation

Tree quality: They are conduits of life force.

The Birch in the Natural World

Let's forge the way by making positive connection. To ensure that our work is based in the greater natural world, and not just dreamed up in our heads, we'll examine the actual birch tree—a silver birch for preference.

What does the birch look like? Does it grow in your area? Maybe the beautiful swaying tree in the park doesn't look like a tough little fighter, a pioneer, but that is what it is. And it is ubiquitous—so if you struggle to find the living tree, then it is almost certainly in a building near you, as timber in construction or furniture. Let's start by seeing it as it is: in nature, folklore, and wisdom.

Find a picture of the birch, or look at the one in this book, with a pen and paper by your side.

Discovering the Birch: Exercise

The best possible way to do this exercise is by sitting under an actual birch tree. Go ahead and try it now with the picture, then find a real birch to visit to repeat this exercise, if a birch is near and in a place that seems safe and sensible to rest in for a relaxed few minutes. Whether seeing the birch in nature or through pictures, you should know what it actually looks like *now*, in whatever season you're reading this. Know the look of the birch in spring, summer, autumn, and winter: the leaf, the bud, the flower, and the silhouette.

Now, settle down for five minutes. Breathe three deep, slow, conscious breaths: the first with your body, mind, emotions, and spirit, the second with the world around you, and the third with the spirit of the birch.

Look at the picture, or stand (or sit) next to the tree, and just allow images and feelings to fill the space that you have made. Then allow questions to arise ...

What does the tree say to you? This will become apparent by what it *evokes* from you, with what images and feelings you respond. That is how we filter the messages from the natural world. (If you think that the natural world can't affect your state of mind, imagine for a few moments, as strongly as you can, walking by yourself in a forest with no one else around as the light is fading. Something is probably telling you to search out your car keys even as you hurry to the car park. Do you get the point?)

So, you are in the presence of the birch, in that you are putting your whole, relaxed attention towards it. Its characteristic is to "forge the way." How does the birch embody that idea; how does it forge the way? Is it forging upwards, through its growth, or downwards, or sideways? What messages do you get from its shape, its leaves?

Allow plenty of time to consider what we might learn, simply from the look and habit of the actual tree in the landscape. By doing that, we are following in the footsteps of our ancestors, who discovered their relationship with the natural world through observation, trial, and error.

Jot down your immediate impressions. Draw the tree, or leaf, or twig; scribble in key words from the experience. This work could lead you on to explorations and discoveries about the trees in your locality, whilst you're advancing through the book. Delight in the process!

The Super-Natural World

Beyond the world of the five senses, there is a larger, more ephemeral explanation of life and its connections. And within the understanding of that world, every tree has its dryad, its tree spirit, a nymph of the trees.

So the next step is to imagine the spirit within the tree. Ask yourself the question, "If this tree is a spiritual being, what would its spiritual essence look like to me?" Suspend disbelief, get your pencil and sketch its fluid lines. The birch lends itself to this sort of imagining; slender and graceful, it has been called "the lady of the woods." There will be an opportunity to meet and communicate with the birch dryad later. For now, imagine its form in a way that appeals to you; there is no right or wrong; you are in the process of devising your individual approach.

You are now starting to forge your own way into your future.

You have studied the look of the birch, the way it grows, and you have evoked within yourself a sense of the birch as a sentient being that you can contact, from whom you can learn.

This is the first step into a magical interpretation of your life. And, like the birch, you are not waiting until your life is perfect, until the Ice Age of your current stuck thinking is a distant memory and the earth is lush and green: you have decided to be proactive. No matter how unpromising your surroundings appear to your rational senses, you have glimpsed a small window of opportunity, enough for a seed-thought of the magical possibility to germinate.

Now it is time to become acquainted with the specific magical gifts of the birch. Through all the facts, all the rationalisations, we will hear the whisper of the birch dryad, the breeze through the leaves. So breathe deeply, and feel the pure air of the forest and the clear blue sky entering your lungs, invigorating you.

As you perform this simple breathing with awareness and imagination, notice the feeling that this evokes; feel already the magic of anticipation.

After the Ice Age, the birch transformed the world from white to green. *So can you.*

The birch dryad speaks:

The shiver of the breeze shakes my seeds, scattering them far across the world. Life pulses through my being, from root to twig. Sap fuels my clean limbs as they thrust upwards. My beauty shines in the forest: my silver trunk, my reddish buds, and the brilliance of my young leaves unfurling at the end of black twigs in this bright new spring world, full of possibilities, make all who see me glad.

The breeze through the birch branches equates to the shiver of anticipation everyone feels when life is full of magical possibilities. And if the birch is going to help you, you should be asking in what way it is qualified to do so.

Well, what qualities would you look for in a spiritual or magical teacher? You would look for *health*, a mysterious emanation of clean, clear wholesomeness, and the birch is associated with health and hygiene, as you will find out. And, no matter how young or old the teacher, you would expect them to have the vitality and zest for life that we associate with youth, coupled with the wisdom of maturity. The birch, in its habit, its physical characteristics, and its folklore, encapsulates these qualities.

So when all we would-be magicians are feeling that we would transform our lives *today*, if only we had the energy to get out of bed, we can tune into the whisper of the birch dryad.

The birch dryad speaks:

The world is eager for your seed-thoughts and plans. There is a bright new day awaiting you. How will you grow?

Developing Your Sense of Your Life Force

Do you remember the list of tree qualities in the introduction?

You share the first quality: *you are a conduit of life force.*

Life force—whatever that is—flows round, through, and in each one of us, as essential as the blood in our veins. We recognise the withdrawal of this intangible essence when someone dies. It interacts with the subtle atmosphere around us and feeds us in a more-than-physical way. It is the reason we feel that some people drain us and some support us. It is why we feel that interaction with our cousins the trees, such strong conduits of life force, will be nourishing.

Yeah, yeah, you say, *but I'm still in bed…*

A simple way to attune to a new way of thinking is to start each day with an exercise to key you in, to get you onto the right wavelength.

Consider the birch and your connection whilst in bed. Start to act upon it, stretching to the sky as you lever yourself into a sitting position. You can think, say, or intone these words:

From root to shoot, I stretch,
From heartwood to bark, I breathe.

The heartwood is the dense core of the tree, so this is an expression of stretching gently not only upwards but in every direction. To begin the magical process of evocation, stretch your arms and legs before your feet even touch the bedside mat. Any small action will lead you in: to rising, to looking out at the weather, to noticing the outside world. Allow yourself to evoke the feeling of being sustained from deep within you. From that starting point, you will begin to attract and notice those same qualities in your outside world.

Through repeating a morning meditation over time, even if just in snatched moments, you are setting your internal wavelength to notice and appreciate the loving and stabilising influences in your world. And, from thence, you can begin to cultivate the attitude of *anticipation*.

But hopefully there will not just be snatched moments for this work! Here is a version for you to experiment with each morning. All the movements will be intuitive; you will be "tuning in" to your body, so just adapt as seems right. Some days it will take thirty seconds of slow movement, and other days will take thirty minutes; both are fine. Just keep practicing to slowly build a connection between yourself and your body, yourself and the trees.

A Simple Morning Birch Attunement

Breathe deeply, and move slowly. Imagine that you are a moving tree. Feel your toes grip the ground, and as they lift and fall, imagine your thousand small shallow roots lifting from the ground, shifting and being replanted. Feel them stretching out to beyond the extent of your arms, which have become your tree canopy. Gently allow your trunk to sway, moving to whatever extent is comfortable for you, and lift your arms, circling them in slow stretches to imitate the upwards surge of your branches, and then lowering them at full stretch to delineate the extent of your growth. Move with the breeze. Have your eyes in soft focus, and your attention within your body.

Things that you might imagine as you do this—maybe to some music, if that helps you:

See yourself in a glade of birches, all moving with you. Feel your skin as bark, silver and shining, catching the early sunlight. See the clear dawn and hear the singing of birds. Feel your life force being nurtured.

Now imagine a long movement of energy from the earth, through your roots and under your bark-skin, to your extremities. Feel your tender young leaves absorbing the energy of the sunlight.

When the image is strong and potent within you, gently stop so that you can absorb fully these sensations. Devise a short affirmation, prayer, or mantra for yourself, the simpler the better. Allow words to filter down from the clear sky, up from the earth, from the life all around you. Your subconscious responds to simple phrases, not great verse, so don't feel self-conscious; no one else will ever hear them. Start with one or more of these if you find it difficult:

- Roots grow, life flows.

- Branches soar, my life is sure.

- As the birch grows, so my life is sweet and slow.

- I have time like the trees, to fulfil every need.

All the feelings you evoke should be of gentle, accepting relaxation, supported by the earth. You should be left feeling poised, confident, and happy.

There is a full-length morning meditation at the end of this chapter which hundreds of students have used since it was first made available. Mix and match; be inventive; keep your sense of anticipation and aliveness.

The Magic of Anticipation

There is a magic in anticipation that all esoteric workers recognise. It is the opposite of neediness. That feeling is an expression of lack, which seems conversely to push away the very things that we want to attract. Be glad, be grateful, and anticipate the best. Then, no matter what happens, you've had the joy in the present moment!

Anticipation comes from being able to appreciate, and being happy with, what you have, and in using where you are now as a springboard to where you might go, to what you might create or produce.

The birch dryad speaks:

My shallow roots can cling and draw sustenance from the poorest soil. This gives me all I need to grow and thrive in the poorest of conditions, shining in my beauty, and producing my seeds, which will populate the earth.

Although the birch is the tree of anticipation, it has decades to grow, to develop. We need to cultivate an understanding that *so do we*; we can grow in grace and beauty whilst the changes we start making now slowly develop. The birch had an awe-inspiring task to inspire us—

> **The birch dryad speaks:**
>
> When the ice receded from the lands, I was the pioneer. Within my being is a thrusting urge to root. From earliest times, I have taken every opportunity, no matter how unpromising, for growth.

One could say also that bare and disturbed earth holds within it the anticipation that it will soon be covered—with daisies, dandelions, groundsel, bramble, rosebay willowherb, and copses of birch. That is the nature of nature!

So no matter where we start from—actual poverty or just poverty of aspiration—from all the knocks the world has given us (and I am not making light of them) we are going to cultivate the attitude that what we have, little as it may be, is nevertheless sustaining us, and we will grow and develop into our true selves from this place.

Newness: Each Day, Each Week, Each Month, Each Year

The birch has a special symbolism as the tree of new beginnings, and it is the first in the tree calendar developed from the work of Robert Graves. By simple observation, we see the spring as the time of the earth's renewal, and the birch also carries within it a sense of seasonal anticipation for whole communities. In Scandinavian countries, the start of the farming year was traditionally indicated when the birch buds opened into leaf. So birch speaks of newness: a new aeon, new growth, and the new farming year.

As the birch is the tree of new beginnings, its time is the morning, when we rise, when all the possibilities of the day are still ahead of us. Practicing the birch morning exercise will give your body a gentle stretch and help tune you in every morning. Look out for ways of making your life new, every day, every week. Use the man-made calendar or the ancient view of the moon and sun phases to chart a perpetual cycle of new beginnings to help you adjust, grow, and develop.

Prolonging Youth: Your Magical Guide

We all admire mature people who are young at heart, and one way of staying young might be to maintain the ability—or is it a discipline of thought?—to be amazed by life's possibilities. What a perfect state of trust to be in, to promote a state of anticipation, an eagerness to get up and get on, well into our latter years.

As a magical guide, the birch is our wise, older person who still has this sense of anticipation, and, by working with the exercises, you will gently encourage this quality to unfurl like a young leaf within yourself.

Have you ever wondered why we get bored and depressed? Why life is "same old, same old?" There is much more to life than just what we can understand through our five senses, and this is what you are keying into when you take the leap of faith that says you can learn from a tree! It promotes wonder: if this is possible, then what else is? And life becomes a fascinating exploration.

The mundane answer to the question of boredom is probably that our very intelligence kills off our natural childhood sense of anticipation: being able to argue in our busy brains from cause to effect, we think that we can predict what will happen. And what a bore that makes of life!

Why do we persist in the arrogant illusion that we know what life holds, even though our predictions about life are so often wrong? We didn't predict the car breaking down, being snowed in, being bored at the long-awaited party, meeting our true love at the event we dreaded, or being moved to tears by a song from childhood. And those are aside from the big things—personal accidents or astounding good fortune that comes out of the blue. You can make a list of all that has happened to you over the past week, month, or year to remind yourself that, despite our expectations, we can never know what life has in store. So why do we presume to predict even the next minute? It is our duty to be like the birch—to know we are sustained and to anticipate infinite possibilities in a positive way.

We maintain this point of view by witnessing, relaxing into what the day might bring, and keeping a seed of joyful anticipation deep in our hearts—connecting to it, reminding ourselves, frequently.

So, each bright day, whatever the weather, we will be ready to *notice* and draw sustenance from wherever it might come, the great life events or the simpler—glorious weather, praise at work, the bus arriving on time, having a cup of tea made for us; a cheering phone call, or the sense of satisfaction from doing a job well. We should keenly anticipate these small happy events that build so surely and incrementally into a contented life.

That doesn't seem very grand, very much to aim for? Rest assured, this is the foundation of your magical life. Life is made up of small moments: awareness and gratitude for every wonderful little thing that is harmonious is the beginning of magical change.

Performing a tree meditation in some form each morning, and allowing the feeling it gives to well up at intervals through the day, will remind you of that other vital quality which all trees can give us: a strong sense of *extended time*, time available for us to relax and enjoy fully each anticipatory moment as our lives unfold around us. We will surely move forward at exactly the right pace, whether we're on a jet plane or in a traffic jam, so it is sensible to stand back from the angst and enjoy the ride.

There is no apology for the constant repetition of this point throughout the book; it is vital.

Enter imaginatively into the suggestions of the birch dryad now to remind you of how easy it is.

The birch dryad speaks:

By evoking the qualities of my tree, you will enter slow time, so allow them to flow through you, and feel that you are time-rich.

Human time is not relevant for now. Forget how old you are, let go of your feeling of wasted time; it was all for a reason, which needn't concern you now... Your stress is slipping from you. Tasks will wait for the few precious minutes it takes for my tree to sway in the breeze—to respire, to transpire, to be. Witness your current situation from my green perspective, and see the overview from the forest. When you return to your human concerns, resolve to relax and do one thing to alter your state... Turn your attention back to the outside world, and do that thing now.

There's no doubt that accessing a sense of anticipation can be a real challenge. It is difficult to pull yourself up by your own bootstraps. Evoking that feeling will become easier with constant, small attempts, and will set a good grounding for you.

Take a moment to think of how easy you found that last small exercise. Or was it difficult? Then remember the intelligence and reasoning faculty really can hinder this process, so just trust, relax, *stop trying* and *start allowing* the feelings to well up.

Magic of Fertility

The birch is known for its stimulating qualities, and traditionally it is associated with fertility. The leafing birch heralds the burgeoning time, when birds, bees, and flowers are busy, busy, busy—producing, working, making the most of the sun's influence to grow, fertilise, and reproduce. In folktales across Europe, lovers frequently meet or stay in silver birch groves. Practically, the attraction of an easily identified tree is obvious, and the bright bark and delicate sheltering boughs and twigs shining in the moonlight set the perfect scene for romance.

Medieval herbal tradition links the birch firmly with the goddess Venus. In ancient Welsh lore, the qualities of shining and whiteness indicate the divine feminine influence emanating from a magical place. Guinevere, King

Arthur's queen, is a famous possessor of this glamour. The earlier Welsh spelling, Gwenhwyfar, can be interpreted as the White Enchantress or Ghost—both names that might equally apply to the otherworldly white birch in the depths of the green forest.

The birch witnesses the fertility of humankind: it is the choice for the maypole, and the traditional wedding of European tribal peoples involves "jumping the broomstick"—the witch's broom of story—with its brush of birch, shaft of ash, and bindings of willow. So, with the blessings of the natural world, with the birch as witness, fertility was anticipated and celebrated in times gone by.

Fertility and Creativity

These days, fertility is not the imperative that it was for our forebears. Fortunately, we have the unique privilege of expressing our urge to manifest in the world through our fertile *imagination,* our creativity, which can be expressed in many thousand ways. So the spirit of fertility is always relevant and vital for us, irrespective of our relationship status or age. Creativity is a natural instinct; it is how we key into the natural growing season throughout our entire lives and how we feed our souls by active engagement with life.

Take five minutes to visit the birch again, and this time, whatever the season, let your magical imagination form the pictures of a late spring scene.

The birch dryad speaks:

It is evening, and as you approach my copse of birches, you feel that each tree is emanating a pulse, singing with life. Soft moonlight strikes our silver trunks; the whole glade is lit with a soft gleam. Our branches twist and stretch like limbs, and in each graceful tree you can see my sister dryads, the creative spirits of the trees, each distinct and different. One dryad expresses its tree-creativity by growing tall and straight; another in music, through the continuous rustling of its leaves. Another's branches dance at the slightest breeze, with abandon, as if its roots would pull from the earth; yet another stretches to caress its partner tree, expressing pure love and connection. Every expression of tree-life is there, and, in response, images of all your creative impulses drift into the magical life in our grove: you as artist, as lover, as craftsperson, as worker. There are no dull areas to life, for everything you do, even the most mundane chores, adds to the magical whole. The moon and the spring breeze suffuse your being, activating your creative urge, even if you do not yet express it in the everyday world…and you bring back that feeling with you now.

A Last Word on Rationality and Common Sense

You might still be wondering: why not just de-stress with normal breathing exercises, meditation, and so on? Well, meditation is a wonderful tool, but for its benefits to affect us profoundly, it requires a commitment of time that many of us find difficult. Through the exercises in this book, we are consciously choosing to believe that we need a new way of thinking, and we are actively creating this. It's an approach that weans us away from concentrating on the minutiae of our human relationships—our families, our partners, our work colleagues, niggle, niggle, niggle. If we feel divorced from nature, if we exclude the wider world, we dive headlong into our human relationships, making our lives into soap opera melodrama. We need to get back our sense of perspective, to get off the motorway and back onto the track ways.

Awareness of the trees' longevity and role as witness allows us space to regain focus and balance quickly, by just stepping back. It can make a real change at a deep level—so we are not trying to "overlay" our emotions with a gloss of calm whilst we are still seething inside. It is a system that can lead us to a state of genuine congruence, where what is inside of us and what we present to the outside world can agree completely.

Remember: we can't fix any problem from the same mind-set that created it, and magic is the art of changing consciousness at will. The trees can help you build these two realisations into your way of relating to the world.

Further ideas and exercises are in the study section below, and just before that is the structured moving tree meditation promised earlier. Feel free to adapt and personalise the suggestions throughout the book. This is an adventure, so evoke the anticipation of the birch and feel light and free.

A Druid Tree Meditation

This is a formal tree meditation composed and written by the chief of the Order of Bards, Ovates and Druids, Philip Carr-Gomm. It is widely used by members of the Order, and many students of varying religious persuasions practice it daily and can testify to its efficacy.

In the Order of Bards, Ovates and Druids, we learn many methods of meditation. Here is one inspired by the trees that you can practice, either as a spiritual exercise in its own right or as a prelude to other meditation or movement work.

Its purpose is to help you feel centred and grounded, and to help you deepen your experience of being in your body and in relationship to the natural world. It encourages the flow of life force (known as Nwyfre in the Druid tradition) and harmonises the flows of earth and sky energies within you. The movements help to gently stretch certain muscles and they also work energetically with the chakras, moving from the base up to the heart, brow, and crown—encouraging the process of opening to love and wisdom, and of harmonising heart and mind.

Each element of the meditation may be experienced for as long as you wish, and once you have mastered its simple sequence, you might like to try deepening your experience by dwelling for some time on each part of the meditation for an extended period.

Ideally the meditation is undertaken standing up, with the feet sufficiently apart for you to feel stable and well planted on the earth. Standing upright like the tree helps you to become aware of the sensation of gravity and the feeling of being embodied and grounded that this brings. It also enables you to gain the maximum benefit from the simple stretching that the meditation entails.

If you cannot perform the meditation standing up, it can also be practiced seated. If you use a chair, use one without arms. If you cannot perform the physical movements of the exercise, you will still benefit if you remain still and imagine the movements.

Begin by standing or sitting, closing your eyes, and becoming aware of the environment around you. If you are not outside in a natural setting, you might like to imagine yourself in one, such as a forest or woodland grove.

Now move your awareness to your body, to a full appreciation of your embodied being. Move your awareness slowly down from the top of your head, relaxing into your awareness of your body as you do so. Relax your eyes and mouth, release any tension in the shoulders, and gradually move your awareness down through your torso and legs to the soles of your feet.

Feel your feet planted firmly on the earth. Imagine roots travelling deep down into the soil, and sense these great strong roots spreading wide and deep beneath you.

Feel the nourishment and energy from the earth travelling up those roots now until you sense again the soles of your feet. Feel that energy flowing up your body as you move your awareness slowly, with love and acceptance and openness, up your body: up your legs, your thighs, your torso. And if your mind drifts off, just bring your attention back and continue this pilgrimage of consciousness up your body—up your arms and chest, your neck, your head.

When you reach the top of your head, just let go of this movement of awareness and rest in an awareness of just Being… still and calm, alive and vital… not denying any discomfort you may feel, just allowing it to be there.

Become aware of your breathing and let your awareness rest here for a while, just breathing in and breathing out.

And now raise your arms, not forwards in front of you, but out to either side of you with palms facing down. Let your arms float up effortlessly as if they are doing so of their own volition, floating up until they are parallel to the earth. As they reach this position at shoulder height, turn your palms to face upwards, and as you do this, move your arms back a tiny amount—just a centimetre or so—and enjoy the sensation this gives of opening your chest, your heart. Imagine your arms and hands are like the first great boughs that mark the beginning of the crown of your tree. Sense the branches and leaves of your crown, gently moving in the sunlight and sky above.

Stay in this position as long as you like, and then slowly move your arms up until your fingertips touch above the top of your head, sensing as you do this the top of the crown of your tree. Enjoy the stretch of this movement, and then retrace the movement: slowly lower your arms down to either side, palms facing up until they reach shoulder height, at which point they turn downwards, and continue in one flowing movement down, until your fingertips meet at the midline of your body. As you move your arms down to this position, allow your awareness to move towards the earth and a sense of your roots, and then sense the energy of the earth flowing up the trunk of your tree (in other words, your legs) until it reaches your hands, at which point your hands begin to travel, fingertips touching, up the midline of your body to your chest. Pause at the chest and let your fingertips touch your body. Or you can flatten your palms and press them gently against your heart and chest. Then bring your fingertips up to the brow to touch there. Then raise the fingertips right up as high as they can go, to repeat the stretch above your head to the top of your crown.

Stay there as long as you wish, and then repeat the sequence twice more: separating your fingertips and sweeping your hands down with palms up, flipping your palms to face downwards at shoulder level until your fingertips meet just in front of your body, then bringing them up again to touch heart and brow before stretching up to the crown.

On the third and final sequence, lower your arms to either side and just rest in stillness for a while. Open to your awareness, sensing yourself breathing in and breathing out.

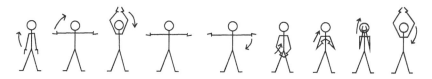

A Druid Tree Meditation

When you are ready to finish this phase, give thanks to the trees, and gradually allow any sense of having roots, branches, and leaves to dissolve as you become fully aware of your own body.

At this point you can choose to finish the practice, or you may want to enter deeper into the stillness, either by sitting down or by staying upright, and using whatever technique you prefer for this phase of meditation. Alternatively, if you are using this practice as a preliminary to a movement meditation such as yoga, t'ai chi, or qigong, you can now move into that phase of work.

Lessons from the Birch

Anticipation

The birch dryad speaks:

When conditions are right, my seeds germinate. With great anticipation my shoots break the soil, ready for their growth, to take their place in the world as new, strong trees.

Forging the Way

Now comes the time to decide in depth what you want to do. To the suggestions in this chapter, we add the following ideas for further work. All that follow are *suggestions*—you are in charge, so do what feels right to you. After all, evoking the right feeling is what this is all about.

This section is split into two main branches. The first encourages a generic sense of anticipation, so that this can become your natural way of being and relating to the world. Don't worry if your factory setting is "glum" or "pessimistic;" this will not require hard work—in fact, the opposite. Instead, you will gently develop an awareness so that you check in with your mood, and then access anticipation through imaginative evocation. In the second branch of this section, we will apply the energy of anticipation to a specific project.

Developing the Attitude: Affirmations

To develop a larger perspective, we must stay aware. Look back to the introduction to remind yourself of tiny, positive phrases that can help transform the way you view life. Remember, saying them by rote will have no effect: we are aiming to evoke the emotions.

Here are two preliminary suggestions for affirmations, both in the present tense:

• *I am filled with the anticipation of the birch.*

Feel the truth of it, a joyful feeling welling up inside you. Remember a happy time when this was true. Repeat the affirmation, breathing the feeling in and out … repeat and breathe … and so on, until your present state of mind reflects the words.

• *Like the birch, I reach to the future with bright*
   expectation.

Repeat, as with the first, then ask yourself, how does saying those words make you feel? Does an appropriate emotion reflecting these words arise within you? Your feelings might be of lightness, expansion, or joy, as well as anticipation. Notice them all.

Enjoyment is the aim. If the words feel slightly wrong for you, adapt them to suit yourself. Keep them simple and keep the original meaning. Repeat each out loud, allowing the feeling of them to well up within and amplify your mood. Don't *try hard*, just tune in to yourself and allow it to happen. Resolve to do an affirmation a set number of times every morning to prime your mind for a wonderful day ahead.

Use the same technique with any or all the affirmations below. The lightness of birch can support us in many areas, so adapt them for every situation. Vary them so you stay interested; the aim is never to get stale. And, again, check at regular intervals: how do the affirmations make you feel? Does an emotion that reflects these words arise within you?

BIRCH AFFIRMATIONS

To relax and stretch your physical body; combine with movement:
From root to shoot, I stretch.
From heartwood to bark, I breathe.

For anticipation every morning:
Like sap, anticipation runs sweetly through my being.

For support:
The strength of the natural world surrounds and holds me.
I am in my perfect environment.

For a sense of your essential nature:
My slender twigs dance in freedom in the moment.
All that is right for me is possible in my life.

To relieve stress and enter timelessness:
I sink into the time of new beginnings, of possibility.

To feel in charge of your life:
I am the prime mover who transforms by my actions.

To relax in the middle of a busy day:
I share the timeless, serene anticipation of the birch.

Think of some activity you don't usually enjoy, then devise a new affirmation connecting you to the birch energy. Make it something really simple to start, without too much emotion attached—shopping, for example, rather than a stressful meeting. Repeat the affirmation often; you are creating building blocks that will lead to a practice to support you through every life event.

As an example, let us say that "I love shopping," is currently untrue and evokes only disbelief. It is a product of the rational mind, so useless. The secret is to trick your rational mind, to approach the problem at an oblique angle, to sneak a positive approach under the radar of your rationality!

Using the first quality of the birch, anticipation, anticipate pleasure in approaching and dealing with the situation in an optimistic way—for example, "The birch spirit is with me" (this should start it welling up inside you). Then one or more of these suggestions:

- Like the birch, I am in the right place.

- I cope efficiently with every aspect of life.

- I enjoy witnessing my grace as I complete the shopping effortlessly.

- This situation is just a part of life; I welcome it and deal with it calmly.

- My energy is contained and I complete this task simply.

Then try the activity—don't fall into the trap of thinking that reading is doing. Use the affirmations beforehand, rerun them in your mind, then evaluate how it went.

How did positive anticipation work for you? Were there other practical factors that could have made it easier, like not shopping just as the shops were closing? The result is not as important as the fact that you have approached something with a different attitude. Be gentle; be firm; be honest and write the results in your book. And keep adapting and practicing.

Getting into the Neighbourhood

Now the first practical work—although you may have enjoyed the taster in the preceding section. This system is grounded: we are supported by the natural world, so you must go out into the neighbourhood, as far as is possible. Round up the family or a friend if you want, and go out for a walk. Seek out nature books that make a game of who can spy particular trees, plants, and birds. *Your mission* is to spot the local birches. When you do, note their appearance, size, and so on, depending on the time of year. If there are no birches, are there any trees that seem to share the same qualities of lightness and airiness, straight growth, delicacy, and beauty? You might take a sketch pad—and it doesn't matter if you're no good at drawing; most people feel the same way! These are notes and sketches just for you.

First consider your tree: is it leggy and tall, or sturdy and well shaped? Has it had to fight for space and light? Look around the location—it should tell you why that is. And when you draw your conclusions, congratulations: you are beginning to read the natural world.

Concentrate on your tree. Does anything grow underneath it? What is the ground like? What other plants and trees are growing near? When you have looked at a few in different locations, you will get a fair idea of which plants, trees, and fungi tend to be found together. Is your birch on the edge of woodland, standing alone, or in the middle of other trees?

When you have answered these questions, take a quiet moment under the branches, a refreshing canopy of delicate green. Feel a part of yourself responding to the tree. Breathe in thanks for what you have in the moment, and in anticipation of more joy throughout the day. Then whistle the dog, or catch up with your group, and enjoy your walk!

As a continuation of this, remember to keep a lookout for birches when you're out or visiting new places. Note each sighting in your notebook.

Daydreams and Visualisations

Remember the Guidelines for the Inner Work (page 25–26) whenever you devise your own visualisations. In the introduction you were encouraged to relax into the imaginal realm, to drift and dream. Now see how much further you get when you allow more time: you can judge this by how much richer and more textured your response feels.

Visualisation: Dreaming the Birch Dryad

Try this right now, or substitute twenty minutes of television, reading, or radio time later. Because this book is about *doing,* resolve to do this today. Read the following through a couple of times before trying it. Use all the guidelines you have read, and those that are below. Make sure that you are safe and comfortable in your physical space. Having allowed time, you can extend the relaxation period if that seems right to you. As you relax, affirm to yourself that you will have a pleasant experience and will come back to your normal state feeling refreshed and positive.

Take your time settling comfortably and then gently take three breaths— this will soon become a welcome signal for a focussed and pleasant imaginative exercise. Sense or feel or imagine with no effort or stress… Allow your imagination to "drift" into a copse of birch trees.

See the colours of nature, so relaxing on your inner eye. Feel the cool breeze… engage all your senses. Smell the freshness, feel the bark, hear the rustling leaves. How rich can you make the landscape? What is the weather? How warm is it? What season? Take time to evoke the feeling of space and peace and refreshment within yourself… Drift towards a particular tree that attracts you, and imagine the spirit of the tree as a dryad, who is willing to share her wisdom.

Look at the tree or sit or lie beneath it as you think of the tree spirit. What does the dryad look like? From thinking and imagining in your earlier reading, you are now feeling with a deeper part of yourself.

Take time to let your own mind-pictures build, to make your own connection, evoking within yourself the feeling of the beauty, grace, and eager aliveness of the birch.

When you have a clear image and a sense of the essence of the tree, develop this into a profound realisation of the support of the universe, and a feeling of anticipation. Send a loving message to the tree. If you don't know what to say, remember that we all like receiving a compliment, and the birch is a tree of great beauty. Stroke its bark. Admire its colour, its shape, the texture of its twigs and leaves, and so on. Get a sense of communication from the spirit of the tree ... As you do, imagine the dryad shyly emerging from the trunk, or climbing down from a bough high above you. See yourself dancing with the dryad in your inner world for the joy of life and sharing a wordless sense of loving, shared experience.

Soon, you feel that it is time to return, and you want to, for this encounter will have given you gifts which you can bring back to your everyday world.

The dryad drifts away and becomes more transparent, sinking back into the trunk of the tree, and you feel the impulse of your physical body—the need to stretch and move and get on with life ... and as you feel this urge, the whole scene starts to fade. You are aware of your breathing, and with every breath the world reasserts itself, and the scene is gone, completely, and you gently open your eyes and move.

Remember all the guidelines for coming back quickly and easily to the apparent world, and always use your own common sense as well. Ground yourself; assert that you are back, have a drink, having allowed time to reflect and enjoy the positive feelings you have brought back.

Using the Visualisation Exercises

- Perform a tree visualisation every morning. Use the informal moving meditation in this chapter and vary it in content and length according to your needs each day, especially when you are in a hurry. Use more formal exercises whenever you have time.

- Try a night-time visualisation. You will probably drift to sleep during it, which is all to the good. Set your intent to have a sweet and refreshing night's sleep and to wake refreshed. Does this help you sleep soundly? There will be various night exercises relating to all the trees, so you can use whichever seems to fit how you feel.

- Use any of the visualisation examples as templates and adapt for different situations.

- Some visualisations use the image of the dryad as a teacher/ guide, and some do not, to reflect personal preferences. The image will be helpful to some and very off-putting to others. *Trust your instinct* to do the right thing to keep you on course. Adapt as you wish.

Craft Your Own Visualisations

Here are some visualisation ideas for you, for when your sense of anticipation seems to be hibernating! Do not worry about creating wonderful descriptive phrases. Just know what associations you are going to draw on, take your time to sense and feel, and relax.

By the magic of your inner understanding, you can freeze-frame a scene or speed up natural processes so that trees can travel from spring to autumn in the blink of an eye. You can use visualisation to travel through a complete season, and let your mood change in reflection, if that is appropriate. Follow the guidelines for beginning and ending, and don't think that visualisations have to be long to be intense! Quality is the important thing; use the examples below to craft "mini-visualisations" to fit into your routines.

Visualisation 1:
When you are depleted, connect to the energy of spring
Images that might be helpful: Winter turning to spring; the earth warming and the tree waking, the air softening and warming. Night changing to a beautiful dawn. Buds on twigs swelling and unfolding—by the magic of time, see this happening before your eyes until they reveal their perfect green spears. Green catkins dangling. Connect to the energy of spring and the promise of new initiatives through your breathing simply by setting your intent and allowing it to happen.

Visualisation 2:
Before a project, access your energy
Images that might be helpful: Young leaves unfurling. The birch as a living, decorated maypole, with ribbons flowing from it, a community dancing around it, and you joining in, setting the season for growth and new work. Lovers making birch twig tokens as they start their relationship. The sun through the leaves bringing the promise of summer. The earth warming, ready for growth. Connect to the burgeoning, fertile aspect of the birch, and through this, imagine creative energy welling up through your being.

Visualisation 3:
When you feel unsupported, connect to the strong growth of the birch
Images that might be helpful: A tall, mature birch; following the trunk down to the roots, and then imagine the roots snaking down through the earth. The root system spreading out into the stability and nurturing of the earth. A million tiny threadlike white roots feeding into the huge fibrous network, all feeding

into the tree base. The roots drinking in nutrients, and the nutrients carried to the whole tree. Through the pathways nourishing the tree, travel up the trunk to the canopy. Look out at the immensity and stability of the world—land, sky, topography, and weather all supporting growth.

This inner work will become a special time for you, so how many visualisations would you like to do in a week: one, two? Have you worked out which days suit you best? Will you do the morning or evening visualisations as well? Try different permutations for a week, and then, as usual, review and adapt to suit you.

Here is a sample of Visualisation 1. Try it if you wish to compare when you have crafted one yourself from the notes above. Then ask yourself: which do you engage with most deeply? Which was most effective? There is no sense of "better or worse" to your comparison; it's just interesting to see how the visualisation from your own brain is a product of exactly what you need at this time—and that is why you will increasingly adapt all that is written. Just remember to keep the overarching *spirit* of the tree quality to the fore, along with its essential benevolent nature towards all beings.

Sample Visualisation: *The Energy of Springtime*

To try when you have completed Visualisation 1, as a comparison with your own first experience.

> *As you approach your copse of birches, your eyes are filled with the blue of the sky, green of the grass, and shining bark of the trees. Feel that each tree is emanating a pulse, singing with life, making a reverberation that prompts a response from you. With your deep senses alert, you approach a tree and can hear a birch dryad, who describes the perfection of what you're seeing… listen to her:*

The birch dryad speaks:

On the edge of the copse, the hawthorn is opening into flower, and the scent of its creamy flowers steals onto the fresh breeze. In the heights of my birch tree, delicate flowers are dangling from my twigs, a promise of the invisible seeds that will later scatter in the breeze. Bees buzz and as you stretch with my tree, the sun warms the length of your body, imbuing you with the energy of springtime.

This burgeoning resonance evokes a deep response... of the imminence of new things, new initiatives, new impulses, buried in the fertile earth of imagination, but needing only the right conditions to be brought safely into the world. Do not speculate, just bask in dappled warm shade, in the feeling of your creative potential, which is in tune with the land and the trickle of life-giving waters. The creative urge is evoked joyously for change and transformation; we need to dance, to sing, to write, to garden, to explore, to cherish the things we love. This urge is deep within us all, heralded by the singing of the birds, and blown to us on the soft winds of spring. Fill yourself to the brim, and then feel the urge to make your goodbyes... and, in the usual way, allow the scene to fade and the everyday world to reassert itself.

Cultivating Simple Habits

As well as your short daily visualisation, aim to set your alarm to repeat affirmations at break times through the day. Have a specific image of spring which you can call up in a moment, to evoke a feeling of anticipation at any time. Carry a small notebook to record small happy thoughts and events, then review them each evening to send you into sleep in a state of optimism and anticipation. This is an important part of conscious noticing and being grateful in the moment.

Making Specific Plans

Now choose a small change that you wish to make in your life—nothing that you feel too emotional about, so you can easily maintain your "tree stance" of dispassionate witness through the process. And nothing too complex, so it can be easily achieved. Get used to making small changes that you complete successfully so that you develop a habit of success. Here are some *aides-mémoire* to help towards a successful outcome.

Keep a piece of birch handy so that you see it often and it can remind you of your project. Evoke the anticipatory energy of the birch within yourself every day and make a tree map of your intention. A tree map is a creative way of exploring any situation, and making visible its associations, using a tree as a template. It is easiest explained by a diagram.

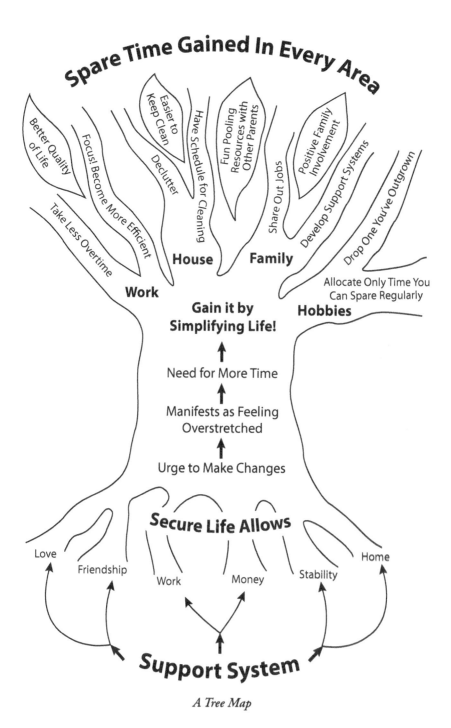

Spare Time Gained In Every Area

Better Quality of Life

Focus! Become More Efficient

Easier to Keep Clean

Declutter

Have Schedule for Cleaning

Fun Pooling Resources with Other Parents

Share Out Jobs

Positive Family Involvement

Develop Support Systems

Drop One You've Outgrown

Take Less Overtime

Work

House

Family

Allocate Only Time You Can Spare Regularly

Hobbies

Gain it by Simplifying Life!

↑

Need for More Time

↑

Manifests as Feeling Overstretched

↑

Urge to Make Changes

Secure Life Allows

Love

Friendship

Work

Money

Stability

Home

Support System

A Tree Map

Approach this in a relaxed frame of mind. Draw a tree (we are going to work from the roots to the leaves), then write under the ground all that supports and stabilises you. All these factors allow you space to be aware of the urge to change rising within. On the bottom of the trunk write what the change will be and how it manifests—the state you're in at the present.

Work up the trunk to the boughs, which denote areas of your life. List easily achievable steps, tiny adjustments and improvements—as many as you need—to change through these areas and to achieve your goals, which you can picture as leaves or fruit. The roots feed each part of you; do name them—there will be many. The soil is ultimate nourishment, containing resources such as love and peer support to draw on. Doodling with different coloured pens helps you to group sections until you have put down all the associations with the steps to achieve your goals.

If you feel reluctant to do this, then put those feelings on your diagram as well, perhaps in a specific colour, and then connect to solutions. Remember to keep your optimistic connection to the birch anticipation during the exercise.

As an example, suppose you feel *laziness*; feeling that *it's easier to keep things the same* is a barrier for you. Smile, then enjoy finding how to sidestep that attitude. You might draw lines leading from it entitled *small steps* and *reward*, and then leading from that, the miniscule first step and one or two rewards itemised. These might include simple reminders of feelings of wellbeing you'll get from achievement, or promising yourself tea and biscuits when a task is finished. All this is entirely up to you. Have fun!

Your tree diagram should ultimately result in a few key steps towards your goal, each easily achievable. Examples of easily achievable steps might be:

- To improve social/work/life contacts—ring five contacts/businesses/clubs every day

- To research family tree—email all known relatives over the next week

- To develop a positive family routine—read the children a bedtime story every night

Each step is simple. Each is achievable. Each gets you nearer to the stated goal. More steps can be added until you reach your objective. When you've done this for your aims, put the steps on the fridge or by the bed.

Look at your tree diagram every day, after your birch morning meditation, and decide which steps you will take that day. If mornings are too rushed for this, then check it every evening and plan for the next day. Then sleep sweetly, knowing that you are moving incrementally towards your aims. You are moving steadily, with lightness and anticipation: it's a wonderful feeling.

Birch Night-Time Visualisation

To finish this chapter, here is our first night-time visualisation of the birch. At any time during it you might drift off to sleep, and this is just fine. Sweet dreams!

As you relax before sleep, remind yourself of your true inner feelings, and with each breath, begin to evoke them—contentment, stability, and gentle anticipation. Do not struggle or strain; just allow the maelstrom of surface feelings to quieten down so that more peaceful impulses can arise naturally in your body and mind. Without emotion, let yourself drift along into a waking dream, so that, with all your worries left behind, you are walking towards a large copse of mature birch trees.

You pause, admiring the focus of each leaf searching out its own patch of sunlight, planted on the sandy soil, and the shallow, exposed edges of the roots that anchor the slender silver trunks.

Your sense of relaxed anticipation grows as you approach, and then you are in the centre of a circle of trees with sunlight streaming down on you, and the edges of the drooping thin black twigs and green spear-shaped leaves making a curtain around you.

Take your time, and look around the circle at each tree; see their different shapes, heights, the markings of their bark . . . each is unique and beautiful. Each has grown in response to natural conditions, just as you have. The tree that gets the sun first in the morning will have slightly more mature leaves. The tree that takes the brunt of the prevailing wind will be the most bent and asymmetric, whilst those on the sheltered side of the circle will be most evenly grown. Each has adapted; each is flexible; each is uniquely itself. So are you.

Ask the circle of trees for support, in words, in a gesture, a movement, however feels right to you. Open yourself to the blessings of the trees, and feel a response from one in particular . . . as a welcoming breeze, a rustle of leaves, or just a feeling . . . relax and wait, a response will come. In your dreamlike state of pure contentment, climb until you find yourself safely sitting on the tree's first major branch, with your back leaning against the trunk. Maybe you are usually scared of heights, but in this scene you feel completely secure and in charge, and enjoy the novel sensation. The leaves are now whispering very near to you and are half-concealing the view. Below you are more leaves hanging, and past them you see the ground, with its thin grass. Through the leaves above, the blue sky shines. This seat is the traditional resting place of the spirit of every tree, and here you feel closest to its green wisdom. Whisper to the tree; thank it for its help. Relax into rightness, contentment, and harmony you imagine becoming the mainstay of your life, allowing you to move creatively to the place where you should be.

And when you have spent long enough in your tree-sanctuary, thank the dryad spirit of the tree, and effortlessly swing down to the ground. You are once again in the centre of the copse, bathed in the green-golden glow of sunlight through leaves. Feel it wrapping around you as you drift off to sleep, smiling in anticipation of a wonderful day tomorrow.

2

Birch and the Magic of Intent

Tree quality: They are not judgemental.

The birch is the "pioneer" tree: it has a mission.

So do you.

From the ending of the Ice Age to the present day, the birches' tiny air-borne seeds were and are the first of the tree-seeds to colonise new or disturbed ground. Change—sometimes miniscule—prompts their germination and growth, and opportunities in our lives activate us in the same way. Like our ideas, birch seeds will not germinate unless certain factors are in place to nurture and encourage growth. The tree's opportunities are clear soil and the right temperature and climatic conditions. Our opportunities might be physical and practical—offers of work, of relationships, changes in status and finances—or they might be internal, triggered by books and ideas.

Every day we scatter, as the birch does its seeds, not only physically as fragments of hair, skin, and expired breath, but millions of ideas, thoughts, impulses, remarks, and emotional reactions to the day's events. And almost all of our mental and emotional "scatterings" are reactive, emerging from past conditioning and expectations automatically: we "play the same record." As we get older, we can even recognise ourselves going through our script of responses, and we can feel exhausted and despairing in equal measure.

The Intent to Change

To change anything, we consciously dream our future in our inner reality. Each of our acts started as a thought, so first we activate our imagination, lest we restrict ourselves by the poverty of our aspiration.

To be blown by the winds of life takes no energy, but shaping our futures requires intent, and maintaining that intent takes energy and commitment. The birch's mission might seem simple as its intent is already set in the heart of every seed: to grow and reproduce. But at the most basic level, *so is ours*. From the millions of life choices we might make, if life is to be meaningful, our mission is to develop the inner sense urging us to grow and express our creativity.

We can go off on a new path simply on the basis of whim or inspiration. A sudden offer or opportunity allows us a thrilling "what the hell" moment that can change our lives irrevocably in a flash, and these impulses can be inspirational or destructive. Positive lasting changes, which affect the way we grow as surely as the prevailing wind shapes the young tree, require our *intent*.

Scattering ideas without thought every minute is the habit we are starting from. Wedded to this is a classic habit that stops us achieving and keeps us in our present reality. It's wishful thinking, and it's non-specific, colouring our daydreaming in a rosy glow, a brighter future that is a retreat from reality. Most importantly, this saps our energy for actual change.

Why would we want to escape from our lives when we can transform and enrich them? And the first thing we need to succeed is *clarity of intent*. To know and recognise success we must know what we're aiming for in the first place. Unlike the birch, whose life will take a prescribed course, we must make choices to decide where we want to go, the shape our life will take, and what the fruits of that life will be.

For clarity, we realise the need *for space*. For new ideas and initiatives we have to clear the ground in order to give the new seed a fighting chance of growing up healthily. Our lives are crowded—we feel time-poor and space-poor, loaded down with demands of the outside world and the abundance of our possessions. Simplifying and prioritising, whilst being fair to all and maintaining your place and contacts in the outside world, form much of the work you will do.

Intent—Clarity—Space

Write these three seed requirements in your notebook—give them a page each or put them into columns for comparison. Play with the ideas they bring to mind. The work is underway.

The Birch and Spiritual Hygiene

Cleanliness and hygiene are associated with the birch, and are necessary components of our getting clear for the work. The very name of the birch, coming from the proto-Indo-European root *bhereg*, means white, bright, to shine. Repeating the word whilst visualising its bright beauty can help evoke within the bright clarity we need to forge our path. Do it now, and then listen to the message of the birch dryad.

The birch dryad speaks:

I am the white one, a marker you can look to. In your own world-landscape, I remind you of your individual uniqueness, your gentle, sure ability to claim your space, to clear the way for your future growth. I reach to the sky, but my journey started as a tiny seedling. See yourself as a clear, shining, healthy being, growing in the landscape. Stand or sit straight now, and evoke within yourself an energy glowing with clarity, which you can breathe in and out. Your skin is shining like the bark of the birch. As my birch has one instinct—to grow—so you can fill yourself with one intent, fresh and clear, which fuels your impetus to grow and fulfil your destiny. All else will spring from that intent.

When we are getting down to the work of change, we must feel that the specific ideas that will change our lives to aid this intent are reasonable and within the scope of what we can achieve at the moment. Otherwise we're just back in the world of daydreams. We live in a world of restrictions—of age, gender, finance, and culture. These are part of the human condition and should be viewed as exciting challenges that shape our journey through life. Regarding them as negatives simply doesn't benefit us. For good or ill—but most certainly for growth and development—they have formed us, and we are here now and ready to change. Be glad. Every restriction can help to guide you or can be a challenge to be overcome. Welcome it all; embrace your humanity!

Remember the tree-quality for this chapter: They are not judgemental.

The place where we are now is the result of the choices we have made so far. So we will be grownups, honouring those choices and working within their restrictions. Harsh judgements are useless. Directed at ourselves, they keep us stuck, diminished, and guilty. Directed at others, they keep us self-satisfied and small-minded. So we must lose the habit. Here, the regular quiet contemplative practice of "being as a tree" will allow us the mental and emotional space gradually to ditch the judgemental thoughts, which suck energy from our lives as the undertow of the wave sucks the sea back. Let's get on and get clear.

Getting Ourselves Clear for Action: The Birch as Cleanser

Folklore marks the birch out as vital to the health and hygiene of many traditional communities, on both physical and magical levels. It is an astonishingly versatile tree and has been well used by many cultures. Learning about its particular gifts and associations can spark our imaginations, and we can develop an individual way of working with these gifts to further our intentions. But first, the practical applications of our pioneer.

Kitchen bowls and artefacts were made from birch wood because of its natural antiseptic properties. It is astringent and has been used seasonally as a cleanser. Learn its manifold gifts to health from any herbal book. The leaves are diuretic, anti-inflammatory, effective for urinary tract infections, and rheumatic complaints. The sap can guard against kidney stones and treat gout and skin ailments, whilst as a liquid applied externally it relieves muscle ache. The bark can promote healing of wounds.

Its sap runs so strongly and sweetly in the spring that it can be harvested for wines and cordials then, giving its gift prolifically without harm to the tree. Many winemakers today eagerly anticipate the spring sap, setting their intent and preparing carefully to harvest nature's bounty.

Birch's association with spring and new beginnings spills over into its more esoteric uses. In the spring of our lives, cradles traditionally made of birch wood protect babies against the glamour of the faery folk. Many tribes combine the twigs with red ribbon for protection against evil or, more prosaically, against lightning, the illuminating flash that can be so destructive—like our sudden impulses when we are in our favourite "what the hell" mood!

The clear astringent properties of the birch are enshrined in many customs. "Beating the bounds" is a strange practice in England and Wales, which predates the Norman Conquest and is still carried out in some parishes today. The parish boundary is walked, led by a priest, with regular stops for boys to beat the boundary marker stones with birch boughs, whilst prayers are offered for protection and blessings upon the parish. What a fabulous ancient example of maintaining the integrity of a whole landscape and the community living within it.

The witch's broom, already mentioned—with its ash handle, willow ties, and a birch twig brush—has cleansing implications way beyond the simple removal of dust. We can assume that any cleaning it does will resonate with the healing, antiseptic qualities of the tree on a magical level, cleaning the house aura at the same time. As well as acting on the landscape, and our own houses, birch is used to cleanse our bodies—Scandinavian saunas use birch twigs to stimulate the cleansing processes of the body.

One more aspect of the birch is relevant here, especially if we are considering it as we set our magical intent. The tree has a common neighbour. A distinctive, brilliantly coloured toadstool, the poisonous and psychoactive fly agaric (*amanita muscaria*), grows beneath it, and because of this the birch is associated (particularly by Siberian shamans) with magic and the underworld. So let's allow a little magic into our process of change!

A cluster of these red-capped, white-flecked toadstools nestling in the bole of the silver birch is a magical sight. Picture it now, the colours so exotic that they might indicate a portal to another world. They do, for they can lead us into the world of the imagination, where our active engagement can provoke real transformation in the real world. And, given the very dangerous nature of the toadstools, in the imagination is the safe and only way that we will study them!

Defining Your Intent

What path will we take, what ideas will we use to manifest our deep intent to grow, to change, to be creative? Wealth, for example; it's widely understood that we all want it. But is that true? It's worth repeating that goals are not daydreams. Goals are specific and achievable, so they come with new sets of responsibilities. In my daydreams, I can be a millionaire without any responsibility. But if I set it as a goal, then I must be clear that

I must develop the kind of business-mind that will find it stimulating and enjoyable staying in charge of all that moolah.

The birch has its intent built in, and *so do we.* But we have so many possibilities, we need to search for what is going to feed us and allow us to express ourselves perfectly in the world.

Go into reverie and identify the goals that are most important to you. How to do that?

After the birch movements, when you have gained a degree of tree-detachment, sit quietly and allow your deep feelings to well up. See which feelings you most need to have as a constant in your life. Allow them to drift as cloud-words across the blue sky of your imagination … security … challenge … stimulation … love … warmth … and think of how these already manifest in your life, to a greater or lesser extent.

Make It Simple and Specific

Security can be very simply subdivided into physical, financial, and emotional. Respectively, we meet these through home, job, and friends/family. Let us assume that the second is slightly lacking; there is always too much month at the end of the money, or never quite enough to treat your children as you would like to or to return hospitality to your well-heeled friends.

It might seem simple to set your intent for this one: to earn/obtain more money. But there are a lot more creative ways of looking at this. The situation might prompt you to examine your lifestyle and expectations. After all, a really simple way to feel wealthier is simply to move to a smaller house that is cheaper to run. One definition of wealth might be never having to worry about the size of the heating bills!

One way of being hospitable is giving people a creative alternative to the boring round of drinks parties and dinners that are their norm. Example: making a date with another family, or a group of singletons, to mix up Christmas cakes together. Everyone would be involved in the preparation, weighing and stirring, and with a simple snack to help the work along; it might be a refreshing change from expensive entertaining. And you see what the example has done? Using an idea already in our culture, you've made your event seasonal, just as the first and the last picnics of the season are. All these are social activities that do not stretch the budget, and you will accrue golden memories of simple times with friends that can make you feel very wealthy. We are responding to the rhythms of the natural world, just as the trees would expect us to. Consider these matters for now, and work on them in the study section.

Now, after thought and working with the study materials so far, we have honed down to a specific end goal to make a change in our lives. The next stage in keeping clear is to break down the way we will achieve it into small, doable stages. Holding a new seed in your hand, it is impossible to say what it will become. Yet, viewing the mature tree first, the journey from seedling to sapling to tree is logical to us.

So, when you have dreamed your aims, with all the emotion and expectation and anticipation you can muster, fast forward in your imagination a year and see where you want to be, what you want to have achieved, then plot the course there by logical steps.

Set Your Seed for Success

Make step 1 *so simple* that you can do it now, or today, or this week, with one phone call, one decision, anything to get you started. And then plot out from step 2 to however-many-it's-going-to-take in a diary and check it each week. Keep your intent alive by evoking anticipation every day.

The birch dryad speaks:

As I grow, I dream. The sun, the wind, the rain, the snow, the earth all nurture as my dream manifests into a mature tree of stature, beauty, and grace. Dream your intent, and keep hold of your dream in your heart. My dream translates daily into bud, leaf, branch, bark.

Similarly, your dream will manifest in action, in change, in development, in new relationships and directions, *if* you can hold that dream, that intent, and keep referring back to it. As you do your regular tree meditation/movement, whisper your dream to the natural world; clear your mind each morning to keep your intent shining like birch bark gleaming with rain. Then go about your everyday jobs, confident that by honouring your mundane obligations and making mental, emotional, and physical time for your objective, you are furthering it.

Resolve-Sappers

Sap is the life-blood of the plant. What might leach it, draining your energy, your resolve, your intent?

How can we not be judgemental, when we're basically so flawed and are constantly making mistakes? If you have transgressed your moral code, or acted in a way that makes you feel ashamed, you have to acknowledge it, but then don't waste energy on judgement: recognise that it wasn't the first and won't be the last time. In easy stages:

- Acknowledge your mistake.

- Put it into the wider context of your life— get the tree perspective.

- Do your utmost quickly to put things right.

- Do something to affirm your intent to do better in future.

- Move on.

But what if putting things right is more problematical? Or someone will not accept an apology? That's a pity, and asking them just what it would take to move you both along positively might, if it doesn't get an answer, at least show your sincerity. But if it's a no-go, then you just have to remember that what goes around comes around. The reparation you decide to make—of time, commitment, or money to a good cause, perhaps—might not ever be known by the person you've wronged, but in the invisible reality of life, your *sincere recognition* of an imbalance and *intent* to square your accounts is all-important. Leave the other person to their situation; you will be clear.

Magic starts from feeling clear and comfortable, so keep yourself in that state. And outstanding issues? Your life is too full and exciting to give time or energy to them; keep clearing!

Intent and Expectation

I love paradox, so it makes perfect sense to me to say that, whilst setting your intent, you should not expect anything! Here's an example:

Home life is stressful, so you set up your intent for it to improve. *(This is assuming non-abusive relationships within the parameters of acceptable behaviour, of course.)*

You do a birch visualisation; you fill yourself with the possibility for transformation. But in doing so you set up a series of expectations: that your partner will become helpful, your children polite, your parents less judgemental, and your siblings friendlier.

This is an example of how not to do it! Putting the responsibility for change onto anyone or everyone else *never works*. And your inevitable disappointment makes the situation more stressful, because it is compounded by your sense that "It isn't fair!"

Now let's rerun the example. For true transformation, you would do the work but dismiss any expectations of others.

So you imbue yourself with the birch spirit of transformation, and visualise the steps that might help you achieve it, recognising that the people around you will be what they will be, and that we're all basically trying to do the best we can. Allow people to be what they must be, and support them by thinking the best of them.

Some of the steps might involve asking for help, of course. And your knowledge of your loved ones will show you how slowly you have to go with this! But the trust for magical transformation comes from and is carried by *you*. *You* must: get up earlier, clear the paperwork, instigate "work hours" to share the cleaning, make cooking a fun activity, establish kids' bedtime routine to give you grownup time in the evening. Why not establish a personal bath routine to gain physical, mental, and emotional space for yourself? Or use your time on public transport for this!

Keep On Keeping On

You can adapt the points above to whatever is relevant to your situation. Do the real-world work gently, firmly, and with the support of your dreaming and imaginative work every day. Miraculous results have occurred from such simple beginnings. But a great occultist once said that given the choice of hard labour or magic, the former is the easier! "Keeping on keeping on" requires not so much effort, but constant awareness. Keying into the birch tree's remit for witnessing and allowing events to take their course, removing the human anxiety, and simply watching your progress day by day—without judgement—will help keep the end goal in sight. It's worth it.

Some days you will forget, or slip up, or not live up to your own high expectations. As you drift into sleep, review the day gently: sit at the base of the birch tree and be cleansed and made ready for a sweet night's sleep, to start again tomorrow.

Along with anticipation, think about not expecting anything—it's very freeing, and really adds to your sense of gratitude for every positive happening. Just accept.

The birch dryad speaks:

Through the seasons I grow. My intent stays sure, and every year I am higher and broader. The rain soaks my trunk and drips from my leaves to feed the ground. As I bend in the gales, I am strengthened even as my leaves tumble in a shower of gold. I dream through the cold times that give me rest and rejoice in the slow movement of my life through the winter. I welcome the promise of spring, and the falling of the sugar snow that aids the running of my sap, before I wake to the new year. Each is a part of tree-life, and I accept all and keep my intent.

You might think ruefully that the life of the birch is more predictable and therefore easier to accept than that of a human! But, thinking back over life, your human patterns are not that different. Take the example of falling in love, making a mistake, messy emotions, becoming disentangled, falling in love again … we've all done it.

When we know what our intent has been, then we can understand our lives so far. And most of us have very simple aims; after meeting our needs for survival according to our cultural conditioning, then we need affection and connection. Hopefully, working with the trees will broaden our understanding of the myriad ways that can be fulfilled, so that we lose our desperate need for approval and *any* romantic attachment, no matter how unsuitable. We have an intent for a clearer life, connecting not only on the physical level, but on the imaginal, the emotional, the magical— and not only with our fellow humans but with all the natural world. It does take the pressure off having to be always in a relationship.

The growth of the birch is straight and tall, the trunk bare for much of its length before putting out branches. Its lesson is of new beginnings, and of focussing, to get where we want to be. Clearly marked on older trees are deep fissures in the bark like arrowheads pointing upwards, a visual reminder that along the length of our lives, we must maintain our focus. Enjoy the growth, celebrate every season as it passes, but keep awareness always on your ultimate intent: to develop in a way that feeds your deepest needs.

The Human Grove

Unless we're hermits, living alone in our own grounds, we're all in a human grove. In similar circumstances the sociable birch still rises upwards straight towards the sun.

Your life might be very overcrowded with people—physically in your home, mentally in your job, emotionally with family demands. If so, remember and visualise regularly those tight-packed birch saplings we've all seen on the side of the road. It seems as if they all spring from the same small piece of ground, yet as they grow, their intent to find their own share of the light and air they need to sustain them sends them up straight as an arrow to their goal.

This is the way you can grow with intent.

The birch is exposed in the landscape. It battles with the winds; it is hardy and resilient. *So are you.*

The birch burns hot and needs no other wood or lighting help. Its bark is so flammable that it can burn by itself without firelighters, supplying its own tinder and then strong logs to sustain the fire. It is ready. *So are you.*

Cultivate that self-sufficient attitude—not to exclude others, but more in a sense of always being personally ready, always prepared to make the effort, always enthusiastic.

The birch is light and clear; its leaves and boughs dance and shine with the elements. Lose your expectations. Lose your importance. Simplify and clean up your life. Take a leap of faith and follow your intent for a bright, shining future.

Lessons from the Birch

Intent

The birch dryad speaks:

The sun and air call to my shoots and saplings. My every instinct
is to focus into strong growth, to assume my proper shape.

You are familiar now with that sense of anticipation that makes life so vibrant,
and by feeling that way, you are attuning yourself to exciting and positive
developments.

If you have forgotten to jot down small instances of happiness, then
take a moment and think of five now, with maybe just a smile from a stranger
as the first. It is part of a magical process of recognition, for our experience
is made simply from what we focus on. A million impressions are there
for us every moment of every day, but the optimist and the pessimist will
allow very different images to come through—rainbows or dirty streets,
it's our choice. But it's not an escape from the world to notice the positive; the person who sees the rainbow is most likely to get busy and start
working to protect the environment. When you start to notice, you start
to care, to make connections, and to want to make a difference.

Hopefully, anticipation is becoming your default setting—even if it is a struggle on a cold wet morning. It is essential to be able to access this emotional response, for without it our energy plummets and all our good intentions fly out the window.

All the following are suggestions to get you started on this second phase of holding your intent. It is important that you own your work and develop it as appropriate to your life and circumstances.

Affirmations: Promoting the Mind-Set for Intent

I hope that you are finding affirmations to be valuable tools for maintaining focus, and that you are becoming creative in thinking them up. Have you tried putting different affirming words to favourite songs? Dancing round the kitchen as you sing?

Here are the suggestions to build on dealing specifically with the ideas in this chapter. Never do them by rote, automatically: take time to *feel* the reality of what you're saying, of your intent growing straight and strong. Allow the change in your mood to well up and become reinforced with every repetition. You might use boring tasks—such as ironing or bed changing—as a background to affirmation practice. Mix and match those below, which are all geared to natural change, growth, and focus. Which appeal most? Which help you to key into the feeling you want? Then make more affirmations specific to your focussed new projects.

Birch Affirmations

For anticipating new growth:
From seed to tree I grow.
I set my intent to grow into my true shape.
As I think, so I grow. I set my focus for _____ .

For peaceful anticipation:
The landscape is still and quiet.
My thoughts grow like seeds in the soil.
Through natural stages I grow, guided by my intent.
I relax into growth.
A new focus for life is expanding within me.

To make space for focus:
I inhabit clear space to focus, and I grow towards my goals.
My focus shines like the birch bark.
I focus like the straight birch.
I hold my intent in every cell; all my functions feed it.

Clarity and Cleansing

When setting a new intent, we first look backwards, and then around us, evaluating past projects, making a tree diagram or mind map to show exactly what worked and what didn't. Don't be scared to draw dead branches on your tree or to have the trunk struck by lightning to indicate profound failure. It is all a learning experience if you just take time to notice and learn the lessons, thus setting yourself up for success next time. Perhaps you are already having some successes after the new project exercise from the previous chapter. If so, you can fine tune that now, using some stages of the visualisation below if that is useful, but with pen and paper, grounding your ideas in a diagram.

Get into your birch-thought, then. Check that you are in tree-witnessing mode, so you don't get involved emotionally. Look backwards to past projects (learning an instrument, giving up smoking, and so on). Have you had lots of false starts? Have you had unreal, woolly expectations—more like dreams than plans? Have you overestimated the time or effort you can commit?

If you feel you have identified a pattern of behaviour, then the next stage is important. Before starting any new project, or the next stage of your present one, look critically at how you are tackling it and amend it by doing three things that reference the birch:

- Simplify the project. Lose all complexity; get down to your real intent.

- Imagine the clear landscape.

- Clean up your act; get some clarity to find simple solutions.

If things look too complex, then break the stages down further, attaching to them simple acts. For example, "Straight after _____, I'll do five minutes of guitar practice." Better still would be "*Before* I _____, I'll do five minutes of guitar practice." That should be simple enough to manage, so if you still can't stick to it, you can go back to the drawing board and work out just why not. There is always the possibility that you've chosen what you think you *should* do, and not what you really *want* to do. If that is the case, why would you persist? Give in gracefully; it could make you feel immediately lighter. Overestimating how much time you can commit is the biggest mistake, and one that almost everyone makes, so do be realistic. Five minutes every day is better than a guilt-ridden half hour once a week.

Remember the clear landscape of the birch as she grows. There is no undergrowth, and you too must make space if you are to succeed. Clear away extraneous things that will get in the way of achievement—that might be as simple as cutting down television viewing by an hour, or cutting one shopping trip each week. Physical cleansing is symptomatic of mental and emotional cleansing, so if you feel mired and stuck down, then clean and clear something; throw something away. Clear physical space encourages us to spread ourselves mentally and emotionally, which is why we tidy our desks ready for work the next day or wash the pots before we go to bed to get off to a good, clear start.

Set your intent ethically, with a full regard to all your family and work obligations, none of which should suffer from any new turns of your life.

When you are clear that you are acting fairly to all, then allocate your time and, with clarity, do something *every day* to forward your intent, no matter how small—and keep the birch in the forefront of your mind.

If you've tried this sort of thing before, why should this time be any different? Well, you've never had the support of the trees before now. You've always tried with a more limited perspective. Think of a time—not a strongly emotional one, just one of those many small disappointments—when you didn't succeed. Read the following, and then put down the book and take five minutes to think it through:

Connect to your tree-awareness now; let it evoke within you the strong sense of witnessing, of a larger perspective. You are standing in peace and timelessness, in acceptance of the seasons and of steady growth and development. Continue to breathe slowly with this feeling, until it fills you with serenity and loving detachment.

Then, holding that feeling, think back without any emotion at all to your small example of plans not coming to fruition—that feeling that life circumstances stop you from pursuing your intent. You seem to get scuppered either by other people or your own attitude. Be kind and smile to yourself whilst you're doing this: trees are compassionate!

When you look back, chances are you will see all the human interactions that muddy the waters when you are trying to achieve. You'll notice how you respond when you should just let go; how you are deflected into disagreements; how your ego demands that you stand up to something that your soul would say is not worth the effort, or that is demeaning to your sense of yourself. Love that person that you have been; bless every success and every failure. Then re-evoke within yourself the core feeling of the birch—the simplicity of growing as you should, making your way and allowing everyone else to do the same. Affirm your boundaries, knowing that you are not eroding your loving connections by doing so, but are putting in place a harmony of being which all will benefit from.

Then allow the scene to fade, and return to everyday activity, feeling wonderful.

This is the way to make plans: allow drifting time for the inspiration you can get from dreaming with the birches *before* using your logical mind to define and focus your intent.

Evoke the feeling of intention for your new life, and, on the screen of your imagination, see what images support that feeling. You should be able to move in imagination into the birch copse, or sit under a mature tree, or make your way through a plantation of living silver trunks, very easily by now. Never neglect this inner dreaming process; it keeps you on track.

Doing things in threes seems to be both pleasing and symbolic, so don't think that these changes will happen only in your physical mundane life; consider also your mental and emotional life. Then think of intents that support each other and that are easily doable—and if these evoke a positive, expansive response, you will know that you're on track on your spiritual journey!

Just as you did before, when you have had your dreaming time, then ground your ideas by producing a tree-map of what you've learnt. Intertwine the different sections sinuously, like the branch system of a tree, so that each has its own space for light and air.

The Reality Behind the Reality

If you're ready to try another of these exercises, then this time, instead of small, easily achievable objectives, we can place intent for more nebulous qualities— quality of life, or more love or companionship, for example—which demands a much longer focus and requires regular reviews. In this way, we go deeper into what we really want from our practical changes. But every aim, no matter how nebulous or seemingly ambitious, will still be broken down into simple, achievable steps.

An example might be setting your intent to enjoy harmonious relationships at work. This is the deeper need, which might manifest practically as a wish to get to the job you should have, with colleagues who respect you—an idea that usually never gets beyond the realm of wishful thinking.

The Physical Plane

- Firstly, decide to do your present job as best you can; have clarity around your responsibilities and abilities.

- Next, be happy with where you are—and if you're seriously discontented, then do make an effort to count every single blessing. After all, many people can only dream of the security of a job and regular wage or salary.

- Determine to respond from your new "tree-stance" when you are in the workplace.

- Distance yourself from human pettiness by connecting to a larger perspective every morning—two minutes on arrival at work, in the cloakroom, reinforcing your birch connection.

- Allow time to evoke harmony and security, so it can flood through you throughout the day to maintain your intent. Devise a simple affirmation to support this process.

You now have the support of the forest to keep you in balance throughout the day. A simple rhyme that can easily be brought to mind might help you to key into it. Don't worry, anything that occurs will do—your subconscious is not a poetry critic, and actually, the simpler the better. Two examples:

I'm in tune with the team,
Work goes like a dream.

With birch's help I work with ease,
My colleagues help me; the job's a breeze.

I'm actually embarrassed writing doggerel so dreadful; my only excuse to the reader is that I've found that such jingles do work.

The Mental Plane

- Start a study/reading course that will enhance your job prospects. By not being so emotionally involved with work processes, you will have freed up the mental space to do this.

- Read up on your present job—doing things well can become addictive!

The Emotional Plane

- Engage with work only on a professional level.

- But do always be professional!

- Remember, even if your job is your vocation, it's still not your life.

Do not fight every tiny point; do not get involved in power plays. Do your job to the best of your ability. Work in a way that gains you a reputation for fairness, consistency of performance, and reliability. Be a good team player, but remember that it is just a work team. Don't mix up your responses—you don't have to act as if colleagues are friends. This also applies to the volunteer work you do or the school duties with other parents. These can require more tact, as such groups often contain people who are looking for friendship and support, but extend it wisely! This alone will save you a huge amount of energy.

Then, to save even more energy and improve your quality of life: leave work behind when you leave work! If your job won't fit into a box, then at least have designated work times at home and stick to them. Allow quality time every day with friends and family. This is essential to increase the harmony of your relationships, which are also a part of your focus.

Maintaining a balance allows you to be fulfilled in all aspects of your life. Allow time for gratuitous acts of care and thought—sending a card, ringing someone, making a favourite cake. This habit will spill over into your work life, making you more considerate and generous to colleagues—a sure-fire way to promote harmony and make the workplace pleasanter. And then maybe your mental work might not result in you leaving your present job, but in applying for promotion within the organisation. Who can tell? The important thing is that, by setting your intent, you are taking incremental steps that actually improve your life situation *now*.

So keep at the forefront of your mind:

No problem can be solved from the same level of consciousness that created it.

A Quick Check-In

Are you really changing the way you view the world? Think back over a few days. If you are drawing on new areas, such as the imagination, evocation, checking bodily responses, trusting your feelings, and broadening your horizons so that you take the heat off of your human contacts, chances are you are beginning to. Well done!

This sort of work is deceptively simple, for it puts you in an attitude of awareness of intent, an awareness you can build on for more ambitious aims.

If you enjoy tackling your work via mapping and diagrams, you can play with any initiative and the stages of how to achieve it. How does that work for you? Do you prefer lists and a more structured approach? Remember, it's all down to you—choose a method you can enjoy, to help you throughout your life.

Visualisation Suggestions

Play with these ideas to support and help you maintain your intent. Work on feeling your focus running through you, as sap runs through a tree.

Visualisation 1:
In difficult circumstances, connect to the hardiness of the birch
Images that might be helpful: A crowded thicket of birch; the ground choked with brambles and undergrowth. You as a sapling, stretching up to your own space. Birch hardiness and endurance running through you; roots reaching deep down. "Veins" in a living layer under the bark feeding you, supplying what you need; the beautiful bark which protects and shields the living fibres of the tree. Effortlessly, grow past your restrictions. The wind in the upper branches; the promise of a wider world.

Visualisation 2:
When you lack enthusiasm, connect to birch focus
Images that might be helpful: Bright spring days. Sap rising and increasing and pouring through the tree, pulled irrevocably by capillary action. A sweet, reinvigorating river of nutrients. Spear-like leaves unfolding, catkins and seeds in a cycle of life which includes you. The sun pouring down, energising your physical body. The moon flooding you every night with magical silver inspiration.

Visualisation 3:
When the job seems too big and you can't find your way to the next stage, connect to the witnessing spirit
Images that might be helpful: The birch copse in summer. Contact the birch dryad. Distinguish every separate spot of green—leaf, blade of grass, herb foliage. Your perspective returning; the glory of the green world and your rightful place in it.

Observing dispassionately; no need to understand and know. Trusting the wider universe; the natural world; loving and appreciating your life exactly as it is. Trusting that all change will be for the good, as the living world unfolds its pattern to you.

Remember, the time of the birch is spring, and you can always access this energy, for any purpose. This is when the birch is focussed on producing new growth, flowers and leaves. And it is the time when it is most unencumbered: the undergrowth that will smother the forest floor later in the year is not yet not sapping other living things.

So, no undergrowth to slow you down, clear skies, clear ground—ideal opportunities and great starting points for developing your own visualisations. Trees do not grow in the same way all through the seasons; spring is the time for them to reach upwards, with intent, and only later do they increase in girth.

Practical Work

Grounding with practical work is a necessary part of the process, so keep walking round your neighbourhood and lingering under your favourite birch tree. Nothing can replace actual experience of the natural world. Other suggestions for connecting to the practical energy of birch:

- Take a cleansing bath with birch essence before a new project.

- Have a sauna and a detox, especially in the spring.

- Imbibe the essence of the birch; breathe it in through use of the imagination. Flower essence manufacturers credit the birch with the ability to broaden your vision, losing your worries in a wider view of the world, which gives you empathy and serenity. All of which sounds very much like what we are gaining by connecting to the tree in our inner vision.

- Clean your space physically—you can make a birch broom for this.

- Keep a straight birch stick visible to remind you of your intent.

- Write your intent on a piece of birch bark.

- Take a walk to your nearest birch regularly; align yourself with its trunk and feel your focus.

- Light a birch fire, using the bark and twigs as tinder. See the bright flame leaping straight up to its goal. Watch how cleanly it burns, with hardly any ash. Think of intent and clarity. Think of simplicity.

- Look at clumps of birch, or pictures if there are none in your area. How do they accommodate each other? How do they transform to their true shape when they have the space?

- Press birch leaves and make spear and arrow collages for cards.

- Use spear-shaped leaves to make prints.

Being Non-Judgemental

Judging others and situations takes too much energy that we need in order to keep focussed on our intent, so we need to practice letting go of that attitude, which is incredibly deeply ingrained in all of us. It's a real challenge, but those negative responses are meaningless from the trees' perspective, so viewing things from their standpoint can support your new intentions.

Start by looking again at your birch morning meditation. Take time now to customise it to include this component. It is important that you take charge of any changes; put your full intent into crafting the right thing for you—you know your own weaknesses and what needs most work. Consciously decide to shed your critical judgements of people. Does any particular person or behaviour spring to mind?

This doesn't mean compromising your ethics or sense of morals. You might be surprised at how many judgements you make that are about completely surface things, and underneath, the people guilty of them are lovely human beings, kind and generous. Other people are allowed their life choices, just as you are allowed yours.

Losing judgement, losing unreal expectations that others will conform to your view, that your way is the only right way, is very freeing. When you lose your sense of entitlement and feeling let down when your expectations are not met, you become sensitised and appreciative of all help actually offered to you. It's another of those glorious paradoxical ways that the universe seems to validate your new way of looking at things.

Suggestion for visualisation:

When you think of your loved ones, put them in their own birch glade, adjacent to yours. You can see them clearly through the twigs, but allow them the space to be whatever they must, without having any opinions about it. Perhaps, it occurs to you, they feel as weighted down by your expectations as you do by theirs? Then see the green, harmonious aura of the birches surrounding you all in loving, non-judgemental energy. Take your time to see yourself clear and full of intent and anticipation, ready for the day ahead.

As always, this is just an example to try out when you have time. The more you enter the imaginal realms and allow time for these ideas to surface, the more creative you will become in creating your own adaptations.

Collect a piece of birch with catkins, each one representing a family member. They grow from the same twig, and are fed through the same system, yet all develop individually to produce the seeds of their own immortality. If it's not spring, then sketch them, copying a picture. Name your catkins!

Lastly: The Magic

Remember the connection between the birch and the fly agaric mushroom, which finds the perfect habitat amongst the birch roots. Even the most open, light, and dancing of trees has a core of mystery and magic at its base, and hopefully you will be getting a clear sense from your tree meditations of the vast scope of the worldview which is available when you expand your vision of what is possible.

Magic does happen—non-manipulative, totally natural magic, which shows that we are in tune with the flow of our lives. Becoming aware of this, it is surprising just how often we will make or hear a chance remark that sets our feet on a different path, or opens a door, or points us in the direction in which we should go. But we must stay aware, for at the moment these chances are passing us by every day, unnoticed. To start the magical process, we set our intent sincerely and intending the good of all, and send it winging out into the universe: through our breath, through our actions, through our inner imaginings. We see it whispered through the land by the leaves of the birch and spread wide with her seeds. When we visualise the birch and our intent, and we imagine a red toadstool with white spots shining out from the leaf and twig litter at the bole of the tree, we are keeping attuned to the possibility of magic in life—the sudden revelation that mystery and difference can bring to transform us. And isn't that secretly what we long for?

But beware: the active principles of the fly agaric are very dangerous; only work with it in the inner world, and respect its dangers in the outer!

Lastly, imagine ten impossible things—doodle, map, or draw them. Have fun. Let's not be serious all the time. The imagination is activated by joy. And a life fuelled by limitless imagination tempered with common sense is a life where your magical intent can successfully manifest.

Night-Time Visualisation: The Birch Fire

In your imagination, walk into a copse of birch trees. What season of the year is it? Imagine clearly their bright trunks, branches, and dark twigs; are they in leaf, bud, or flower? High above, the sky is a clear blue, and you hear birds singing. All is calm, all is well, and, like the trees, you know you are in the right place. Relax and lie down under a tree. Look up into the tattered green curtain of birch leaves and twigs above you, with the blue sky showing through. The scene evokes a sense of timelessness; there is no rush. Your stress and worry leave your body and sink down into the forest floor. Breathe in timelessness with each in-breath; breathe out stress.

When you feel ready, rise and walk around the copse, saying hello to your cousins, the trees. Stroke their silken trunks; run your hands over the deep, dark furrows in their bark; look up the trunk to the junction of the first large branch of each tree, and whisper hello to its dryad.

Take your time.

Tilt back your head by each tree, until you are looking up into its highest branches, growing straight at the top of the straight trunk. At each tree, allow the straight growth and aspiration of the birch to evoke in you a feeling of focus, of sureness, of growing towards your goals, just as the tree grows to the sun and stars.

In the centre of the copse, a fire is laid on the beaten earth. When you have completed the round of trees, you walk to this lattice of birch wood. It is made of thrown branches that are long dead, with an inner heart of kindling of birch bark and brittle twigs.

This is right, whisper the leaves. Man needs trees to live and can coexist happily with them. Treat their gifts with care and respect, and be welcome to them. The trees willingly give their service.

With a sense of the symbolism of the act, you put a light deep into the heart of the fire. The kindling catches, and a plume of smoke rises

straight into the air. Twigs crackle, the tiny flames begin to leap, pulled
upwards in a dance by the air drawn through the lattice of sticks, until
the fire blazes with a hot, bright flame. Feed the fire, and then sit by it,
enjoying the bright heart as the wood crumbles into nothingness, for the
birch makes hardly any ash. Tilt your head to watch the top of the thin
stream of smoke rising high in the sky, straight as a plumb line. Your focus
flows as straight, from the hot, bright energy of your intention and focus,
fed by your actions, into an unknown, mysterious, and wonderful future.
All is well. Take a few minutes simply to be, to receive the wisdom of the
watching trees, whilst your over-busy mind relaxes. Tree wisdom is in
being in this perfect place, sustained, nourished, and focussed, without
any strain, on the rightness that is your path.

3

Birch and the Magic of Flexibility

Tree quality: They are long-lived witnesses to events.

How often do we humans really take the long view? From a tree perspective, rooted and witnessing, it is easier to see all sides of the question. And when we do, it is easier to change and adapt, with grace, with circumstances.

Our responses are instantaneous, lightning-swift, compared to those of the birch. Just think how relaxing if, instead of making split-second decisions, we could take a day, a week, a year to respond. We'd surely make far fewer mistakes! And it's rare that a knee-jerk reaction is actually *vital* to our lives and wellbeing. Breathe with the birch instead of being bounced into snap decisions or responses.

Take a moment now to think back to your last automatic response. Then think about how it could have been improved with a little thought. Resolve to develop and practice some holding phrases, such as "I'd like to think about that," "Oh, I'm not sure how I feel—I'll have to get back to you," "Ah, interesting; I've never considered it. Give me some time with that one."

Remember the trees' relationship to time: roots grow around boulders; trunks bend away from the prevailing wind; a secondary bud shoots where the primary has been worn away by friction. From root to canopy, every birch's individual shape is a mute lesson in what it has witnessed and how it has reacted to the world around. Yet all ultimately fulfil their destiny, growing from the nourishment of the earth towards the sky. If we had eyes to see, we could chart its history through all these signs, just as we know ourselves through our shape, our health, our attitude. We will look at this in more depth later.

The birch has the quality of flexibility. *So do you*. But we all need to develop it. Trees do not have agendas set by ego, but we often use up our emotional energy—energy essential for the evocation of positive change— defending an entrenched position or pursuing a course so as not to lose face. We become stiffer, in fact, when we should be loosening up, to sway effortlessly with the winds of change.

Flexibility and lightness are essential to live a magical life. Time for a quick check of how your customary ways of looking at the world might be changing.

Your mind is becoming suffused with natural images. You are opening up a different perspective on life and when stressed, you are developing the habit of taking yourself away for a few minutes and connecting to the larger-than-human cosmos. This helps you to maintain your equilibrium and sense of perspective, and you are working to keep your mind flexible, moving in imagination to the natural world frequently.

Connect to the flexibility of the trees *now*; feel yourself becoming lighter, and then return, in five minutes, to continue this chapter.

A physical object can act as a trigger to remind you of that connection and your part in the greater plan of life—a photo of a favourite tree, a stone from a holiday as a paperweight, a seasonal vase—catkins in spring, flowers through the growing time, turning leaves, and evergreens in the winter. None of these are overt indications of your inner work: they are well within the norm and can be displayed at home or at work. Only you need understand their symbolism and their use as a focus for your private forest world.

"Worry beads" are well known; make sure that your stone is smooth and tactile, so handling it is a pleasure, as you mentally withdraw for a moment to allow the forest to flood your inner senses. See it nestling at the root of a large birch tree. Hear the birds, feel the breeze, and breathe out your stress before continuing.

The birch dryad speaks:

Just the slightest breeze will set my twigs moving and dancing with grace, as my human cousins can change effortlessly from stress to relaxation. Relax into the dance of life: constantly moving and adjusting, yet always returning to your true position. Like us, you can keep on track, yet bend and accommodate the ideas of others, for, as in the life of the forest, we must all interact harmoniously with our societies.

Grace and flexibility will result in win/win situations, whilst we remain on our chosen course. To pursue our proper path, we must be the mature people who can do this. Easy enough when life is harmonious; the testing times are rather different ...

Take as an example a situation that will affect us all at some time: bereavement. We probably know of families who have lost their bearings at these times, with people losing sight of what is important. We may even have been those people. Stress and loss, divorce and bereavement unsettle us all. And we mustn't underestimate the "mini" bereavements that are a part of life: children leaving home, moving house, changing jobs. At all these times of flux and change your first work will pay dividends. This is when you step back and take time to ask: what are the key points of the situation? When family possessions are being split, especially, what is of value might get lost. If you *weren't* (dis)stressed, which of these would be important to you? An extra buck or the carriage clock inheritance for your family? Insisting on your rights if there's been a misunderstanding? Or seeing all sides of the family embracing before going back to their own lives?

Hopefully, most of us would put the third point way above the other two. Negotiate, witness, see the other person's point of view and have a clear idea of what is really important to you. And, after all, after the embrace, we're allowed to be very glad to wave our relatives off—there's no rule that we have to get on with them 24/7—whilst still respecting the family relationships that we cannot escape. Again, witness and find genuinely worthy qualities in your relatives, even if you'll never get on temperamentally.

Grab your notebook and pencil and think back over the past week. Remind yourself of all your positive relationships and outcomes and your dreaming time in your inner forest, which has allowed you the space to sway and move, to change. Make a list of those things you have tackled maturely and with flexibility—a child's bedtime, arrangements with a spouse, kindness to a work colleague who needs it, and who will return the favour when asked—and keep updating it.

Learn from the mistakes you will make along the way, and then make reparation if need be. Forgive yourself and forget them! The tree is a long-lived witness—*so are you.* Remind yourself each time you are mired in guilt that you have no time or energy for judgements that benefit no one. Entrenched attitudes and fixed judgements are diminishing—be light in your responses, especially when judging yourself. These guidelines are of course for we fortunate ones whose experiences fall within the parameters of acceptable behaviour, so if you have any deep-seated issues around forgiveness because you have been a victim or perpetrator of bad acts, then seek professional help in order to move on in your life.

Clarity leading to lightness and flexibility; this is the way. As we clarify, as we slough off accumulated habits, then, like the birch after rain, we will shine with purpose.

The birch is not only used for cleansing, but for purification. Think of those stimulating birch twigs in the sauna and of incense used to cleanse space. It is used in the scent business to underpin other perfumes, just as its clearing quality will underpin your changes. Bring to mind a fresh smell now. Really breathe it in, and allow it to rejuvenate you.

As you concentrate on flexibility in this chapter, allow the many continuing possibilities of your life, whatever your age or circumstances, to flow through your imagination, sweetening and filling the nooks and crannies of your mind, so that there is no room for negative thoughts.

The Flexible Birch—Uses

Be amazed and inspired by the ubiquitous nature of the birch. As you read the following, allow your mind to wander to consider how many directions your own life might take.

As well as its use in medicine and healing, the quality of the wood suits it to a wide variety of uses. But forget today's practical applications for a moment and allow your imagination to conjure an image of its most ancient use: the grace of a birch bark canoe skimming over a misty lake at dawn into the dim unknown. This resonates with people of all cultures and connects us to past civilisations. The canoe is a symbol of self-sufficient humanity in perfect harmony with nature. And it is because of the flexibility and durability of its bark with its resinous oils that the birch is perfect for the task.

Birch wood has a multiplicity of uses, both as wood and as plywood. With its hygienic associations, it is made into toothpicks and tongue depressors for use by the medical profession. The attraction of the living tree transfers to the cut wood, which is smooth and satiny, with a close grain. Many homes contain birch—as shelving and kitchen units; as floors and concealed in walls in house construction; as fuel; for play and sports equipment, or drums and musical instruments—it adapts to all. From ancient times bang up to the present day, its flexibility ensures that it is important. Birch is a component in wind turbine blades and for skateboards. Truly, the pioneer birch is all around us! And to take its use to the more magical level, paper from the birch has been used in antiquity for many sacred texts.

The variety of uses of the birch can be compared to our use of our time—fitting ourselves to whichever purpose has priority, with whatever label comes with that—mother, father, daughter, son, colleague, worker, homemaker, craftsperson, carer, earner—yet still keeping an essential sense of ourselves and the basic material from which we craft our lives. The birch surrounds us: when we need to key into its gifts, we know that it is not only accessible through our imagination, but that we are never far from the actual physical presence of the wood.

Birch, Our Plans, and the Changing Seasons

So, surrounded by the birch, take a moment to listen to your inner dryad in all her vitality as she fills your mind with the beauty of nature through the seasons. Lower the book for five minutes and rest your eyes, focussing as you breathe deeply three times to allow your mind to drift to the planes of the imagination ...

The birch dryad speaks:

See my tree shining here at deep midwinter, with the dark sky and stars high above, and a clear full moon lighting the snow so that the shadows of the trees stream over the land, and the shapes of the other trees are dim and concealed. An owl hoots, flies past my silver trunk, the arrow-shaped deep fissures in my bark pointing upwards in dark shadows, and my icy branches reach to the sky ...

And, as you blink, the scene changes to high summer, with the sun beating down, making a shimmering canopy of the brilliant leaf spears fluttering in the balmy breeze. The sky is a duck-egg blue, and the green spears of grass mirror the shape of my vivid leaves, making a haze of a green world of wonder—glints of silver and green and blue, gleaming in the golden glow shining from high in the firmament...

With your dryad guide, you have just imagined the polar opposites of nature: the birches at deep winter and high summer. We see change in nature, so we know that it is the natural state for all living things. Through this, we begin to understand and become reconciled to and then embrace the constant dynamic of our lives: the balance of flux and reforming, change and stability.

Goal Setting and the Natural Cycle

In terms of goals, deep winter and high summer respectively represent the deep incubation period of setting our intent and being in the full energy of doing all we can to achieve it. But most of us enjoy four seasons, so what of the others? To many occultists, spring and autumn, the two equinoxes, have been regarded as the times of greatest flexibility and change.

The spring equinox corresponds to our first steps in achieving our goals: that journey from the broad principles of what we want to create in the world and the specifics of the way we will achieve this. The autumnal equinox is the time of completion and harvesting, of learning from what we have done and seeing how much we have achieved: it is the time of wisdom.

Connecting to the spring equinox energy, how many ways will we plan to use to achieve our intent? How many twigs will we extend in different directions, and with what delicacy and flexibility will we move, act, and react to move towards our goal? We don't have to wait until spring to start our projects, of course, but in our inner world, connecting to it can be very helpful. The whole of the energy of birch is directed towards the inception and first steps on our journey.

Birch and Self-Sufficiency

It is worth knowing that the birch tree has both male and female flowers. So, within us, are attitudes that might be considered "male" and female." Actually, these gender attributes are better expressed simply as active and passive qualities, but however you think of them, remind yourself that, no matter how happily settled with relationship or family, you are responsible for crafting your life and have within you all that you need to do that. External support from family, friends, and contacts is the icing on your cake—and sometimes that icing might be in short supply! When you take responsibility instead of expecting help as your entitlement, you will come to regard help as a generous bonus, which you will respond to gratefully each time. You will have grace, like the birch.

Goals and Setbacks

Blockages and setbacks always challenge us to use our judgement honestly. There is a difference between beating our heads against brick walls and persisting in a way that will make for a breakthrough. Remember the witnessing of the tree; use it to take a dispassionate overview before making your judgements, and be always ready to adapt. To humans, conditioned to react immediately, challenge often activates all our worst instincts: battling, one-upmanship, proving our point no matter what—all of which can skew our judgement. Instead, we practice, again and again, keeping the goal in sight and gracefully circumventing the obstacles by taking the long view.

Fear of losing face, of having been over-ambitious and failed, can prevent us from attempting anything. When we do make an attempt, it can make us pig-headedly push on with our first ideas even when we're getting nowhere. In the forest, you can bask in a peace that puts human judgement very firmly in its place. At each setback, harness that serenity and consider your options.

The birch dryad speaks:

Sit under my tree, so relaxed that you are almost an extension of my trunk. You feel kind but dispassionate towards whatever you will see. Look down a long green trackway through the forest and imagine yourself in your everyday life. How do you view yourself? Be kind, take the long view. Gently focus on all the positives. Remind yourself that you are making time to consider your life. Think of what has brought you to here, and how to support your changes … Gently come back to the present in this attitude of detachment.

Back in the real world, note down any thoughts, questions, or answers that occurred to you.

Whatever your goal, ask yourself: should your energy be flowing in a slightly different direction? Although we might have marker trees guiding us through the forest to our goal, the path of nature is not ruler-straight. After dipping into the inspiring cauldron of the imagination, the fertile earth of the forest is nurturing the seed of your idea. But you have probably planned the next stage through your more limited, conscious mind, which is rarely as flexible as it should be, and is not infallible!

It's important to keep the inner connection you experienced when you first set your goal, so return frequently or daily for a short time to that inner place of green wisdom, and emerge to translate your inspiration into action. Focus and relax, focus and relax; this is the never-ending sinuous movement through life to our objectives.

By now you have studied birch trees. Some will have been well grown, standing solitarily in their own space, whilst many will be shooting up from a common plot or spread along roads, full size but thin and tall. Which are you? We are all shaped by the restrictions of our homes, circumstances, and gender, as we've noticed before. As we think of the flexibility of the tree, we look at our present shape and celebrate it.

Consider two students who are polar opposites: in race, colour, gender, expectations, and education. How might they grow to maturity? Immediately, we might think that the privileged student will grow more strongly and into a fuller shape, like a tree with more air, space, and nutrients.

But this is where we must acknowledge our difference from, as well as connection to, the trees. For we can, regardless of—or perhaps because of—our restrictions, draw on indomitable strength of will and emotional reserves that urge us to make our way in the world. Conversely, the most privileged, knowing that life is always secure, can suffer from apathy and boredom. Being born with a silver spoon in one's mouth can sap the will to strive, whilst the urge to rise above our circumstances produces inspirational stories.

Just remember that those overcrowded birches still achieve their full status at maturity, reaching just as high to the sky, having just as many gifts for the world; supplying beauty, seeds, shade, sap, wood, and ecosystems and habitats for other forms of life. Over three hundred species feed on the birch, making it impossible to quantify the degree to which they enrich the environment. The "shape" of our lives ultimately is defined by the effect we have on those around us and our contribution to the world. By developing flexibility and the wish for the greater good of all as a default position, we are ensuring that the ripple effect of our actions is similarly beneficial, in ways that we may never know.

And as the tree is bent by the wind, and gnawed by deer, so our bodies are remembrances of everything that has happened to us: accidents, childbirth, chronic ailments which are our family heritage ... they are part of the flexibility of our miraculous bodies.

Take a moment to remember yourself as a bright, open child. Look back kindly at where you've come from, feeling proud of how you've coped with all your circumstances, physically, mentally, and emotionally.

Diseases of the Birch

As you think of your past, bear in mind that the birch is prone to certain diseases, weaknesses, and pests, *as are you*. And, in avoiding them, awareness is half the battle; they are different for all of us. Don't mistake flexibility for being a pushover, for being deflected by others. Let's consider our tendencies in the light of the diseases of the birch.

The birch is subject to *borers* getting under its bark. Trees that are weak or damaged are most susceptible, and insects can cause vast damage, interrupting the flow of sap and destroying the tree. With a very few changes, does this apply to you? For damage, read knocks from life; for borers, read anyone who "gets under your skin," who encroaches on your boundaries when they are weakened; and for sap, read energy.

Fortunately, as pruning can improve tree health, so pruning and controlling our attitude to circumstances can do the same for us. What attitudes don't you need anymore? What physical activities can you just dump, freeing up the time you now *need* to dream in the forest? "Pointless busywork" is the way teachers can keep pupils occupied and out of mischief, and that is often what we fill our lives with. So how to change?

Make a list, "Essential Pruning," along the lines below. Have fun, be creative, and remember *quality time* with partners, friends, and especially children is always time well spent. Kids remember good times with you; they don't remember or resent having a sandwich instead of a cordon bleu meal.

Activity	Essential Pruning	Time Saved
Basic shopping	Plan and go half as often	_____ per week
Recreational shopping	Only when combined with socialising—a coffee with a friend?	_____ per week
Cooking	Only cook once a day Simplify breakfast and have a cold lunch/soup	_____ per day
Hobbies	How many? If adding to stress, alternate seasonally to cut in half—singing in winter, rambling in summer?	_____ per week/month
Ironing	Do you really have to? What, EVERYTHING?	_____ per week

And then we come on to those pests ...

Pruning gives you clarity; when you make your list, you will doubtless guiltily pencil certain people into the first column as time wasters and people who sap your energy. Honour that intuition. When the people are family members, of course, we have contracts to honour. But our very awareness should help to reframe the way we relate to such people—always with kindness, but with a level of distance that keeps our spirits clear and energetic for what is important to us. Our job is to prune *our own* dead wood—leave everyone else's to them. By letting light and air into our minds, we allow the free flow of ideas just as the breeze serves every leaf and twig of the birch tree.

And what of acquaintances who take up too much time? There is never a need to be unkind or dismissive, but do be creative! Firstly, and most importantly, do you like these people? Will they support you in reaching your goals or do they leave you tired and miserable? Meet them out for a coffee, instead of allowing them to camp in your home for hours at a time. Extricate yourself from the dinner party circuit in favour of a regular phone call or a visit to the cinema, both of which are more time-efficient. Those who claim an excessive amount of your time will soon find others who can supply that need, if you don't.

We, like the birch, should grow with a strong central trunk, and any damaged branches or any growing in the wrong direction can be carefully cut to encourage our health and increase our vigour, which we can then apply to our soul-felt aims. Check yourself regularly as you would check a tree: nurture your growth and feel your spirit expand.

And after getting clear, avoiding the traps of judgement and blame, there is forgiveness. Forgiveness is not saying that what's been done is okay if it's not; it's about recognising that holding on is bad for you, and that it is time to allow the negative emotions to dissipate harmlessly, for your ultimate good, as gently as birch leaves flutter in the autumn wind. The bark of the birch helps to heal wounds and burns; incorporate its healing properties into your meditations, so you can put your past actions into the storehouse of memory.

What do we want to be *now*? How do we want to move and dance? In what shape do we feel completely comfortable? We are crafting the shapes of our lives. Soon, knowing that we can always return at will, we will be leaving the birch copse.

Let us move forward free and unencumbered, as we grow in grace and beauty.

Lessons from the Birch

Flexibility

It is time now to internalise some of the secrets of flexibility.

Remember a time when you went outside after a high wind or storm: there were probably branches and twigs littering the ground. When even flexible structures are subject to sudden violent movement, they will break. We transfer this knowledge and apply it to our own attitudes. We must not be rushed, badgered, or bulldozed into decisions, or we will probably make them from inflexible and entrenched positions. Get a clear mental image now:

A stormy evening; a sudden gust of wind through a stand of birches; a dead, inflexible tree and a branch snapping. Crack!

Practice bringing this instantaneously to mind over the next few days before going into new situations—team meetings, family gatherings, whenever the phone rings—as a reminder to count to five when you need to. Practice the mind-picture with the phrases suggested in the chapter that give you breathing and thinking space, "I'll have to get back to you…" and so on. And see yourself as the birch tree gracefully bending with the wind of others' suggestions, and then assuming its own proper shape.

We're not paranoid—we know that the majority of people are not *trying* to bulldoze us—but we do notice that some seem to get their own way more than others. That's because we sway constantly as we respond to different opinions and can easily lose our own focus. The art is to understand the constant dynamic between flexibility and focus, then learn to *slow things down* to allow our true responses to shine through.

The most usual approach is a knee-jerk reaction, so that, as well as being buffeted by forceful people trying to push us in their direction, we can be our own enemy, pushed by the self-generated gale of *wanting to be the good guy, wanting to fit in, wanting to go with the majority opinion*, and so on. And then we find we've agreed to work under that project leader, go on holiday with those cousins, or buy that house. Crack! Part of our self-sense and our plan for our life—even if it's just a couple of holiday weeks—has been damaged by bad decisions that we regret.

Imagine yourself as the birch, intensely alive and flexible, gracefully coping with the zephyrs, the winds, and the gales. Feel the green life of the sap in your veins as you move. See your branches spreading wide, with every twig stretching to a different direction all its own. Which way will you go? Which way will you grow?

Keep your mind flexible! Be prepared for new challenges! If the birch stayed only in one position, then it, like our minds and bodies, would seize up, and the smallest puff of wind would imperil the whole structure. Trees remember their flexibility even when they are no longer rooted, which is why houses in many earth tremor zones are built of wood, to adapt to the shifting of tectonic plates which would bring houses of inert brick crashing down.

And the first stage of flexibility is to practice thinking differently.

Think carefully about these suggestions: if you don't want to follow any of them, ask yourself why not. And then ask what you might do instead.

Consider taking up a new hobby, going on a course or to a club just for a term, or go along with someone else's hobby. It's good sometimes to seek out new experiences and those that don't come your way very often—even to dress differently. How does it feel? Why don't you try watching a different type of TV or DVD programme? And remember, as your body regenerates regularly, so should your mind, so look back and see how often your ideas do.

The birch is reactive to external situations. As humans, our instinct also is to react, even before we fully understand a situation. Often, by stepping back and becoming a witness, as if a tree, we will become sensitive to situations and will go forward with trust. And then we might look back later and find, as if by magic, that we have made an accommodation with events almost before they unfold in the real world. This is how to be in tune with life; accessing this intuition is the gift of the trees. This has a knock-on effect: the birch, as pioneer, actually improves the soil. And you will sweeten and nourish the life of your nearest and dearest as you become more satisfied with your own life.

Do review regularly—why not look at your family and work relationships every year, to see how you and your colleagues have all developed and grown? Many people turn round in middle age and suddenly realise that they've lost touch with the world they thought they knew. Stay flexible and responsive to what is actually happening in your life. Don't be afraid to let old attitudes and old relationships go, to allow new and more enriching experiences to unfold.

Set the book aside for five minutes and try this exercise:

Relax in your tree body and see your life situation as a forest around you. What overshadows you? What smothers your lower branches? What supports and companions you? What needs pruning in your life? What new paths need to be made to make you more accessible? How are you preparing for the next stage of your life? Gently adjust your internal landscape; other trees will adapt here and respond to your needs, without any emotion or violent chopping... See any tree that is

too large, too close, gently withdrawing to allow you more space. See
shrubs in need of nurture blooming and developing under your care.
Stretch and flex, and feel the blessing of each touch with nearby trees.
Feel wonderful about your life. Make notes in your notebook, and
decide to act to adjust things as necessary.

Draw some sketches of your life, as if all humans are trees in a forest. First, draw birches intertwining: win/win situations between people and situations in your life.

Remember the lightning-blasted tree from the last session? Draw it again, and this time put lots of growth and health into the living part of the tree that is left. This is you! Mark the boughs—stunted and living—as parts of your life: see how to circumvent damage by flexibility and subtlety. With hindsight we realise that most past mistakes were not too serious, so don't let fear of making one stop you from trying new things. Enjoy crafting your life!

Draw an overview of your life as a map of a forest; divide it into areas of life, some of which will overlap: cul-de-sacs, highways, small private trails and tracks.

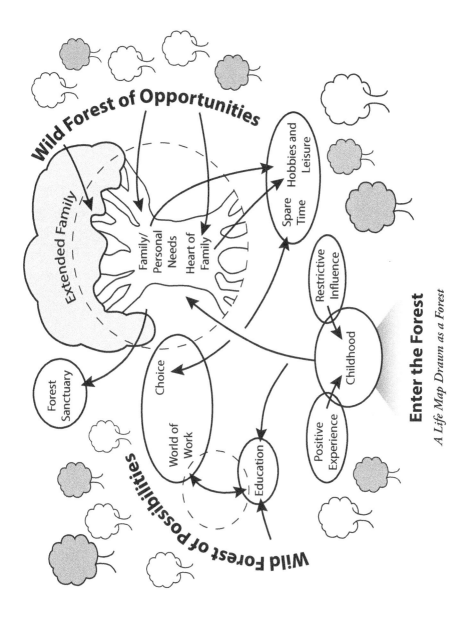

Wild Forest of Opportunities

Extended Family

Family/Personal Needs

Heart of Family

Spare Time

Hobbies and Leisure

Forest Sanctuary

Choice

World of Work

Education

Positive Experience

Childhood

Restrictive Influence

Enter the Forest

A Life Map Drawn as a Forest

Wild Forest of Possibilities

Your Morning Meditation

For this session at least, even (or especially!) if it takes you out of your comfort zone, add on some movement before, during, or after your morning meditation, as far as health allows. We cannot separate body and mind, and becoming more physically flexible will remind you to keep an open attitude. Devise the dance of the dryad, even if only with your arms and hands. Keep a favourite piece of music close by so you can dance it regularly.

Fill your mind with the images in the chapter of the birch throughout the year. You could coordinate this with the time of day: in the morning, think of the birch in the spring; at noon and in the afternoon, the full-leafed copse in high summer; in the evening imagine the autumn wood; and at night-time, the bare-branched trees of winter, stripping back the cares of the day to leave you free and clear for sleep.

Flexibility

- Consider kindly and gently how your upbringing has influenced your life. Decide *now* to be light-hearted and generous.

- Practice creative thought. Suppose you were a different person, how would you respond? Well, what's stopping you, if it's a better way?

- Who would be your birch role model? A teacher? A public figure? A family member?

- Read up on lateral thinking and creative solutions. Start with the old chestnut: how many uses can you find for a brick—or maybe a branch? Write them down now, and don't stop until you reach twenty!

Flexibility of mind, body, emotions, mentality, and spirit are all wonderfully intertwined. No matter how restricted your body, make the most of it. Know that working on one aspect of yourself will and must have a knock-on effect on all the other parts.

Affirmations

You are used to affirmations now, but before you think of these new ones, remind yourself every time that you're *evoking for change*. Take time to think of the meaning of the words; feel the truth of them deep within; feel their influence relaxing you and causing a feeling of wellbeing to permeate through you. Enjoy!

BIRCH AFFIRMATIONS

For lightness and joy:
As I stretch daily, I grow in flexibility.
I dance with the joy of life.
I reach for a million possibilities of life.

For noticing and acting:
As I witness, so I respond to my life: I sway and move with grace.
I prune my twigs, so that other areas of my life may thrive.

For moving forward graciously:
I am astringent like the birch; I heal and clear my life as I grow.
I am freed from dead and outworn parts of my life.
I forgive and move on with clarity.
I allow others to dance to their own tune.
I take joy in the dance of life.

Now make up your own or adapt those above to be perfect for you, each day.

Visualisation Suggestions

The visualisations that you craft yourself in this session should invite you to extend your flexible mind into flights of fancy. Really stretch your sense of the lives you *could* live, even within the constraints of your present life.

Visualisation 1:

When circumstances are proscribed, connect to birch freedom

Images that might be helpful: A noble tree growing strongly, in a confined space; the strength of growth upwards; the joy of finding space to spread wide. The interaction with the wind, sun, rain, and moon; all the elements of all the seasons. The perfect shape the tree has become. Your spirit stretches and becomes its own perfect shape and your body reflects that; let it sink deep into you. Bring back and respect that feeling in your life.

Visualisation 2:

When you feel cut off from possibilities, access birch connection

Images that might be helpful: The birch and companion trees—oak, elder, maple—whichever you wish. Ask each how they all interact; hear answers in their whispers and rustles. Undergrowth protecting the birch from the deer; oak shading it; elder nourishing birds. Keep listening. Your birch touches branches with the nearest tree, communicates the vibrancy of life. Microscopic life forms connect all. Branches touch and squirrels leap between them. Deep below, roots mingle. All is accessible; breathe in the connection of the forest.

Visualisation 3:

When you feel damaged by life, connect to birch healing

Images that might be helpful: A huge, old, damaged birch, relic of gales and woodsmen. Wounds long healed; the astringent oil of the birch cleansing and healing each lesion when it was new. No emotion, no expectation; observe the process of life as it is. Every organism, including humans, has its healing mechanisms for wounds of the body, mind, and spirit; know this is true.

The tree's perspective. An old tree humming with vibrant life; witnessing all; tranquil as it reaches to the sky, fulfilling its destiny.

Remember, your rational mind must find your plans credible; to be a tightrope walker might be a tough haul if your chronological age is seventy-plus and you have arthritis. If that's always been your *daydream*, of course focus on it in a visualisation—absorbing the sense of freedom will be nothing but beneficial. The main thrust this month is to be bold, but not to push your bounds of probability beyond the limits. Who knows what might manifest as a result? Any suggestions I make might just point you in a direction that *limits* your own imagination, so over to you …

Practical Work

Try some or all of the following suggestions to help to ground and implement the ideas of the chapter into actions in your everyday life. Even if your fingers are all thumbs, craftwork is good for you—I know, as I'm so bad at it! Use any time you've gained so far to have fun, before it gets absorbed back into everyday activities again. Here's a list of suggestions:

- Try making paper from birch bark.

- Paint and draw on bark.

- Cover a jar with bark to make a birch bark vase.

- Make a miniature canoe with the kids.

- Birch was used in antiquity for making footwear and hats—
  be creative!

And then you can work on yourself, on improving your mobility or level of health, maybe taking a dance or exercise class. Get inspiration for your movements by studying the birch on a windy day; sketch its movements and then go home and dance and sing with the dryad. And remember *why* you're staying so light and flexible: to be ready to implement all those exciting plans you've thought of. So make an aspirational scrapbook—how many possible futures can you envisage? Cut and stick any pictures that indicate possibilities for your life or different ways that your life might take. Paste in pictures that make you think of the qualities you're trying to access—a gymnast, a horse, flocks of birds, and a role model who changed career in midlife might all make you think of flexibility, strength, focus, and success.

Make a mind map, drawing out and using the many uses of the birch to stir your imagination. Add on their correspondences with your life (e.g., broom—cleaning duties; waterproof oil—adventure weekend; sacred texts—spiritual study, etc.). Think back over a year with your key moments and flexible developments in all areas of your life, and find a spreading branch of birch as an *aide-mémoire*—twigs springing from the end of a branch, with catkins perhaps. Put it where you need a remembrance of your own flexibility: around your home or office, or on your children's bedroom door.

And just in case these wonderful, joyous grounding exercises have little effect on your entrenched attitudes—and we all find it difficult—devise exercises that allow you to practice seeing both sides of the question. Get a different newspaper; argue on the other side of any argument to your habitual stance. Talk back to the news as if you have the opposite political opinion. Use your birch flexibility and witnessing qualities *not* to judge, and practice when looking round in the streets. Suppose that group of suspicious-looking youths helped you when you had an accident? Suppose that a well-dressed, charming man conned you out of your savings? How would your habitual attitudes change then?

Such things happen every day to those with closed minds, who formed opinions many years ago and will never change them. Be sensible, use your life experience, but still remain *open* in your opinions. I was furious when neighbourhood kids jumped down into my garden, until I went round to their side of the wall and realised that it was an open invitation; any self-respecting adventurous nine-year-old—including myself at that age—would have done it! Being flexible often means looking through another's eyes. By understanding their point of view, you can make it easy for them to do what suits you, or your family, or your business, and difficult for them to annoy you. This is not manipulative; it's just a way of ensuring people get on harmoniously. Remember, people are rarely prompted by malice, as my neighbourhood kids weren't: most people sleepwalk through life, taking opportunities where they see them and happy when others make life easy for them.

Don't discount any way to encourage your mind to be flexible. The humble crossword puzzle invites you to make connections, and, if you stick to one made by the same compiler each day, you will soon tune in to their way of thinking so well that your clue-solving will become lightning-fast. Compilers are very clever, but how predictable they are! Can that be a wake-up call for you? How easily can people tune into *your* thought processes? Do you *want* to be so predictable? If you find the idea too limiting, then practice daily exercises to become more flexible.

Look around your home with the eyes of a toddler, a teenager, a worker, and an old person. What conclusions do you draw, and are you happy with them? Children remind us of the birch; if you have any in the family, dance or get down on the floor to play with them. Go to nature for examples of cooperation; watch flocks of birds as they wheel and fly (there are plenty on YouTube)—they exemplify individuality and harmony in action.

Look around your home to see if there is any birch wood in your furniture. Traditionally, planting a birch tree at the front entrance of property would protect the inhabitants; today, if you have room, planting a birch would be a reminder of the guidance and protection of the trees. There are also many tree charities that need tree sponsors, and it's nice to be responsible for a planting.

Each evening, reflect on the day. Be your own witness, and recall every positive attitude that shows how you are combining flexibility with maintaining your focus. Through alternating inner and outer exercises, you will balance flexibly between your enquiring and active being and your times of reflection.

Visualisation: Getting in Tune with the Birch

As you breathe, you remind yourself of your true inner feelings and with each breath begin to evoke them—contentment, stability, rightness. Do not struggle or strain; you are flexible and generous. Just allow the maelstrom of surface feelings to quieten down so that peace can arise naturally in your body and mind.

These feelings lead you into a waking dream, so that, with all your worries left behind, you find yourself walking towards a large copse of mature birch trees.

Pause to examine the scene, admiring the focus of each reaching bough, searching out its own patch of sunlight. See them planted on the sandy soil, and the shallow, exposed edges of the roots that anchor the slender silver trunks.

Your sense of anticipation grows as you approach, and then you are in the centre of a circle of trees, and joy wells from deep within you, spilling out almost like an energy that connects you deeply to the scene. Sunlight streams down on you, and the edges of the drooping thin black twigs and green spear-shaped leaves make a curtain around you. Around your feet, the crimson caps of the fly agaric fungus glow like otherworldly jewels.

Take your time, look around the circle at each tree; see their different shapes, heights, the markings of their bark ... each is unique and beautiful. Each has grown in response to natural conditions, just as you have. The tree positioned to get the sun first will have slightly more mature leaves; the tree that takes the brunt of the prevailing wind will be the most bent and asymmetric, whilst those on the sheltered side of the circle will be most evenly grown. Each has adapted; each is flexible; each is uniquely itself. Each is a result of its life circumstances. So are you.

Ask the circle of trees for support, in words, in a gesture, a movement, a dance—however feels right to you. You are bathed in the sunshine and greenness of the copse. Open yourself to the blessings of the trees, and feel a response from one in particular… as a welcoming breeze, a rustle of leaves, a feeling that the energy of the tree is drawing to you, or that its aura is opening to admit you… Relax and wait, a response will come. In your dreamlike state of pure contentment, drift to the base of your tree and ask to be taken to the place of the dryad.

As you do, you find yourself safely sitting on the tree's first major branch, with your back leaning against the trunk. You feel completely secure and enjoy the novel sensation. The leaves are now whispering very near to you and are half-concealing the view. Below you are more leaves hanging and the view of the ground, with its thin grass. Through the branches, the blue sky glows. The breeze is stronger, energising; breathe deeply. This seat is the traditional resting place of the spirit of every tree, and here you feel closest to the green wisdom that will keep you balanced and give you a clear view of any problem or situation. It evokes from you a sense of excitement, a feeling of being in a place so very different, but one where you feel completely in control, with the strength and integrity of the tree aiding your own endeavours. Whisper to the tree; thank it for its help. Relax.

Without engaging your emotions, call on the beauty of your surroundings to evoke true loving energy until it fills you. You simply love life, but want to do better—to feel more harmonious, to waste less *time on trivial things. Decide now to relax into being in tune with the rhythms of your life.*

You flood loving energy out to all your family, friends, colleagues, enemies, and strangers indiscriminately. With every relaxed breath, pour your love and intent into your life, and see pictures change in your mind's eye as you craft your life with anticipation, focus, and flexibility. See contentment; your successes are mirrored in the lives of others, and all are happy. Rightness is in the contentment and harmony you imagine becoming the mainstay of your life, allowing you to move creatively to the place where you should be.

And when you have spent long enough in your tree-sanctuary, thank the dryad spirit of the tree, and effortlessly swing down to the ground. You are once again in the centre of the copse, bathed in the green-golden glow of sunlight through leaves. You are so full of understanding and love of the birches that now you feel the need consciously to reassert your sense of yourself as a whole autonomous being. At that thought, the scene gradually begins to fade, the birches swaying to you in farewell, and you whisper thanks into the air.

And then your body reasserts itself, and you feel the need to move, to stretch, to yawn, and to open your eyes, asserting firmly, as always, your name and that you are fully back and present in the world, feeling refreshed, alert, and with a happiness that only connection to wonderful experiences can bring.

Finish this study session with the next visualisation when you are ready to retire for the night or to drift into reverie at some quiet time.

Night-Time Visualisation of Birch Flexibility

Remember, night-time exercises are to relax, not to over-stimulate you. Take your time, and don't fight the urge to drift off to sleep if that should be right for you. Set your intent that the end of the visualisation will find you on the verge of sleep, happy, relaxed, and secure.

Settle yourself as usual, checking the comfort of your physical body with each breath and allowing tension to seep out with every out-breath. Evoke the feeling of sublime peace and allow time for it to fill you ... You are flexible, in your mind and your ideas, so do not focus on any one plan, just relax into the knowledge that throughout your life there will be many projects, which will be successful by virtue of you focussing and then allowing the flexibility for them to manifest as they should.

Imagine that you are walking by a stream on a soft and warm spring day. Take time as usual to see, feel, smell, and hear your surroundings. Notice particularly the life of the stream—ducklings with a mother duck, a kingfisher flashing past, small fish in the deep pools—and the fresh greenness of spring growth. From round a bend, you see a convoy of small birch bark canoes drifting past—each of them a possible project, travelling far along its appointed way. See how bravely they bob on the current; how well made, flexible, and graceful they are. Enjoy the show ...

On the bank of the stream you find a miniature canoe that represents something your deeper wisdom knows is right for you at this time. Climb down to it and name it "Trust in Life" and set it on the water to sail confidently on its way with your blessings.

Continue walking by the stream, over which hangs a birch tree. Pick up its twigs, walk onto a bridge, and idly drop them into the fast-flowing water, naming each for any goals that spring to mind. Then take your ease ... rest between water and land, between earth and sky, and see how sinuously the twigs glide with the current, taking the path of least effort, helped onwards by the current of life. Relax into that journey yourself; now it is time for sleep.

Moving from Birch to Oak

You will soon journey from the sparse terrain and scanty cover where the birch finds its home into the oak forest. Take a moment, a day, or a week to see how far you have travelled.

The wisdom of the oak will wait whilst you check that you have internalised that of the birch. Look back over the preceding chapters: remind yourself of the practices you now follow. We humans have a great ability: we adapt quickly and tend to take all positive changes in our stride, and just notice the negative; so take a moment to celebrate your progress.

As an example, we hardly notice how well we are recovering from accident or illness, how fit we're getting, until someone else comments on it. And then we see our former pain and suffering through the dim curtain of memory, as if it all happened to another person. So we must review to see how much we have improved, how far we've come along the way.

Take time to congratulate yourself on how well you've taken on the book's suggestions. Read the practical chapters on this material again, ticking everything that you now do, underlining everything that you have tried but that hasn't become a regular habit yet. Put question marks by anything you're still not sure of—and remember that these are broad guidelines. Every journey is individual and will be handcrafted by you in accordance with the general principles.

Ask yourself a few questions along these lines before you continue. Can you hear the voice of the birch dryad in your imagination—supportive, encouraging, reassuring? Are you working consciously with your sense of anticipation, focus, and flexibility every day? Is your connection with the birch reminding you that you too can be a witness? That you can step into a calmer appreciation of time passing? That you can observe and use your observations?

Does what you know of the physical growth of the birch support you in your efforts when you are forging a new path? Can you access that strength of purpose, of reaching for your goals? Can you dig your roots into shallow soil, bend with circumstance and yet maintain your true growth towards your goals?

Can you evoke, call up, a magical feeling within yourself, one that connects you to the wonder of a wider life?

Think about what you have *done*: first in your imagination, or your inner world, and secondly in the actual world—the walks, the craftwork, all the physical activity that grounds the work of the imaginal world and helps to make our internal changes *real* to us.

Then, before you move on, celebrate with the birch!

With friends or family, have a feast or any sort of get-together. They don't have to know the reason. Invite adults to contribute food—bring-and-share is a wonderful way to ensure that everyone "owns" a party. You can supply birch candleholders or birch bark on which they can draw their own place settings, or paint a cheap paper tablecloth so that it resembles birch bark, then serve birch wine or cordial, either bought or homemade, for the truly adventurous! Wear a grey/silver scarf or garment and key into the atmosphere of the birch dryad. Feel the cool stillness of the birch copse around you as you set aside the time for your preparations: there is time!

Look back at the practical ideas in the lessons sections and see which you can use for this occasion. Do a moving meditation before your guests arrive. Theme the party to "beginnings and gratitude." Invite people to bring photos of their younger selves and enjoy looking back and forwards.

Focussed plans take time and work—it's important that we allow our new ideas to sink deep within and become part of our new way of thinking. And these periods of consolidation are an ideal time to dance with the joy of the trees in regular celebration.

You have worked hard in the preceding chapters; relax with the birch. And when you are ready, on with the journey…

The Oak Tree

Inhabiting Our Space

Oak Qualities:

They are authentic; they present themselves just as they are.
They are nuturing.
They are of service.

Optimism

Accountability

Knowledge

4

Oak and the Magic of Strength

Tree quality: They are authentic;
they present themselves just as they are.

Moving from birch to oak, we are turning from our purely individual plans. It is time to put them in a wider context and consider how we relate to our environment.

The oak abounds with magical symbolism, yet it is conversely the tree that emphasises the importance of being of use in the everyday world and relating well to others. And this is the essential balance between the magical and the mundane that we will incorporate into our studies.

The oak is one of the longest-lived trees in the forest. Trees like the birch, which nourished the soil for the dominant tree species, prepared its way. The oak has grown and adapted to fit its conditions, and the result is an embodiment of strength. When you go out oak-spotting, notice the huge canopy, the crown. Look at the lower branches to see how the leaves are spread to catch maximum light. Oak is often used as a marker tree: once we start looking for it, the shape quickly catches our eye from a distance, and it has always been regarded as a tree of status, because of its imposing presence, its generosity, and its myriad uses.

The oak dryad speaks:

Imagine my large, mature tree now. Admire my balance, my sturdy branches thrusting effortlessly from the thick trunk; my perfect canopy of rich green, with vibrant clusters of acorns nestling underneath. What beauty and wealth I bring to the world. See the first massive lower branch, where I have my being. Your fingers feel the furrowed cracks of my bark, imagining the strong, green life pulling upwards continuously, feeding my tree to its uttermost extent.

Look high to see me overarching the other trees in the forest. Feel solar energy pouring down, to be caught and stored in each lobed leaf, and listen for the hum of a thousand insects. Birds and squirrels hide in my branches: the strength of my tree supports a multiplicity of life forms.

The world needs a whole forest of diversity, with every tree bringing its different qualities and gifts. But each can only grow and develop in its own way: *just like you*. Life tries to bend and constrain us, and if we have no strength, we will get pulled out of shape. So for our ultimate health, we have to develop a strong core. There is only one proper shape for us to grow into so that we inhabit the perfect physical, mental, emotional, ethical, and spiritual vehicle for our continuing growth and fulfilment. As we connect to the oak, as we study it and observe its silhouette, its very shape gives an impression of a quietly growing powerhouse. And like the oak, our inherent strength will come from quietly growing into being our own authentic selves. When we are not strong, we try to cover our own inadequacies, and this wastes a lot of time and energy. There is a simplicity to strength. Every tree, like every human body, is intricate and miraculous, but all its complexity is for a purpose. There is nothing convoluted or artful in its interaction with the world in our bodily actions, and we do not need it from our emotional or mental processes either. Strength comes not from covering up, but from accepting and acknowledging our own failings. The nature of the oak, by its size and height, is always to reveal its true shape to the world. Disguise is impossible.

If your regular practice is activating your powers of evocation and feeling, you can gain from the strength of the oak in many ways.

Use the dryad's words to evoke a response within you, and you should feel supported and fortified just by these quiet whispers from the forest. Take a moment one, two, or twenty times a day to access it. Think of vibrant green leaves, glowing with life force. We can gain a sense of mental, emotional, and spiritual strength from sitting under an oak and using it in visualisation work: from connecting to our inner oak and accessing all the oak qualities we have within ourselves.

Don't worry if you don't yet feel yourself a strong person. Remember how different from the oak the acorn looks—who could possibly imagine that the one would grow into the other? It's quite miraculous, a potential to change magically from a perfect tiny green egg-shaped seed in your hand to a mighty tree-cousin which will shade you and your descendants. You also are transforming every day, to become a person of simplicity and strength.

The oak dryad speaks:

My leaves will shelter you; lean against my mighty trunk for your support. For hundreds of years this has been my role, to use my strength to nurture all of nature's creatures, and you also are welcome. Rest by me, allow me to lend you my vigour. Relax completely and be refreshed.

The oak tree is a resource, both within your mind and in the landscape. You can both *evoke* oak vitality, stability, tenacity, force, or any aspect of strength that you need from within, and rest in those same feelings that the actual tree will give you. Cultivate your local oak and rest under its canopy frequently, watching it closely so that you can bring it to mind in your inner world whenever you need it.

So we can act both "as the oak" and also with the help of a large tree as "oak supporter." Both of these ways will allow you to inhabit that space that is meant for you, and reinforce the determination and daring to present yourself just as you are.

Strength and Understanding

The word "strength" might make you feel uncomfortable: it can have worrying connotations. Our world is full of examples of the misuse of strength, so we must divorce it from any unpleasant associations with domination and coercion. Most people will not achieve all they can: why is that? Because they fear that growing up and outwards into all their abilities, being focussed, and achieving above the common run is not possible without a dominating attitude. They think others will see them as bossy, pushy, or aggressive.

But true strength obviates the need for aggressive tactics. People who are strong at their core, who have emotional maturity, share the qualities of the oak that help our development into the well-socialised humans that we should be. It is accepted that inappropriate behaviour in the workplace—the pushy, bullying attitude that we might fear manifesting—can be helped by assertiveness training. The message is clear: it is the weak, or those who perceive themselves as weak, who are most likely to be aggressive. Strength in this context is only positive.

When we evoke oak strength, that word encapsulates the qualities of authenticity, moral integrity, a good self-image, and a mature sense of what is right for us in the world. From this sense of ourselves can flow empathy and understanding, reinforced by the knowledge that comes from our life experience. What a great way to be, to feel, and what a gift for us and our communities. And it all starts from strength.

Slow Growth and Development

The oak is slow-growing to achieve its rightful place in the forest. We need to come to terms with the necessarily slow progress we make towards our goal to become the motivated, focussed person who will spread to achieve their full potential. And we have probably noticed that there is a certain charisma to the person who has already achieved this.

Take a moment to think of a colleague, role model, or formative influence who has this charisma. There is something in each of us that yearns for focus, for a plan, for a feeling that we are on the right track, and we find those qualities inspiring in other people. We want to sit in their shade awhile, to bask in the power of their aura, and let their strength of purpose remind us of our own capabilities.

We lean towards these people, whilst we back away from those who appear needy. We fear how many demands those weaker people might make upon our resources. Beware such relationships; sometimes our own neediness is fed by being needed in this way. If that is the case—and it is very easy to slip into this sort of co-dependent relationship—then awareness is the key to help you gently withdraw and instead move towards relationships that help you grow, rather than keeping you in the same place. Relating to other oak people, in fact, not the tangled, climbing creeper-folk whose nature—needing the support of stronger people—is to surreptitiously sap your strength.

Normal, healthy relationships are where the interaction of creative energy feeds all parties. They help sustain us over the dry, stale periods of our lives.

As the dryad is filled with the sense of the plan of the growing tree, so we allow ourselves to imagine we are filled with the plan of our perfect, future selves: that we are growing according to our very own spiritual template.

"Why should I believe this in the face of all the evidence?" you might ask if life is particularly difficult at the moment. We should keep faith with this belief precisely because we yearn for it. We know it is worth "keeping on keeping on" because, when we review our lives, we can see how very far we have come already. Our steps might be tiny, but they are all choosing the path of our life journeys. In choosing the way to view our lives, we are committed now to relaxing, to acting "as if," instead of thrashing ineffectually. As within, so without: as we imagine, so we direct our lives, and so the universe responds in kind. Eventually!

From this standpoint, allow this feeling of rightness with life to fill your senses in regular practice over the days and weeks. Remember the slow progress of the oak. Consciously slow your breathing, your thinking, and notice how it makes you feel. Does it help change the way you view things? Does it make a difference to your magical and actual reality? Are you beginning to feel that each imagining feeds the outer world, that each joyous everyday occurrence sparks a response and evokes your feeling of living a magical life? Joining inner and outer impressions is acting as a tree, where every impression informs our growth.

The oak dryad speaks:

I look down from the topmost branches of my tree, and far below I see a sapling, grown from one of my acorns. Its thin trunk has been buffeted by the winter winds, and its bark nibbled by deer and rubbed by forest animals. The bracken is tall and the small tree seems to be fighting for space. From my great height, I remember when its first tender shoots broke through the soil, and as I look now, I see its energy spread and expand to become a ghostly giant—the template that anticipates the mighty tree it will become, the shape that it will attain in many years, strong and robust. At that time, I will be a huge fallen giant, still giving of my strength when the men come with chainsaws to chop my wood for your fires.

Myth and Kingship

Mythic study shows the association between the oak and king/queenship. Oak reminds us of the positivity of regal strength, which maintains order and harmony in the kingdom, and it does the same in our personal kingdoms, of which we are sovereign.

The tales of the Celts and later stories of King Arthur speak to us on a deep level of these matters. Although mainly about men's adventures, they are not sexist tales, but simply reflect the mores of past generations. We must remember that the qualities of king/queenship transcend gender and are equally accessible to all, and that legends are purveyors of symbolic truths that we recognise intuitively.

When we read stories of kings and knights and ladies, of mythic men of the forest, we can see the nobility of the oak in each hero and heroine. And the same is true in fairy tales—doesn't the woodcutter, a man whose life is entwined with that of the forest, often bring about the happy ending? A modern heroic figure in films who exemplifies these qualities might be the fire-fighter—strong, in control, upright, and gentle.

We can all apply these four qualities to ourselves, and how we manifest them in the world is our challenge. Take five minutes to remember how you have shown your strength by giving comfort or service to others lately—kissing a child's hurt knee, caring for your neighbourhood, helping an old person, or making time just to talk to a neighbour.

These are all random acts of kindness that spring from us when we are in our most expansive, generous mode. And it is the security of our strength that promotes the generous urge to share. If this is the effect of strength, we understand that it is our duty to have a confident and strong sense of our morality and the way we want to interact with life. And isn't "duty" an interesting word? It's a bit out of fashion, but it is associated with kingship. It is our duty and our delight to live up to our highest expectations of ourselves. When we expect a lot, we can achieve hugely.

The Oak and Sovereignty

The oak's association is indelibly with sovereignty. The oak is the king of the forest! His blue-sky eyes gleam high above shrubs and smaller trees, through the forest canopy. Oak leaves have been used through millennia for crowns, for religious and military insignia, on badges and shields, to confer status on us humans and to identify us with oak's robust, honourable, and long-lived nature. Individual families and clans through the ages have also claimed connection to the oak, and it is represented on many coats of arms. The fortunes of some noble families are so entwined with the oak that its destruction will herald the end of the family line.

But with oak's status and sovereignty also come obligation, responsibility, and a sense of duty. The oak speaks of *service*, and in identifying with this huge and powerful cousin, you learn to manage in your own life the balance of the severely mundane—exemplified in the myriad practical uses of the tree as timber—and the iconically mythic. You dance with the dynamic of your responsibilities to your family, colleagues, and work, whilst living as a magical person. It appears that this chapter is particularly concentrating on the mundane, but until that is sorted, clarity of spiritual purpose will be an uphill struggle for us all. The study session on this will reinforce the magical aspect of your path.

A Last Word on Weakness

If we are weak, we are in deficit, and life is a struggle to maintain on whatever level. Relaxing into a position of strength allows us to empathise with others, to show true understanding. Strength allows us to be vulnerable without feeling threatened by difference.

Take a moment to feel the truth of this.

We no longer need to make an effort to be all-knowing, invulnerable, in charge, having all the answers. A weak teacher might belittle a bright pupil as a way of staying "in charge." But inner strength allows a mature teacher to welcome the awkward questions, knowing they are essential, and feels comfortable saying, "I've never thought of that: let's explore that idea. What do you think?" In this way, our strength in knowing that we have a sound structure of "selfness" allows us to be comfortable that we have weaknesses without feeling "less"—and we allow others to blossom and flourish.

The oak dryad speaks:

I am a symbol of strength, and yet I am constantly vulnerable to the elements, to wildlife, to man, and changing with the magic of the seasons. In late spring, far later than my cousin the birch, see my tiny, russet-flushed leaves unfolding like delicate fingers, tenderly opening to the sun; a child's fingers could tear each one. Feel the interaction of my thread-like roots with the earth and its organisms; each could be severed in a moment. My trunk teems with insects and moss; the galls on my twigs and the nests nestling into the crooks of my branches all use me and I am open to them.

I know three truths: I am connected, I am vulnerable, I am strong.

Support and Longevity

A part of the strength of the oak lies in its longevity, which is real and evidenced. Optimistic tradition says, "500 years to grow, 500 to mature, 500 to decline." Or, to push the oak even farther back into mythological time:

Thrice dog's age, age of horse. Thrice horse's age, age of man. Thrice man's age, age of deer. Thrice deer's age, age of eagle. Thrice eagle's age, age of oak.

Julius Caesar wrote of the vast forests of Europe, within which a man could walk for sixty days and not reach the periphery. The oak was a dominant species of those ancient woodlands, and it has a special place in the hearts of modern Druids, for the tree was especially revered by the Druids of old, known for worshipping in forest glades. The most complete ritual we have from those times is an elaborate rite for cutting mistletoe found on an oak tree. The oak's connection to spirituality goes back to our most ancient history.

From its long-lived habit we can absorb to a deeper level the idea of ourselves as beings who need not be at the mercy of a ticking clock.

The birch has inspired us to new beginnings through accessing our natural states of anticipation, focus, and flexibility. The oak tells us that as we pursue our new way of looking at the world we must have strength to "keep on keeping on."

The largest obstacle to embracing a new paradigm, an entirely new set of references in the way we view our life, is our tendency *simply to forget.* We sleepwalk through life, repeating our age-old accustomed patterns. The oak inspires us to stand firm, and to remember that our small, daily acts and efforts of tree-consciousness will benefit us for the rest of our lives. A daily oak meditation—moving or still—will remind us of our true shapes as mature and magical people. We grow into strength in the same way as the oak, taking *time* to become. Slow progress brings us stability and resilience. Remembering the continuity of life's realities—birth, death, life rites, loving relationships—keeps us focussed on the bigger picture.

If thinking of your life is enough to make you feel tired, remember the oak supports us not only when we identify with it but also when we are in its presence and we can rest in its strength. On the days when we want to pull the bedclothes over our heads and let a cosmic mum just pick up the pieces for us, the oak is there. As the oak draws nourishment from the soil, air, water, and sun, so we draw from our immediate environment—families of blood, spirit, and vocation—strength of community and continuity, and strength of memory, all as resources to sustain us.

The oak is especially useful when life gets to be too much, possibly because of your own high expectations. The famous Bach flower remedies offer an oak remedy for strong people who are nevertheless struggling and are bravely keeping optimistic. When the pressures of modern life threaten to overload us, and yet we have no choice but to keep going, we can obtain respite simply from keeping an acorn in our pocket, meditating by an oak, or taking an inner journey to connect to it on a spiritual level. There is a restorative meditation for sleep later, but, for a couple of minutes now, allow the oak dryad to support and direct you, reminding you of timelessness.

The oak dryad speaks:

Allow yourself to sink down so that you are sitting on the exposed roots of my tree, which make a perfect seat for you. Lean back against the furrowed bark of my huge trunk. As you gaze up at my thick branches, you realise how ancient I am—well over seven hundred years old. When the Mayflower set sail from England for the New World, I was alive and thriving. Some of the mature trees that sheltered me whilst I was growing were cut down to make those pilgrim ships. Let your mind drift and see time circling, spiralling, season following season, year following year, each at its appointed time and each unique in its expression. Within my trunk is the ghost of the sapling I once was. Deep within your psyche you carry the child and the adolescent you once were; they are still there, eternally a part of you. You, like me, hold memory of all you have been. How strong and calm you feel, as a witness to your past. And in some intuitive way you understand that your future is also within you, as surely as the capacity to produce next year's leaves is within me. Breathe your future in; be strengthened by it. My tree will always be at your back when you need it.

Strength of History

The oak has been revered by successive generations down the ages, and today, as we are aware of our shrinking natural heritage, ancient trees are protected. It's good to remember that protecting them is not a modern phenomenon.

Wood, as a resource, has traditionally been carefully monitored and guarded by laws. But it is the tree groupings of the ancient Brehon laws of Ireland, as chieftain, peasant, shrub, and bramble trees, which make specific connections between trees and society as a whole—and the punishments for unlawful felling are as stringent in some cases as those for killing fellow humans.

Oak, of course, is a chieftain—one of the seven noble trees—and the laws tell us that cutting one is a danger from which there is no escape; it carries a penalty of three cows.

Undoubtedly, the life of a tribe could be inextricably bound with a specific tree. It is both an acknowledgement of our tree-connection in the modern world and a way to key into ancestral memory and association when we commemorate a family birth or death with a tree planting.

Ancient oaks were given status as:

- Council places
- Religious meeting points
- Scenes of celebration
- Venues for life rites
- Meeting places for hedgerow schools
- Trysting trees

One of the most famous in England is the Major Oak, the meeting place of Robin Hood and his merry men in Sherwood Forest. A behemoth of a past age that seems to link us directly back to mythic history, it grows still, its massive branches supported by huge props.

These landmark oaks carry a deep message and arouse fierce protective feelings, and for this reason have been targeted by those who want to harm the community. For reasons ranging from religious fervour to revenge over sports, oaks have been damaged and destroyed through the centuries. Examples range from the Romans cutting of the sacred groves of the Druids after the massacre on their stronghold of Anglesey (Mona) through tree felling for religious reasons at the time of the English Civil War to present-day attacks such as the poisoning of the Toomer's Corner oak trees in 2010 in Auburn, Alabama. Wilful damage to iconic trees arouses feelings as strong as would an attack on a beloved human elder and unites whole communities. And anecdotal evidence often says that the perpetrator of violence against trees suffers ill-fortune—often blinding—or death as a result.

Oak is a prestigious wood used for high-status furniture, including our last resting places, and the reputed disinterment of King Arthur and Guinevere by Glastonbury monks in 1191 was from an oaken coffin, or perhaps a giant hollowed oak trunk, which contained the bodies of a large man and a woman, whose golden hair crumbled when touched.

So, the message is of strength, status, and endurance. There are many royal oaks; this tree supports monarchs, and we shall see more of this in subsequent chapters.

In the study sessions, we checked with the birch each day that we were still on course. With the oak, we check that our strength is flowing freely through us: the authentic flow of our life force through our physical, mental, emotional, and spiritual bodies. Like all strong people, it behoves us to be kind, to use our strength to help others where appropriate—and to be strong enough to resist demands that pull us away from the way we should be growing.

In our mundane lives, the long-lived oak tells us to take the long view, whilst keeping the birch anticipation, intent, and flexibility active. With the oak's strength, we affirm ourselves and our right to grow into the shape that nature always intended for each of us.

With the support of the oak, we assume our true regal, noble natures.

Lessons from the Oak

Strength

The oak dryad speaks:

Open your heart and embrace the paradox of connecting to my tree in the inner world to increase your sense of strength in your everyday life. You are feeling deeper into the life of the forest and the resonance of the trees.

The First Steps

We have taken time to read, to dream, to anticipate: the energy of the oak is considered, but always relates us back to the real world and our place in it. These study sessions reflect our current reality, being notes and suggestions to ground in the busy world the wisdom you find within the timelessness of your visualisations.

As usual, you will start by finding the oaks in your neighbourhood, especially those that are mature, whose huge branches, almost parallel to the ground, proclaim their age and strength. Sit under these large oaks; give yourself permission to relax totally into their strength. How do you feel?

Imagine waking tomorrow with strength and energy coursing through you—as an athlete at the peak of his physical prowess must feel. Imagine that everything you put in your body, and every movement and exercise, feeds into that strength. Read the whole of this section with an eye to the underlying energy and patterns that go to make up what we perceive as strength.

Take a moment; take your usual three breaths, and feel deep inside to the strong core within you. Then, with every breath, evoke an expansion of that strength. We can call this "stoking the boiler," which you can imagine as a cauldron, cradled by your pelvis. Fill your body, to the tips of your fingers and toes, through your bones, sinews, muscles … Try this in your home and then under a tree: see if it amplifies the effect by connecting to the tree as well as just your human strength. Do this exercise regularly. Search online for any oaks famous as meeting trees, totems, or with a special place in the community, and visit them if possible.

The oak dryad speaks:

Listen … My children people all the land, and I am the focus for your hopes, your dreams, your continuity, and a thousand meetings, generation on generation. I witness your love, your commitment to each other, and the promises you make. Lovers carve my bark, and their youthful hope becomes part of my skin. Leaders commemorate their agreements under my grave gaze. Babies play in my shade.

Affirmations

After the flexibility of the birch, these affirmations are to reinforce a healthy and realistic sense of self, of who we truly are and how that leads to what we may become. They deal with becoming aware of and maintaining our own strength, then with conserving it as we interact with others in a loving and giving way. And they are a reminder to enter into a tree-sense of timelessness, to reduce stress levels.

As always, take time to evoke the feeling of the words within you and fill your mind and senses with them for them to be effective. Remember to use your few moments of private time during the day to reinforce the message.

OAK AFFIRMATIONS

Every morning:
Like the oak, I grow daily in strength and understanding.
The strength of the natural world surrounds me and is within me.

When you feel depleted:
My strength flows through every organ of my body.
Strength pours through my veins, my sinews,
my brainwaves, and neural pathways.

To remind you of all the support you have, past and present:
Like the oak, I bless all who have made the way clear for me.

When you feel stressed and out of time:
I am imbued with the timeless, serene strength of the oak.
I sink into the timelessness of the oak.

For clarity and strength when dealing with others:
My strong branches touch many others.
I can lend my strength, knowing it will be returned.
I thrive on challenge.
My inner core of strength is inviolable.
It regenerates my whole being.
It is right to grow into my true shape.
I nurture my core of strength.

Doodling

A doodle is a rough sketch or scribble which is done absentmindedly—and that is a key to helping to turn off the logical left brain and allow a free flow of ideas from your right brain, with its faculty of intuition and creativity.

A small drawing pad and pen that you can carry around with you is a worthwhile investment. Your doodles should be of the natural world—you might even be getting expert by now at cartoons of birch leaves and twigs. The good news is that after the serrated spear of the birch leaf, the oak leaf is a dream of a doodle—your pen should just flow round its lobes in a natural waving motion, to produce a perfect outline. Then add some veins, and voilà! Try it now. And by your relaxing chair, keep another pad, and then one more for by the bed, for those late night dreamy moments of inspiration. Take your sketch book out and draw an oak as lines of strength and growing energy, or see yourself dressed regally and think of the noblest aspects of your character. You might draw your family tree, and add a crown or a leaf to all your relatives who have come into their true strength, or doodle an oak insignia for yourself, with your initials entwined in the design.

Crafty Projects

- Pierce acorns (take care: they are tough, but too much pressure and they'll split) and gild or varnish them before stringing, for seasonal decorations.

- Find a small oak box to keep precious things in.

- If you're competent, hollow a length of oak bough to contain something precious.

- Have you made your oak crown yet?

Make Some Lists

Thinking of natural king/queenship and its responsibilities, take a light view of the following exercises. Which duties are your joy and performed through love? What are the payoffs for each loving task? Be grateful, whatever your state. List the "duties" that come with your present position—wife, husband, mother, father, niece, nephew—then play with and adjust that list after an oak visualisation. How does it change?

Who Are You?

Real inner strength comes from knowing yourself, accepting yourself, loving yourself. To get you started, why not sketch a diagram of an oak with *you* superimposed on it. Surround it with your main qualities, and remember that most are neither good nor bad, they are simply *who you are*, so there's no judgement allowed in this exercise. Now, on the figure, write your hidden weaknesses. It is right to be private, but ask yourself how vulnerable it makes you to try to keep them secret. So many things just might be hangovers from childhood and no longer really important. Trying to appear strong takes a lot of energy. Would it be easier to share more with your loved ones, your colleagues, and the world? It's fine to say an emphatic "no" to this question, so use your sense and judgement to ponder this aspect of yourself. And at least admit weaknesses to yourself. Take out this paper regularly and allow yourself to reflect dispassionately on the true meaning of weakness and strength after your oak visualisations—and keep amending it as things gradually change!

Ask and Imagine

If you have a particular need for strength for the day, *ask for it.*

Who or what are you asking? That depends upon your belief system, if you have one, but it is simplest to imagine that you have a "higher self" who is always in a place of wisdom that can connect to all the support the universe can give you. Ask for support from a generous, open, and loving heart, and imagine your coronet of oak leaves on your brow. Mentally picture the situation for which you need strength as if you are a witness, quite dispassionately observing, and see yourself coping perfectly.

Make a "Habitat Check"

Like the oak, you live in an environment, a neighbourhood, a habitat.

On birthdays and anniversaries, draw a sketch or write a list of support and sources of strength in your current "habitat" and compare it to where you were one, two, three years ago, then repeat the exercise for your imaginary ideal future.

Mind-map your relationships—which sap your strength? Write them in pencil, faintly, as you imagine your journey away from them. Write positive relationships in pen, beautifully, and embellish them. Draw around and over them the enclosing canopy of a huge oak, keeping all safe.

Of course, positive relationships with family and friends can be pretty draining at times as well! You must take the tree's witnessing role and evaluate sensibly which ultimately feed your spirit and make you strong—all that energy you're spending raising the children, for example. Or coping so professionally at work, in order to achieve your goal.

Visualisations: Further Refinements

You should feel perfectly comfortable with the visualisation technique that you have developed—relaxation, ensuring and affirming your safety, outer and inner, releasing the outer world, focussing on the inner, and returning to stability and good health after your experience. Just remember that you're always in charge.

Working with the oak invites you to craft visualisations that deal with specific everyday situations and people. When it comes to strength and energy, intent and a sense of inner integrity are vital. It can be interesting viewing your everyday situations from the safe place of the inner forest, and imagining a dialogue to sort a problem. If you try this, it's important to assert beforehand that *you will make a connection through your higher self to the higher self of another person.*

The higher self is beyond emotion, temperament, and personality. So although the person "in the flesh" might rub you up the wrong way, or irritate or annoy you, these factors become irrelevant when you imagine both of you in this way. If they are an issue, then you are probably daydreaming an argument to justify yourself, which is not the way forward! This higher connection is the way that you have been relating to the trees, though you haven't articulated it before now. That practice will help keep you on the right lines, and you will check that the emotions you evoke are all positive, and deepen your understanding of profound love and connection.

So, secure in the knowledge that your higher self will remain dispassionate and compassionate to any situation that stirs up emotion for you on the physical level, see if you think that any of the following visualisation suggestions will be helpful. If not, well, you are in charge; just leave them or craft your own. All should result in you feeling more complete in yourself. Affirm before each that you will finish and come back to your everyday waking reality feeling strengthened, invigorated, and optimistic. Here is a ten-minute visualisation exercise to try, in which you view your imperfect younger self.

You have found spare time and have settled yourself safely and comfortably, and as you breathe gently, the oak dryad's whispers are calling you to your inner forest…

Allow your sense of the outer world to fade as you approach your usual safe forest space; pause and go no further until you feel your strength and maturity flowing through you. You are about to gain an insight into yourself, and you engage all your higher senses to view that with equilibrium, as if watching an old film.

In the distance, see your younger self next to a sapling oak in the chilly sun of early spring. You look vulnerable, as immature beings are, and the sight evokes in you a profound compassion; you would love to

*protect both the youngster and the young tree. With every breath, you
feel your strength growing and you pour loving energy towards the two.*

*Think kindly of how well they are reacting to their environments,
and love all the imperfections they might have. Use colour and all your
senses to surround them with a golden-green aura of tree serenity and
strength. And as they respond to it, stretching and growing, see spring
turn to high summer, and feel the love you have sent returning to you,
from the sun and from the mighty oaks of the forest, untwisting cramped
parts of your psyche, spreading an enhanced sense of wellbeing which
comes from ultimate acceptance. Affirm to yourself your connection to
the mighty oaks—that yours is the path of simplicity and nobility, and
that it is your right to return at any time.*

*In the luminescence, the youthful you and the growing sapling
fade from view, screened by a magnificent oak that shelters you. Sense
deep within the constant strengthening cycle of energy as you shelter
and are sheltered, protect and are protected, give your strength and
have it returned... as in your inner world, so in the outer. You will
never know all who are involved in this process, and you don't need to
know; every one of your actions is like a pulse that ripples out into the
world. Be thankful and gently detach your awareness from the scene,
allowing your body the need to move and stretch. Turn and walk away
from the scene, full of vigour and optimism and faith in the world.*

Craft Your Own Visualisations

Now, here are suggestions for creating visualisations that are uniquely your
own.

Visualisation 1:
When time races away from you, connect to oak timelessness
Images that might be helpful: A clock ticking; fading and changing
into natural space. Sitting on the stump of a grandparent tree.

The life of the tree; use "time-lapse photography" technique. Accelerating the footage over many years: the oak as acorn, sapling, a young tree, a mature tree. The markings, scars, and burrs on the trunk; what has caused them? The tree recovering from wounds and thriving. Sights it has seen; feel its witnessing timelessness. The ticking of a wren—natural time passing. The time scale of the natural world within you; peace and timelessness deep within. The clock silenced: a relaxing sense of tree-time.

Visualisation 2:

To affect how you act in the world, connect to the Regal Oak

Images that might be helpful: The oak at high summer, glorious and golden-green. The nobility and inner strength of the tree. Your king/queenship awake within as a privilege. Low boughs whose leaves make a crown for your head; ask the tree for inspiration. Heroes and heroines from myth, fairy tale, famous art, or films rest under the tree, flowing into and out of it. Like a pageant, role models appear, aspects of your ideals and aspirations; respond to them. Place those noble aspirations safely in your heart.

Visualisation 3:

When circumstances are mundane, connect to oak magic

Images that might be helpful: An ancient oak at midwinter, in the snow. Leafless, a long scar down its length. The violent storm and transforming connection of the lightning strike that split the bark. A green ball of mistletoe high in the tree; white berries gleaming in moonlight. Suspended between heaven and earth, alive in the dead midwinter. Muscular boughs connect it to the host tree. The magic of connection and otherworldliness; what might grow into a new and unexpected reality in even the most prescribed of lives.

Visualisation 4:

When you feel isolated, connect to the strength of community

Images that might be helpful: The inner space in the forest; yourself as a baby, in a cradle made from a huge bough of the oak. The most ideal support and upbringing, loving and supportive just for you. Growing in the shade of the huge tree; the trunk ringed with figures made of light—all your strengthening influences, loving ancestors, those who are in tune, although you might not have met them yet. Your youthful self becoming you in the present; absorbing the strength of your unseen community within the larger environs of the oak forest. Each tree's aura flowing into the others. A bell jar of light and love—the spirit of the forest.

As a strong, mature presence in your life, the blessings and gifts of the oak are always just a thought away, the perfect antidote for when you feel overloaded and stressed, as if your strength is leaking from you. We are our feelings; take time to be with the oak, take on its viewpoint, and return full of vigour, with an inner awareness of the mistletoe, the plant of magic, which you, by your attitude, can nurture.

Practical Ways to Keep the Qualities of the Oak to Mind

Forgetting is the main obstacle to progress. In what has been called "the war against sleep," we need constant reminders. Try some of these ideas:

- Carry an acorn in your pocket for your potential, and make a crown of oak leaves at midsummer to wear whilst meditating or to hang in the garden.

- Did you plant a birch tree? Why not contact a tree charity to plant an oak, to mark a personal life event—a birth, or the anniversary of a bereavement?

- Find a piece of oak wood to keep for strength in your home or buy an oak walking stick to support you.

- Look out for oak furniture in your home or civic buildings.

- Search online for old houses and churches and be inspired by the ancient beams and exquisite carvings. Visit them if possible.

- Find, make, or draw a gold coin for sovereignty inscribed with an oak leaf or acorn.

- Most importantly, evoke strength within in your morning tree meditation.

Night-Time Visualisation; The Strength of the Oak

Help yourself drift into restorative sleep supported by images from the oak. Here are some to prime your imagination. There are lots of alternatives, but ultimately you will craft this to your personal specifications. Gently, without emotion, tell yourself a story along the following lines:

Lie in bed and breathe steadily, feeling yourself relaxing and attuning to the wider world of nature just beyond your window … Think of the two-way process of support in life, as if from a distance. There will be no agitation over current problems, just a witnessing as if from the perspective of a tall oak tree. Look with love and compassion, and see energy flowing from and to the tree in equal measure.

And you find yourself under that tree, which has a broad trunk and sturdy limbs near the ground. It takes you back to an imaginary childhood, the one you should have had, in a perfect world, where you were nurtured and loved and felt the freedom of the forest, to run and play. Relax deeper as you engage with your youthful spirit and start to climb the tree, joyously and easily up a rope ladder, making your way to the tree house of your childhood dreams. Soon you are at the top, with your head brushed by the drooping leaves.

Stand on the tree house platform by the rustic door; go through and you are in a small room, safely nestled in the crook of the trunk and a huge branch. Low on the floor, made up just for you, is a small, exquisite bed whose headboard is the tree trunk itself. You feel irresistibly drawn to lie down and pull soft covers over you, gentle as a mother's embrace. Allow your gaze to range around the room; every window and fixture is beautifully but simply carved with leaves and acorns, as if the house is expressing the essence of the tree.

Through the openings on every side, clusters of leaves and acorns press in, against their carved representations, and the breeze in the boughs is a nurturing lullaby of sleep. Through the floor, through the trunk, a nurturing sensation emanates and fills the space, so that you breathe it in with every breath and, like a child, drift peacefully towards restorative sleep.

5

Oak and the Magic of Nurture

Tree quality: They are nurturing.

You will be experiencing the way of the oak by playing with a balance: working on being very much "in the world" and privately developing your inner qualities. Remember, the oak is inextricably linked with community: how do you relate to that? We cannot all be judges, preachers, or teachers, standing under an iconic huge tree to disseminate wisdom—or can we?

Each of us, in our own way, fulfils the role of teacher, counsellor, wisdom-holder for some of our friends and relatives or work colleagues. We may not hold the history of our tribe, but we share in collective memories and can add to the valuable store of knowledge, sane judgement, and experience for our immediate community.

Being out in the world is a challenge: a challenge to maintaining our inner core of authentic self. And the pace of modern life adds to the problem—

circumstances, people, and our emotional responses pull us this way and that like flotsam adrift on the sea. And this is where the exercises, developing the internal strength of the oak, really pay dividends.

The birch exercises are now in our magic bag, a tree resource of connections to draw on whenever we need to. They are invaluable for new projects, envisioning our future, renewing and refreshing ourselves, and giving clarity. And now the oak is safely there too, a strong support, and all we have to do is stay aware and *remember* it is there in reserve for us. The trees can't come to us, but when we evoke, they are there, and accessible.

Take a moment, put the book down, and imagine yourself on the lowest branch of a huge oak tree. It is wide and safe, and you can lean against the trunk, letting the sprays of green leaves fan you with the breeze. Strength. This is what we have learnt so far. The oak sustains us, keeps us strong and on course.

And the strength of the oak leads naturally to its second quality: nurturing.

Previously you might have associated the quality of "nurture" exclusively with mammals. But we have expanded our thinking through relating to the trees as sentient beings. We are opening to realisation of the inspirited world of nature that is activated by a quality of love so profound that we can only stretch our brains to try and grasp its import. If we embrace this idea of the loving, sentient world, then we can also make relationship with landscapes of all sorts—bodies of water, the animal kingdom—but for now, back to the oak.

The huge crown of the tree, the vast spread of its branches ... the oak has developed to be as successful as it can in its environment; and what a wonderful result. There is nothing selfish in its development; the nurturing is not one-sided. As the earth feeds the oak, and the sky allows for its expansion, so in turn it feeds and nurtures others. We need never worry that giving of ourselves is weakening, not if we start with the inner strength of the oak. From this position, the more love and care we give out, appropriate to our circumstances, the more we can absorb. No tree lives in isolation; each feeds into and is fed by the whole of its environment. So we can see the crown of the oak as a huge umbrella protecting and supporting wildlife. We can call it a canopy of nurturing connections.

The oak has it: *so do you.*

Nurture and Gender

Take a moment to contrast the birch and the oak once again.

The birch is of the spring and new beginnings and redolent of the feminine impulse of new life being brought forth. By contrast, the oak is of the high summer, full growth and flourishing, and the active male principle.

Those are useful concepts, giving us associations to help to know the trees, but we must beware of simple labels. Nature in all its diversity is far too complex and sophisticated to be bounded by them—as indeed is human sexuality! To call qualities "male" or "female" is simply very useful shorthand, *not* definitive terms that will limit us.

In this chapter, we will meet, in the "reality behind the reality," great creative energies resonating through the gender spectrum: those that epitomise the nurturing qualities of the oak, through its relationship to the life-giving sun. And as we work, we always look out for paradox: in gender terms, the "feminine" birch also represents supposedly "masculine" action and focus, and the "masculine" oak's supportive nature links it firmly to the "feminine" nurturing principle. You see? Nothing is simple; everything flows and changes, dependant on many factors.

Our tree cousins give us shelter, food, and fire—how much more nurturing can they be? And oak excels at all of these. Go to an old house and you will likely find an oak structure, with oak beams hard as iron. If you prepare a fire to burn slow and hot, you need oak logs. Go on a wilderness course and discover that acorns, which are true nuts, can be used as coffee substitute or as flour.

But the oak, though a gentle giant, is mighty, not a plaything, and this must be reflected in our relationship, which must be respectful. Know your theory, or those oak beams will crush you as you build. Know how to prepare acorns before eating, or you're in for a bitter and possibly toxic experience. Obey the rules or a fire can spiral out of control. Trees are of service to us, but we take all of nature's gifts with respect, not for granted. The world is not our playground, so we act with sense and caution as we step into the forest of our experience, whether of trees or of our fellow humans.

Take a moment to evoke within yourself the *feeling* of the oak's strength, as you practiced it in the last chapter: timelessness, slow growth, connection to the earth and reaching to the sky, spreading to your own shape, rooted in the present, reaching to the future. This feeling we will now develop, expand, and use for our transformation. Understanding connectedness, we want the good of all, and we act to try to achieve this. Our strength, in furthering our own aims, will spread out, expand and transmute into nurturing impulses to benefit others. It is in our nature, when in our power, to use that for the good of all—to nurture. We cannot separate ourselves from others. The bark of the oak and the skin of our bodies indicate both where we separate from everything else and where we can touch. Like the oak, we find our own space and grow strong—and that is good for us humans and the urban landscape.

The Oak Dependants

As well as physically supporting other species, the oak has an honourable history of association with communities. It is indelibly entwined in our ancestral memory with the place of high summer in the procession of the seasons, when it is seen in its full glory. It is symbolic of the regenerative power of the sun—that vibrantly pulsing, eternally flowing stream of life-giving energy. *This source also feeds and flows through us, directly and indirectly.*

A mature oak tree supports more life forms than any other tree in the forest, from over 350 varieties of lichens through fungi and huge numbers of insects, to large mammals, such as squirrels. It is a dominant and unique force in the society of the forest, providing an environment for mice, badgers, and bats, and food for birds as well as deer and boar. Surely this is exhausting of even its prodigious energy? Not at all, because although the nurturing of the oak is apparently a one-way stream, all the life forms it nurtures are instrumental in furthering the germination of acorns and spreading the life of the oak in perpetuity. In considering nurture and interdependence, we keep in mind the word *symbiosis*: a mutually beneficial relationship between groups and life forms.

The ecosystem that the oak provides is a reminder to us, its human cousins, of our connections, obligations, and most importantly the benefits we receive from honouring them. When we first set our intent, we accepted that we are only fully rounded humans when we balance the duty we owe to ourselves and to others.

For a moment, commune with the oak dryad, and then spend some time quietly reminding yourself of those you nurture and those who nurture you.

The oak dryad speaks:

I stand, a giant in the forest, a mighty axis between earth and the dome of the sky. All may rest in my shade, all find refreshment from the bright sun, and shelter from the piercing wind or icy rain, hail and snow. It is my nature to shelter, and I do it without effort, just as I give of my bounty to the small creatures of the forest. Pigs are put out to pannage in my mighty forests, gorging on my bounteous acorns; squirrels bury them in their winter larders and live in their drays high in my canopy. Insects live in my deeply furrowed bark, just as microorganisms live on the skin of my cousins, the humans. And when those two-legged relatives collect my fallen branches for their fires, I know that my wood will release more heat in the burning than any other wood. I dream my slow, green dreams of continuity and the cycle of the years. As a sapling, I was nurtured until I could grow to full strength, and now I nurture in turn.

Oak's Mythic Associations

Mythic associations must permeate every chapter on the oak, if we are to do justice to its resonance and range. The king of high summer, the lover of the lightning, the magical hiding place of the wren and perch of the eagle, the provider for the mystical mistletoe—oak attracts myth as easily as it attracts lightning.

Entering the ancient oak forest we've moved to the summer months. If we see the template of the seasons as an allegory for our own lives, we've now moved from youth to adulthood; we are in the summer of our lives. This is when we really take control of our lives, when we assume *sovereignty*, which we introduced in the last chapter.

King/queenship and sovereignty implies responsibility for ourselves: physically, mentally, emotionally, and spiritually. We will always be on a journey, but in the season of the oak we are sure enough of ourselves and our proper "shapes" to stand up for what we know is right, as a king or queen would, for the harmony of our homes and lives—our particular kingdom.

There is a Welsh story of the oak, king of trees, nurturing the kingly eagle at the time of its sickness, until it could be transformed by magic back into a prince. But the reason for the connection between oak and wren is harder to imagine: after all, one is huge and one is tiny. One stands out from other trees by virtue of its height and longevity, whilst the other is famously hard to spot and has a short lifespan. But both the Welsh and the Irish words for the wren—*dryw* and *dreolan*, respectively—are linked to those meaning "Druid" and its status is explained in a Celtic folk story:

One day, the birds gathered to decide to choose a king from amongst them, and the decision would depend on a feat of power and endurance: the winner would be the one who flew the highest. So the vast flock of birds rose higher and higher in the sky, but gradually all fell away exhausted, until only the mighty eagle was left soaring towards the sun. As the birds prepared to acclaim the eagle as king, from over his feathered shoulder appeared the tiny shape of the wren, who had hidden on its back during its flight. He flew a few inches to hover just above the eagle—and was proclaimed king by all.

There are a number of ways of interpreting this story, but in the theme of this chapter it is especially encouraging to those of us who don't cut a particularly dashing figure in the outside world. The story says that physical impact and an outward show of strength are not necessary to success in life: the quiet, inconspicuous individual can have as much a sense of completeness and regality as the most apparently impressive. It is what is inside that counts; the will, the self-belief, and the wit to work out how to succeed. The wren had all of these: *you have them all too.*

As in the forest, the human grove relies on being enriched by symbiotic relationships between us all, with our breadth of gifts and life experiences. Every one of us is a king or queen, and so it is our job to nurture our "kingdom": the workplace, the home, our internal and external lives. The tiny, hidden wren's nest is traditionally called "the Druid's house"—what a secret and magical place for us to find within us! And it is a place to ponder... if we can achieve without expending effort on showing off to the world, even being invisible to most as the tiny wren is, we will always have strength left in reserve to rule our own lives, in our own houses, and to spend our nurturing efforts where and as our hearts, souls, and common sense dictate.

The Flow and the Power Supply

We do not think of the energy of the sun, or of the oak, as finite. Each day, we bask in the outpouring of the sun's light; each day, the oak draws up nutrients from the ground in a constant stream. Its leaves transpire and respire, gases are exchanged, the process continues endlessly for as long as the tree is alive. A similar process of respiration, digestion, and spiritual food nurtures us, and we process it all effortlessly for as long as we live. When we're tired, it's easy to feel that we're running out of a finite store of energy, but it can actually be fed from a myriad of sources, just as a million tiny roots sustain the mighty tree. Space permitting, the roots can spread far farther than the extent of its canopy, and similarly, the things that nurture and sustain us are more far-reaching than we usually consider. But this is where common sense comes in. Knowing when to step in, when to step back, when to step aside—it is the inner work of the study sessions to help develop and hone our intuitive responses to every situation.

We draw upon all our positive influences to feed us mentally, emotionally, and spiritually, and from that constant flow, we are able to give out the nurturing which others need. And when we are tired, we must allow ourselves to rest—probably the hardest advice we ever have to take!

Many of our "power supplies" will come to mind easily and be in our immediate vicinity, but reaching out to the edge of our terrain for a very few minutes reminds us of acts of kindness or courtesy from strangers, consideration from colleagues when it was most needed, unexpected loving messages from our distant relatives or near-forgotten school friends, or thoughtfulness from neighbours. All of these feed into our sense of ourselves and our position in the world. And it behoves us first of all in our new attitude as tree witnesses, to *notice* when these things happen. Resolve now to really notice—not just in passing, but to gain the full benefit, to accept every act with awareness and gratitude. Let a smile from a passing stranger warm you as you walk, and resolve to be fed by kindnesses throughout the day.

Put the book down for five minutes and think of personal examples. Breathe in the compliments, the courtesies; it affirms you every time a door has been held open and not slammed thoughtlessly in your face! Forget gender—hopefully we would all hold open a door for another human who was heavy laden—and accept all courtesies graciously and in the spirit in which you hope they are meant. Courtesy towards others is not a sexist concept, but is part of the oil that greases the wheels of our society.

Avoiding the Negative

Noticing positively is especially vital in family life, where familiarity with each other can lead to only noticing the negatives. Does that ring a bell? It happens to us all, and we must beware of it.

When this happens, the nurturing imbalance can seem overwhelming, especially for those with young children. That's when gratitude and thanks for every small thing can alter our way of thinking and replace the energy that seems to be constantly draining. Take joy in children, whose own joy in the moment can transform your day. Consciously build on these moments, filling your child-centred time with play and fun. Share in the bond you have with the other adults who look after your children, whether family or child minders. Go walking with kids, and show them the world of nature. Let them play with the sticks on the forest floor, hug the huge trunks, and all come home feeling nurtured and refreshed.

And in every area of life, family or work, forget the simplistic definitions, unless you're using shorthand. Nurturing is not more female than male—the male oak is the most nurturing in the forest.

The oak dryad speaks:

Join me here in the forest, and breathe in the dim, green light. Think of nothing... absorb deep within your being the lesson here, that all is interactive, that the secret of the pattern of all life is that it is interdependent.

Take ten slow breaths: with the nourishing earth; with the trunk of the great tree against which you lean; with the soaring branches; with the vibrant leaves; with the budding acorns, fruits for the future; with the hidden tunnels beneath the bark which echo your arteries, digestive, and nervous system; with the micro-organisms; with the insects; with the birds; with the animals; and finally with the energy of the whole tree.

As you complete this, feel yourself absorbing a new understanding of your role as witness. Know that, as well as fully participating, you can be noticing; you can step back and not expend your energy needlessly in over-emotional involvement. You can be as the tree, free from melodrama, quietly compassionate and nurturing.

If you are practicing regularly, in short bursts, you should be becoming adept at using these short conversations to evoke strongly in a short space of time, and should find that this is nurturing you within, from the imaginal realms. Use the tree imagery from the last chapter for strength and self-possession, and then allow that to expand effortlessly until it fills you and has to turn outwards in joyous relationships. This will show you what is going on around you, in your family or community; it will help you to see how you can nurture others.

Re-evaluating Your Nurturing

From the core of loving compassion fed through your daily contact with all that nurtures you, you now evaluate your strengths: physical, mental, emotional, and spiritual. And then look at the demands that are made upon you, and check that you are using your talents to everyone's greatest good. Are those demands appropriate? They might be right for your situation, but are they right for your character and aptitudes? If they are making you stressful and tired, how can they be altered or shifted to bring you into a more harmonious situation?

Consider this question: how many of our expectations are actually those imposed by society, and how many come from our own limitations?

From your tree-witness stance, take time out to re-evaluate and see how many of your actions are carried out as you sleepwalk through life, carrying along outdated attitudes from your parents and your early years. Habit, especially, accounts for much wasted time and stress, and that is time and energy that you now need for your new projects. So give yourself a gift of time: set it aside for a proper review of your habits. Which do you need to keep to, to fulfil your obligations? Which, with the blessing of your family, can you just dump?

Do not reject the idea of change out of hand, thinking that you know your spouse, your family, your workplace, and can predict negative reactions. That is part of the habit of lazy thought that stops us progressing. Witnessing life and respecting others teaches us that *we can never know other people*; all we can know is that they are wonderfully unexpected and frequently surprise us with their responses.

Do others the courtesy of expecting the best from them—a symbiotic nurturing relationship for the good of everyone. From your timeless tree position, go slowly and kindly. Take the view that people are doing as well as they can—yourself included. Be gentle, and allow people to expand into their true, compassionate natures, to support you in your change, whatever it might be.

The Role of the Ancient Oak

Maybe, still, the idea of fresh energy makes you feel tired? Hopefully, the birch has enthused you, but maybe, because of age or infirmity, the whole nurturing aspect requires just too much effort? Maybe the mature oak seems too big, too strong, too distanced from how you wake up feeling every day? If this applies, then concentrate not on your future plans but on what you need *now*. Focus on how the oak can nurture *you*, and send you out, strengthened, to the world of your responsibilities.

Suppose there was an essence of oak, a tincture that we could add to a bath of green healing, to spread nurturing life through our systems? Well, we are the ones with the miraculous brains—let us use our imaginations and evoke and make it be so! Take time, take time, imagine and be nurtured, and intuit the wisdom of the oak dryad, which will allow you respite when the cares of the world dismay you.

Imagine the oak as an ancient uncle-figure, immensely reassuring and with never-ending resources. Whatever your weakness, the oak can support you to growth and wholeness. Old timber from ships accounts for the bowed appearance of many of the old beams in our cottages. Although they are ancient, they are strong as iron. Be strengthened in your maturity by their solid stability. Let them remind you of your own history and the wonderful continuity of your life. You've been downtrodden all your life? Maybe. But you're still here, aren't you? What does that say about your wonderful resilience and strength? Be proud of it.

The oak has a traditional role in protecting kings and is as ready to perform this service for you. The king of the outlaws, Robin Hood, gathered with his merry men safe from ambush at the Major Oak, and King Charles II was saved from the Roundheads by hiding in an oak tree. For this reason, Oak Apple Day is still remembered in England each April 29th, the day that the king entered London to have the crown restored.

And if you're feeling every minute, month, and year of your age, know that every August, past the middle age of each solar year, a natural wonder occurs on the oak: the Lammas flush, when tender new leaves appear on the mature tree. Amazingly, in the mid-season of its annual growth, it is still regenerating.

So can we.

Viewed in a positive way, the years of our life experience can be a source of strength to us, not exhaustion. Our meditations and associations will help us put out fresh new impulses and enjoy a flush of creative energy whatever our age. Lammas is traditionally the time of the Lughnasadh Games, set up in the Ireland of legend by Lugh the sun god, so there is that oak/sun symbolism again. Imagine the mature August sunlight pouring down on you, encouraging new energy, evoking strength, playfulness, and joy.

In Ireland, the ancient triple Goddess Bridget was associated with fire, the sun, and the oak. Her influence was so all-encompassing to Irish culture that with the coming of Christianity she seamlessly transferred into a saint of unparalleled importance to the Celts, the foster-mother of Jesus, and still linked strongly to the sun and to the oak. She is associated with smithing—a fiery craft—and poetry, likened to "fire in the head." Her saint's day is set at the festival of Imbolc (Candlemas) at the beginning of February, when the sun's return shows in the lengthening days. The floral representative of the sun, the dandelion, is Bridget's flower, and there is also a charming legend that the sun loved her so much that she once threw her wet cloak over a sunbeam, which held and dried it. A powerful oak-supported, fiery woman indeed! Her cell at Kildare, with the flame that was not extinguished for seven hundred years, was guarded by an ancient oak, and Kildare translates as *Cill Dara*, meaning "church of the oak."

Like Bridget, who spent a lifetime serving her community, we are now turning our energy to nurturing ourselves and others.

The Magical Aspect of Nurturing

When we are properly nurtured, when the energy of life flows into us and we are in our power, we set up a supportive, loving current flowing out to others. And soon, as we are noticing the eternal return-flow, we stop having consciously to "allow" this process, and it becomes integrated within us. We let the humans with whom we live off the hook; we stop expecting them to meet all our needs and find other ways and routes and supplies. We lose our unreal expectations and relax into the security that the whole universe plays a part in our support.

The oak dryad speaks:

Sit under my branches; lean against my trunk; breathe in the green energy emanating from my life force—be renewed. Be filled with the love of the natural world. See it stretching back into the past and far into the future: a broad, pulsating golden wave, timeless, accepting. Find your support here, without making any demands on anyone else. With each breath, fill yourself with golden-green light, and breathe it back out to the universe. You, like me, are whole. You, like me, are in the right place.

Without the strain of our unreal expectations and demands, our loved ones and our work colleagues can in turn relax with us, and life can become a graceful flow in perfect balance. And we can take our proper place in the human forest, and contribute our unique gifts.

Lessons from the Oak

Nurture

The oak dryad speaks:

Nurturing others comes from a sense of wholeness within. First feel your strength, your integrity, your faith that all is right with your world, and expansion will arise within you and pour out to all around you.

First Thoughts, First Steps

You might have the personality type that thinks of "nurture" as sickly sweet, mawkish, or intrusive into the lives of others. If we're responsible for ourselves, we might not welcome others' nurturing attempts or want to express that energy to them. Honour that feeling; you are quite right. The nurture we're discussing is on a different level entirely; there will be no awkward interferences into the autonomy of others on the physical level. There's nothing wrong with a shy expression of sympathy or support at the right time— anyone with empathy will feel compelled to offer it—but *trying* consciously to be nurturing will always seem "do-gooding" and strike the wrong note.

The nurture of your tree cousin comes entirely from its essence, from its essential nature. *So will yours.* The stronger you feel, the more happy and grateful, the more alive and full of expectation, the more those inner experiences will translate magically into an expansive, loving, and supporting expression in your dealings with the outer world.

So start by just looking at your particular style of nurture, with your notebook to hand. Are you naturally soft and gentle? Are you brisk and no-nonsense, active and doing, showing in practical ways? Does your nurturing strength emanate from you in a way that makes people feel protected and happy when they are with you? Nurture is one aspect of love made manifest, and it can be expressed in a million ways. The job is to make sure that you express it in a way appropriate for you, and only you can work that out.

When engaged in this fascinating work, consider from whom you learnt your nurturing style. From your father, mother, or other significant adult? We all tend to, and then wake up thirty years later realising that we are duplicating behaviours that might no longer sit easily within us, and have no relevance to our present circumstances in a myriad of social and emotional ways.

A story (everyone with an open heart loves stories) illustrates this, on the most basic practical level:

For generations, a family has cooked the joint by cutting the meat into two, putting both pieces into the tin and roasting them. After this has become enshrined as an ancient tradition, an enterprising child asks great-grandma just why they do it. "Oh, that? I don't know why your mum does it. I started doing it because when I was first married, I didn't have a roasting pan large enough for the joint." Instant collapse of family tradition!

The message is, don't perpetuate anyone else's style or tradition unthinkingly. Don't rerun their emotional responses, or even their cooking style! Doing that is sleepwalking through life. Yes, like the oak, we are bounded by our environment and culture, but not to the detriment of our free will and creativity.

The Nurturing Balance

Being present, withdrawing from the everyday world into the forest, allows the mental and emotional space to question what you do and the way in which you do it. And the way to change those ways if that's right for you.

For example, part of a parent's nurturing instinct has always been to warn children when they were running into danger. But the way they do it has changed over the generations: in times gone, that love could be expressed through a slap to ram the message home. Attitudes—personal and societal—change, and we must too.

Parental nurturing can run you ragged, so, with the gracious indulgence of the childless reader, here are a few thoughts. Try some de-stressing procedures for family life, firstly, by teaching your children about responsibility through giving them chores reasonable to their ages and abilities. Yes, they will moan, but you know that it's really good for them, and they *will feel* very grownup, compared to their friends. And then you will have the energy left over for other nurturing activities—taking them to the park, having fun with them.

When you set rules, make them reasonable and understandable to the child, and then stick to them. Always make time to enjoy your children's company, then they won't need to act up to get your attention. Never introduce contentious subjects or tell children off at family mealtimes; by giving food you are giving affection, so sharing food should always be a positive experience.

As you nurture in every area of your life, you are creating your family's reality or your office environment, and people remember joy, magic, fun, and jobs harmoniously done, not pristine floors and empty draining boards. Only you can craft the right balance.

Approach all aspects of your life from different angles: remember, it's your rational mind and thought processes that have limited you in the past. As you read on, through the visualisations and affirmations, you are harnessing the entirety of your oak connection—to sovereignty, to strength and a feeling of wholeness, to service, and to yourself. Evoke those qualities within you: do it now, just for a couple of minutes.

Imagine that you are sitting on an old oak chair, its wood darkened and polished with age and wear. Take three breaths and allow your inner royal presence to assert itself, that mixture of privilege and responsibility that is what it means to be human. When you really internalise this, it can be life-transforming. Who knows, you might discover you own an oak chair, which can serve as your "throne" for this regular tune-in.

Affirmations

You will now build on the strength of the last chapter to reinforce which-ever changes you would like to make to your nurturing style. These affir-mations only take a few moments, so treat yourself; never forget to *evoke* and feel the truth of what you're saying. And remember, little and often ...

OAK AFFIRMATIONS

Every morning:
I create a nurturing web of relationships with every contact.
I feed and am fed by all aspects of the wider world.

To tweak your existing habits:
I nurture in a way that is appropriate to now.
I can withdraw to set myself back on course at any time.

If you feel cut off from others, or too passive:
I nurture dynamically; I see the right opportunities
    to nurture and act upon them.

If you are overstretched:

**My strong branches touch many others, but I bend and flow with
life, and withdraw from contacts that do not feed my spirit.**

To access the nurturing of the oak:

**My inner vision is always clear to me; I sit by the great oak, and
am nurtured by it.**

For timelessness:

**The ancient nature of the oak nurtures me throughout my life;
I relax into its peace.**

And now we travel from the internal to the external again. We ground
our internal visualisations, hopes, and plans with work in the outer world,
building a bridge—of stout oak boards—so that life is an easy flow between the two realities.

Practical Work

Keep the nurturing of the oak in mind with some of these:

- Give yourself rest and respite by sitting round a fire,
  especially one made of oak wood. It burns slowly:
  enter into timelessness for a magical evening.

- Sit under an oak to perform your affirmations.
  Does that amplify the experience for you?

- Find a piece of oak that speaks of nurturing to you. If
  you've already bought an oaken stick or staff to be a
  companion on your walks, you'll know how supporting
  it is, as well as how strong.

- When on one of your walks, shake wet leaves or deliberately brush under low oak boughs in the rain to be showered with droplets. Imagine the oaken qualities spotting your skin with magic.

- Seek out clean fresh rainwater that has collected in the hollow of an oak tree. Take a tiny phial of it back to swirl into your bathwater before a meditative soak.

- If you're very able-bodied and adventurous, find an outdoor centre offering treetop walks, and take one! If you're not up to it, then try this walk in a visualisation.

A Nurturing Lifestyle

Looking after yourself starts with the physical body, and stems from your love and respect for this vehicle which is essential for your incarnation. This is a thorny issue for many of us...would taking a tree perspective help? Maybe forgetting our outside covering and concentrating on health, not looks, might be a way forward. We all get sucked into thinking that big fingers are wagging at us, denying us what we want to eat or do. And the only response that elicits is straight from our adolescent selves: *I'll do what I want, you can't tell me, you're not the boss of me!*

Forget all that; there is no conflict, no confrontation, no "them" telling "us." This is part of the over-involvement in our soap-opera lives that we're trying to wean ourselves away from.

Without our emotional involvement, changing our life habits becomes much simpler. Like the oak, we have pathways that have to be clear to allow nourishment to reach our extremities. But, lacking the oak's capillary action to pull it through, our complex system relies on the heart for circulation and many large organs for digestion, for respiration, for reproduction...all to be kept in good working order. We are miraculous organisms, deserving of our nurture.

There are many ways of reviewing, checklisting, and otherwise starting to change your habits if they are bad, but this is a sensitive area and not the remit of the book. Just be kind to yourself in developing a system that will support you in your change, and stop beating yourself up! Guilt and judgement take you on an inward spiral of self-disappointment that is never going to be helpful.

I would just say, forget outward appearance; a tree is a tree, and each is beautiful in its own way. If your genetic inheritance dictates that you will never have the silhouette of a supermodel, that's great. Let's hear it for diversity! Let's keep ourselves clean and clear with right diet on the inside, and let the outside appearance take care of itself. Paradoxically, doing the first should improve the second anyway! The oak only takes as much as it needs for its nourishment. In a world of plenty, distributed so unfairly that there is over-abundance for some and precious little for most, let's withdraw to the sanity of the forest and make our peace with our eating habits. Substitute boredom eating with a walk, a meditation, a doodle. Engage with the world creatively, and let's nurture ourselves right.

Nurturing and Preconceptions

To start this work, mind-map all your connections, and embellish your diagram with energy waves in differing colours. This is just for you, so be honest, rather than drawing the ideal; that can come later. First withdraw to the timelessness of the forest: distance yourself, lose the emotional attachment, and draw quite lightly on the paper:

- Your most important people and things will be large and in beautiful colours.

- Those that nurture you will have thick fluid lines of connection to you.

- Those that sap your strength you can depict as dark and uncomfortable.

- Put direction arrows on the lines of connection, so you can see at a glance which way the energy flows. With your loved ones, arrows will usually point both ways.

Spend a few minutes each day looking at and considering it, perhaps after getting into a receptive mood. Do you agree with your initial assessment a few days on? If not, amend the names and lines of nurturing energy until they are accurate. Have you included people with whom you really no longer should have any connection? Is it fair to you both to let them go to find their own more fulfilling connections? Are there a lot of dark, uncomfortable areas and influences? If so, begin to adjust them as you wish them to be. Do you have empty nest syndrome? Is it time, not to let go, but to graciously allow your young ones to lead their lives? How will you portray loving acceptance visually in your diagram?

Spend another few days thinking...

Are you working to change some of these relationships? When you find changes occurring, use your eraser to lighten and minimise what you want to change, add vivid colours to emphasise what you want to reinforce, and gradually include more people and things! Remember from previous work, our support systems are much larger than we at first think, so remember to include peripheral characters, early influences, and courteous strangers.

What about great-auntie who always remembered your favourite flavour of ice cream? The web of connection does not rely on being in contact in the present. That feeling of being special has made you what you are today. Then include the person at the stop by work, who smiles every morning, the tree overhanging your drive, so you don't get wet going to the car in the rain, the mirror on the shop that lets you have a crafty check of your appearance before you go into work. And what about the school's crossing attendant who always has a smile for the children, who cheers you up, the birds that remind you of your parent's farm ... the connections could be endless. Stick more paper onto your original if you need to, but don't leave anyone or anything out. Realising the richness, depth, and breadth of our connections to the real world is the way to realise how well we are nourished and sustained.

Doodling

Are you addicted to doodling yet? It didn't come easily to me, as I'd been taught by the academic system to think in boxes, but I persisted, and it really does open up the mind and make for expansion. I heartily recommend it. For this session, change your tree doodles to include symbolic images of nurture. Here are some suggestions, but really, your imagination is your only limit:

- Hearts and flowers
- A safe bower in the forest
- Branches growing in the shape of hearts
- People sitting round a warm fire
- The wren's nest, filled with tiny birds
- Deer and fawn in the forest
- A celebratory table heaped with food

Keep a notepad by the telephone in your bag or pocket, and use it on the bus or train. Not only will you open your mind, but, with practice, your doodles will become more assured, which will encourage you to continue.

Craft Your Own Visualisations

Craft at least one visualisation of your own before you finish this section; you can make it specific to whatever circumstance you wish. You might like to go back in this chapter to share the connection with the oak dryad again, but allowing more time to go deeper and absorb more.

Visualisation 1:

To rid yourself of preconceptions, connect to oak transformation

Images that might be helpful: A slow-burning oak fire. A drawing pad on your knees; gazing into a fire. Distance yourself, becoming one with the timeless scene; scenes of your life in the fire. As the oak burns, images change into your enchanted future. Drawing or writing a negative judgement that anchors you to your present, filling the page. The words and images fading, losing their hold, disappearing into the past. Tearing off the page and tossing into the fire. Repeat the process for clarity and lightness.

Visualisation 2:

To nurture your internal needs, connect to the wren's safe haven

(Find a picture of a wren's nest to see it, in just the right place, before the visualisation.) *Images that might be helpful:* A wren's nest in the fork of an oak, an intricate globe of interwoven twigs; hear the cheeps of the young within. Another nest, in an old teapot, or in a coconut shell; a wren busily constructing it; laying five pale eggs freckled with red. Wherever it is, the wren makes a safe haven. Transfer that understanding of round, enclosing softness to yourself. Wherever you are in your life, be in a circle of soft, glowing light, of love and strength. Within it, you are nurturing your future. Bask in it.

Visualisation 3:

To develop your sense of responsibility and privilege, connect to oak sovereignty

Images that might be helpful: Connect to the Regal Oak again and the role models who appeared briefly before—heroes and heroines, warriors and kings. The responsibilities and privileges of the king, the knight, the beneficent carer and nurturer. Myths and stories from all over the world: Joan of Arc, Finn MacCoul, Guinevere, Morgan le Fay, Charlemagne, Buffalo Bill, Mother Teresa. Allow as many as you can to show you their gifts of sovereignty. The mantle is on your shoulders, appropriate to your experience; bring back a sense of self-worth and responsibility to the world.

Visualisation 4:
For the simplicity of being nurtured
Images that might be helpful: The cool, green woods: an emanation of love from a large tree. Sit under it, climb into it, and just be. Enter timelessness; feel and absorb, relaxing into simplicity. Allow simple nurturing images to arise for as long as you wish.

Of course you can turn this last visualisation on its head and imagine yourself as the oak, nurturing others.

Magic of Simplicity

The last visualisation could not have been more basic: just let go and be, and allow the beneficence of the trees and the wider world to nurture you. And here's a seeming-paradox: true greatness is marked by simplicity and lack of show. The more we realise our own authenticity, the less we need to show the outside world, and the more energy we store for things of importance.

The wren, king of birds, is small and insignificant. Stop wasting your energy on impressing people—most of us even worry about what total strangers think of us! If I dress up to go out, people might think, depending on their perspective, that I look good, look freakish, am dressing too young/old for my age…but so what? *Most will never even notice me.* We should be true to ourselves: if we're the jeans and sneakers types, then tuxedos and ball gowns are not our thing, and vice versa. There is so much freedom of expression in the world today that we really have no obligation to society except to be true to ourselves and not to offend.

Every time we fuss about what to put on, we should look beneath to see what our anxieties really are. If we are so desperate to fit in, or to stand out, there must be some insecurities attached to that. Ditch the clothes angst and prepare instead by visualising love for awkward family occasions, or by doing your preparation thoroughly before a presentation, and so on. Busy yourself, like the wren, with doing and building and making the best way you possibly can, and know your own worth.

We are cursed with the thoughts that we are pretty dam' important, without doing anything. So, in the absence of empirical proof—the book, the play, the impressive business résumé—we have to expend our energy making sure everyone knows it. Resolve to ground all thoughts in action that reinforces a positive sense of yourself. Within and without, remember the congruent flow where each state builds on the other. Soon you will have built a résumé relevant to your internal feelings. You will have become and will be showing to the world the person you feel you are inside, and that sense of congruence will give you all the assurance that you now seek.

The Timelessness of Nurture

By now you should not believe but *know*, through experiencing these exercises, that to feel fully nurtured is to enter timelessness. There is an eternal quality to feeling truly nurtured, truly in the right place. Whether with family, privately with a loved one, or at work, doing that which engages and feeds your spirit, feeling in the right place at the right time, leads to enchantment. At the end of the busy day, after a family celebration, or a blissful romantic evening, we shake our way back into linear time, having lost all track of it. Being truly engaged in the moment is to live in the timeless state of the trees and the forest. It happens when the real life we are living feeds us on every level; it can conjure a response that we recognise as pure magic.

It's Never Too Late

The time of the oak at its strength traditionally starts at the beginning of summer and continues to the harvest. But we can work with this energy at any time, and we do not need to equate our harvest time with our chronological age. Remind yourself of this each August and if you can, go out to a local oak tree to witness for yourself the "Lammas flush," then return home and meditate on the lessons of this late flowering.

That's it: enough said. Everything in the book so far should be helping you to lose your attachment to linear time. At any time, you can loop back to your childhood and the energy of the birch, or fast-forward to the harvest and the steady sense of slow growth into maturity. And you can retain your sense of fun and magic. The Lughnasadh festival—Lughnasadh is the Pagan version of the grain festival which the Christian church calls Lammas—celebrates the sun god pouring down to ripen the grain. As mentioned before, this festival was traditionally celebrated with games to honour his foster-mother, who brought agriculture to Ireland, clearing the forests and planting grain. Why not have a tea party in August, when the sun pours down on you, encouraging the emergence of new energy, evoking from you your strength, playfulness, and joy?

Whatever your age, allow the nurture you receive from the world to relax you enough to engage with your sense of fun. We should celebrate *every single achievement*, not just grand big achievements, and not in a grand way. A coffee with friends, or a phone call, will serve to mark on your magical calendar the day you picked a glut of beans, received a card from your godson, first felt the wisdom of the forest as a reality deep within your being.

The world is looking after you in a million ways. Be glad.

Within your heart, imagine an exquisitely made wren's nest. Safe inside are tiny symbols of all that you hold most dear, all that you would nurture. Know that it is safe and reinforced every time you care for them in the outside world.

Allow the image to fade … Soon you will make your way to the third quality of the oak, after a restorative sleep.

Night-Time Visualisation: Nurtured by the Oak

Help yourself to restorative sleep by connecting to positive images of the oak. Try the visualisation below or dream up one of your own. This one should be taken slowly, slowly—the idea is not to stimulate your imagination to the extent that you will become more wakeful, but to help you drift away. So, when you are ready for sleep, gently, without emotion, tell yourself a story along the following lines:

The work of the day is done, and you mentally release your everyday concerns … Take three breaths and become comfortable, and then feel that you are climbing into a boat or ship. You make your way either across the deck or down the companionway to the lower deck—you choose—to a bed. As the boat rocks, you become aware that you are floating timelessly on the sea of life.

Allow your surroundings to form around you as you relax still deeper … Craft them exactly as you wish. If you have gone below, you might be in a beautifully appointed cabin in an old sailing ship with a porthole, through which you can see the stars. There is panelling of dark wood, and a desk with the tools of the mariner's trade, and charts so that you could steer if you wished; but now is the time for rest, and there is every comfort for your journey. A small lamp burns steadily. Your bedclothes have never felt more luxurious or more comforting.

Or, if you don't like being enclosed and have stayed on deck, you are now in an oaken bed, bolted fast to the timbers, with sail billowing gently and the sky high above lit by the glory of the constellations shining down on you … There is the north star, showing that you are sailing unerringly in the right direction.

The gentle surge of the sea beneath the thick ribs of the planks rocks you and sends you ever deeper into relaxation… There is an emanation of protective strength from the ship itself, with its solid oaken keel, well caulked, perfectly formed for the journey on which it is carrying you. You are nurtured by that secure feeling; it is as an essence that you can imbibe from the ancient oak planks. Your limbs are soft and relaxed, on the verge of sleep, and you feel the resonance of your essential being nurtured by the security of the boat. You are being fortified even whilst you drift…

You can smell the brine in the air; you hear the waves washing against the side and are aware of the deep-sea life miles below you and the high starry heavens above. You, right here and now, are in your perfect place. All is well, and you drift with the tide… Drift further and deeper, with the strength of the ship holding you and no effort needed from you. Sink deep into a state of restorative slumber… Sleep now and be fed and strengthened as the strong ship of your life carries you peacefully on the journey into morning.

6

Oak and the Magic of Belonging

Tree quality: They are of service.

Our longing for change has been our driving force so far. Using this, evoking the feeling of being already where we want to be, imagining, we have been visualising within the direction of our new lives and seeing ourselves settled in that position.

Retreating to the forest and meditating with the trees daily, even for very short periods, is gradually and surely inculcating a more-than-human perspective to enable internal changes. And we've worked on ourselves—becoming aware of the power of anticipation, of our inner strength and physical health. The longevity of the oak reminds us regularly to withdraw, to relax into the forest space and allow these changes to *take their time*.

Every day, as we practice "being as a tree," we reinforce this within ourselves. We are checking progress in our special diaries, and are integrating and internalising the ideas.

The oak dryad speaks:

> Just be here for five minutes … Evoke the experience of my tree with every fibre of your being and with all your senses. See my whole perfection and then move forward to feel my bark, smell my greenness, hear my leaves rustling, taste the living freshness of the air. Evoke belonging, here in my shade, and then return to your life.

This chapter is about belonging, which is surely where we are at the moment? Well, in a way … So, are we now halting the work of change? No, this is far from the case. But it will flag up some interesting work on *acceptance*.

We must accept that we belong where we are at the present—all our life experience has brought us to this place. Respect and accept it all, even the bad decisions. We are all imperfect human beings, so rejoice in that; we learn along the way, and it's a very bad and rare negative experience that doesn't have, or lead to, some positive results.

Think on this fact now. A lot of our less-than-perfect experience has come about because we made decisions when we were distracted by the world, and so were deaf to the prompting of our authentic spirit. So whilst we must accept where we are, we can also view it not as a static state, but as a jumping-off place to where our spirit wishes us to be.

Being at Home

Like a tree growing and blown by the wind, we have stretched our limbs and found our shape—but what of our surroundings? We might still often feel like a square peg in a round hole: like a birch smothered by brambles, like an oak sapling in a cramped back yard.

The art of life is to get to a place where we truly feel that we belong, on every level.

At Home in Your Body

Starting with our personal kingdom, the body, we should feel comfortable and in control. Many people use therapies to support conventional medicine when they are ill, and most doctors agree that feeling in control and contributing to your recovery aids it. Any mature tree shows how it has adapted to injuries and grown stronger from them: scar tissue from broken branches; burls from stress to its growth. How similar to its human cousins! Every wrinkle and scar on our bodies is a memorial to a time of testing. Every test reminds us to take charge and respond positively. Allow the bad times; let go of the resentments of the past.

The oak grows past old injuries: *so can we.*

At Home in the Family

Then there is the family unit, often a far from harmonious entity. So it is reassuring to remember that nature ensures that seed is carried away by wind, animals, and birds and, in the case of some plants, by explosion, propelling spores or pollen far from the parent.

From the witnessing perspective of the trees, change seems a natural process. We should leave our parents' home, and our children in their turn will leave ours and settle in an environment where their growth will not be cramped by family expectations. Part of our work of belonging might be to remind ourselves of this overview. If this is relevant to you, then go to your inner forest to distance yourself, to cultivate a gracious acceptance of what cannot be changed. There should be no residual pain from this splitting process, but a transmuting of past relationships to a new, mature footing. If you see dealing with the emotional effects of children leaving as a severe block, then it might be worth seeking specialised help to resolve those issues.

At Home in Society

Belonging in wider society has perhaps never been more difficult—or more stimulating and challenging. When we all lived in tiny communities, everyone had, and knew, their place, which was both reassuring and very restricting. Today with far more opportunities to connect, the only place we have as a right is our place in the family—if we're lucky. Every other relationship we must work at—but, excitingly, we can choose where we put our energy.

Start by dividing your life into as many overlapping segments as you can think of: work (paid), work (unpaid), hobbies, interests, clubs, church, connections through the Internet . . . Just consider these areas in passing now, and in the study session, try mind-mapping exercises to show you where most of your energy goes, and whether it's to the right place! If one section is draining, you can discreetly cut back on it, and use that extra time to vision up a life where every part of it will feed your spirit.

As the trees all find their right place in the forest, so we can move and dance to the challenge of today's world, to fit into subsets of our wider society and gain a sense of community from each. The gardening club, walkers' association, voluntary work, amateur orchestra, old school friends group, or knitting circle all bring us into connection with like-minded people. And if you can think of no subset you belong to, then that in itself is a matter to ponder. We are designed as social animals; sometimes it's good to go slightly out of our comfort zone in order to make human connections. We all need that contact for good health, for a rich and varied life. So rise to the challenge of finding exciting activities and companions. No sewing bee in your area? Offer to help make costumes for the local drama group. You don't feel very connected to the group you're in? Offer to help those who run it, letting them know your skills in organisation, accounting, or creativity. There are thousands of ways of increasing our sense of belonging in society, and all of these feed our wellbeing and self-worth. They add to the interest and excitement that we evoked via the birch.

Like the oak, we have symbiotic relationships, and ours too can be with many other life forms and organisms, as well as human. Our sense of belonging depends on connections. Our inner contact with the forest is just one; if you continue this work, you will doubtless find many others.

The office where we earn our money might not seem to give us these connections—but that's not its job, is it? Going into a professional environment might teach us more about being like the solitary oak, as we engage with work to the highest standards and support work colleagues dispassionately and appropriately. These standards will pertain whether we have a seat on the board or are in the humblest job in the world. And who knows, sometimes a like-minded soul does pop up in the most arid environment!

Belonging on a Spiritual Level

Truly to feel that we belong on every level, we must make space for the unseen realms, for the essential mystery of life.

If you go to church or belong to a mainstream religion or follow a Pagan path, then probably you already feel connected on a spiritual level. But acknowledging a spiritual dimension to life doesn't necessarily mean that you feel comfortable embracing a faith system. It is a case of "square peg in a round hole" again: the fit might not seem right. This is where the natural world can supply all that most of us require. Being in nature gives us a sense of perspective; it reminds us of the quiet harmony of the natural world; it shows us wonders we couldn't have dreamed up—the sunset, dawn, a bird emerging from an egg—and feeds our sense that not only is the world a place of harmonious and benevolent growth (even if we are not able to comprehend the larger pattern) but that we ourselves are a vital part of it.

Millions of leaves falling every year remind us of abundance; acorns sprouting every spring remind us of the cyclic nature of life which we share. Learning these lessons, filling our minds with images from the forest, we absorb the teachings of the earth, not through our rational mind but at a deep soul level. We are what we do and what we feel, which influences *how* we think. Turn to the larger life of nature to grow and expand into a spiritual understanding that—in spite of all the ups and downs of everyday life—all is well. For many of us, that deep, intuitive understanding is enough, and we don't need dogma.

Traditionally, spirit is associated with fire, that mysterious element that seems to exist in a slightly different dimension to ours. Folklore tells us that oak was always a component of sacred fires, and one of nine sacred woods for the kindling of the need fire at May Day, or Beltane, from which all other fires in the community would be lit. And it is good to hear the echo of the mythic oak association with the sun king at the height of its strength, when we consider that the oak is the fuel not only for the midsummer fire, but also forms the Yule log of midwinter.

Plenty of Time to Belong: Discover Your Skills

Belonging can seem hard, but the oak tells us not to be downhearted. Remember the oak flower remedy to support us when we feel that way, or sitting in the shade of the tree to experience a profound, regenerative effect. You may have started reading this book with many years behind you and with a constant sense of time wasted. Hopefully, with the growth of your larger perspective, this feeling will now be changing. We cannot reclaim those years, but we can view them differently and kindly. We can learn another way of thinking, one that makes the sense of linear time passing less relevant. The reality of our lives is that we can feel time as our friend; by slowing down and simplifying, more and more is available to us. And by immersing ourselves creatively in all we do, we enter timelessness regularly.

The oak dryad speaks:

I am a mature tree now, and I have spent more than a human lifetime in my growth. I had seen the earth's turning eighty times before I put out my first acorns. I created and produced prodigiously when the time was right, and now I still grow and witness that abundance spreading out around me, creating what will in time become a new forest. I might still be here a thousand years hence, or I might be lightning-struck or chopped down or succumb to disease before my descendants have grown into mature age. But now I am standing at peace, still in my period of fruit-bearing. And now is the only reality I need to acknowledge.

Our imaginations give us the gift of immortality. We can imagine a future both with and without ourselves in it, feeling that, even after death, our benevolent connection to others can support them. If a person thinks suddenly, "What would [any deceased person close to them] have done?" or "Wouldn't s/he have enjoyed that?" are the beloved dead not present with them once again? Won't our loving thoughts strengthen our loved ones when we are no longer around? It might not be provable, but what a wonderful way to view the ultimate mystery.

No matter how far along the path of linear time we are, we can connect into creativity and timelessness to rejuvenate our minds and imagination, and make the best possible use of each moment *now*. We know the shape of our tree; we know how we should grow; it is time to make the most of our skills and talents.

A Role Model

Grandma Moses, the famous American folk artist, took up painting in her seventies and came to the attention of the media when she was eighty. What a role model! We can all do that in our own way by owning our own creativity, by allowing it to belong to us and express itself through us—and success is nothing to do with whether we become famous. Humankind is meant to be creative, so do not waste energy looking back at where you've come from. Be still in the moment, connect to the oak, and allow your creative future to unfold in your mind's eye, then live that as a reality.

Use the oak study session to review your skills, and from them, develop a framework of how you can best use them for your own enriching and then for the benefit of others. Do not worry about the size of your contribution; just do what seems right in the moment. Balance all your needs. As your circumstances change, you can adapt what you offer to your family and the wider community.

"If you want anything done, ask a busy person,"—and anecdotal evidence says that in any situation, 75 to 80 percent of us will be catered to by the active 20 to 25 percent. Now, that statistic allows most of us a huge area of positive, constructive interaction to move into, and what a morale boost to know that we are part of the group that helps things along for the majority. It just takes a shift in attitude—realising that if a job has to be done or a project supported, there is no reason *not* to offer help. If you never have, do try it. A time when this happened to a significant percentage of the population was during the Second World War, when women stepped into the world of work and volunteering to keep industries running and help the war effort. To read of the paradigm shift of those women, who had previously seen their roles solely in the home, can be inspirational. Stretch yourself: you might surprise yourself and all around you.

Belonging in the Natural World

Quickly ask yourself these questions, some of which draw on the study sessions:

Do you feel at home in the natural world by now? Do you know more about your own locality and the trees there? Are you excited to see how the changing seasons affect "your" trees? Have you seen them at different times of day? Are you grounding yourself in the world of nature, so that the images are vivid in your imagination, and can transport you to scenes of peace and beauty? Just thinking about these things should evoke those feelings that arise when you are in nature; take a deep, relaxed breath, and smile!

Do you keep remembrances of nature around you? It's exactly the same principle as putting a picture on the fridge to help you eat with awareness. Do you use natural objects—wooden bowls and dishes, leaf print cards and tree calendars, driftwood and pebble paperweights? Do you have a nature table that is constantly changing?

Answering these questions can really remind you of how far you have come. Reread the suggestions in the practical sections, and feel the spirit of nature within your home. Enough said; there is a world of excitement waiting as you pursue this path. Find organisations that can take you out into the countryside—and especially those that can give you an insight into the hidden life of the wild—deer, badgers, wolves. Put a special expedition on your birthday wish list; it will change your perspective absolutely, and give you a completely different set of references for all aspects of your life.

Belonging and Inspiration

An old oak speaks of continuity and an ordered existence; that might seem a little dull. After all, we are humans, with the capacity for faster movement and thought, and surely we ought to use that? Of course we should, but we are currently aiming for an antidote to overuse of our brain and too-quick thinking—that's the place from where stress emanates as fast as a wink. There is a middle ground between living a soap opera and standing immobile in the forest for the rest of your life, and we are finding it.

When we have systems in place that support our being at home in the world, life is no longer a frenetic struggle to keep up. With family, friends, and a source of income and/or simpler lifestyle in place, we can turn our minds to other things. That's when we look for inspiration, and this is where the oak can be of service, for which tree is most often struck by lightning? The old proverb supplies the answer: *"Beware the oak, it draws the stroke."*

Lightning, and its attendant thunder, has long been associated with kingship, deity, and divine inspiration. Like the king of the trees, the oak, the king of the gods has been associated with a thunderbolt and lightning, with examples worldwide. The Greek Zeus armed with a thunderbolt; Odin and his son Thor, the Norse weather gods; Thunderbird, Tlaloc, and Apocatequil of the Americas—throughout history, peoples have revered the magical energy of lightning's shocking and dangerous strike. Lightning appears out of nowhere to wreak destruction, to transform. It is like nothing else and is as mysterious and otherworldly as the fire that often results from it. It can be likened to the sudden strike of inspiration that hits us out of the blue, transforming our thinking, our lives.

Finding our work, our true ambition that will add meaning and purpose, is one way to make us kings or queens of our lives. And in doing so, we must court the lightning that the oak attracts; we must be open to the strike of inspiration that may direct our paths. Not that I'd advise anyone to shelter under the oak during a thunderstorm—in fact, please don't! There are scientific reasons for the attraction of lightning to the oak in particular, compounded of its height and the moisture content that attracts the electrical charge. Symbolic truth and practical common sense can exist together in our minds, and lightning work is always to be done from a safe place or in the inner imaginal world.

Oak is famed not only for suffering the explosive effects of a strike, which can blast its bark many yards from the trunk, but also for its ability to survive the blast and to heal. Our aim is to free the time for inspiration to spring forth. The more time we spend in "tree-ness," the more we allow it to well up within us and the greater space we leave for it to suddenly strike as an idea that must be followed. Within reasonable limits, we aim to follow these inner urgings: who knows where they might lead? Without following, we may never know. And it's a pity to do all the preparation, to take all the time and trouble to immerse ourselves in the states that will encourage inspiration, and then ignore it.

There is a meditation specifically to visualise the forest in a thunderstorm in the study session, but you might like to spend a couple of minutes anticipating this now.

The oak dryad speaks:

The sky above the field is darkening, and gusts of warm wind blow your clothes around as you shelter by the gate. In the middle distance I stand, isolated in my height, in the middle of the small hedge. You see my huge dead branch spreading out, the only one with no leaves on, and the pale stripe running down the trunk, a scar from a previous lightning strike. Yet my living branches stretch out sideways to their full extent. The rain torrents down and the distant rumble of thunder tells that the storm is getting nearer ...

Atmosphere ... evocation ... can you achieve this imaginatively in a few moments yet?

Belonging and Sustainability

Our search for the unexpected flash of inspiration is held by the structure of our regular work, which makes us available and open to it, like the oak growing steadily to tower over the other trees and so to draw the stroke.

We can count on the reliability of the oak and depend upon it always belonging in our lives. And there is a charming apocryphal story to illustrate this. We don't have to know if it is literally true to absorb its lesson.

New College in Oxford, UK, was founded in the 1300s. Like the other colleges of the university, the structure depended on iron-hard oak beams—giants of over thirteen metres in length. So how could they be replaced when, over a hundred years ago, it was found that the beams of the dining hall were full of beetles? Where was wood of that quality in the twentieth century?

The college forester was called and was not fazed. At the building of the college, a stand of oaks had been planted on college property precisely for the purposes of replacement, when it became necessary.

For hundreds of years, the message had been passed down through successive foresters that the trees were designated for that purpose. And so it happened: the building was restored—and, hopefully, that forester ensured that more oaks were planted for when they would be needed after the next few hundred years.

We connect by our practice to the oak's dependability so that change and fluidity, the unexpectedness of our human lives, will always be supported. Through life's journey our ideas change; we chop out parts of the structure of our belief and ideas and replace with the strong, fresh, and new. This is the way of maturity. If we form a worldview in our teens and never alter it, then how will we suddenly find replacement ideas to make sense of our lives when the beetles of experience attack the structure of our beliefs? By belonging completely in the real world, we keep our minds fresh and open; we nurture our structures and are not afraid to replace and update them as necessary, knowing that we are more than them, that we will always have the resources for change and growth.

Belonging: The Portal to Magical Reality

Lastly, let us look at a primary quality attributed to the oak: as a portal or doorway.

In the ancient Celtic alphabet of the trees, called the Ogham (pronounced *Oh-um*), the oak is called "Duir," which also means "door." And midsummer, the time of the oak king, is also a doorway—the portal to the darkness to come, as the days grow progressively shorter. So study based around learning the wisdom of the forest may be said to reveal a doorway to spiritual truths.

The image of the door is sublimely evocative. As we approach, we have a choice: to gain access or to go another way. If we decide that we want to go through, then we must knock for access, await a reply, make the commitment to moving from one space to another.

How do you interpret these images?

Every time you pass between two same-species trees on your walks, you are potentially going through a doorway—or not. It is all up to you; it is all in your intent. If anyone read your notebook, it too would be a portal, a doorway through which they could glimpse a magical journey—although only through the actual experience of doing the work could they pass that portal to transform themselves.

Doors of high status buildings such as cathedrals, castles, and institutes of learning have always been of oak. We can use this association to imagine a door in our mind through which we will travel to our future of a new, magical reality. This portal could be an oaken door, a door actually in the trunk of an oak, or simply two trees growing together, with the boughs meeting overhead, between which you pass with awareness. Having passed through, we, having integrated the wisdom of the trees, will be able to relate to the real world from our new perspective. What a great reality to inhabit!

Working with these ideas in the study session, we keep in mind that as we step forward, the two upright jambs of the door-frame are there in support. Stepping through we can always access the strengthening, nurturing, magical and noble gifts of Duir, the oak. After the next study session, we will move ever deeper into the forest to meet with our third and final tree.

Lessons from the Oak
Belonging

The oak dryad speaks:

From my heartwood to my bark, from root to crown, I live in the world, whilst my spirit soars to the stars and delves to the deeps for magical sustenance. How do my roots and leaves supply all my wants? How do thin sap and sunlight nourish my massive structure? How did my canopy evolve to catch most sunlight? What wonders! I simply accept; the world supplies all my needs. Some trees from the times before the ice, before humankind, have shrunk over aeons to manifest as weeds today, yet I continue as a noble form to inspire and serve all living beings. I am a miracle of the mystery of evolution and life. I have my place in the forest and in the wider world.

First Thoughts Before Action

Belonging—how wonderful! Both inside yourself and out in the world, you belong, as a right. Take a deep, slow, relaxed, and smiling breath in and out as you affirm this by reading each of these statements:

- I accept myself, warts and all.

- I am happy to relate to the world.

- I know that I have unique gifts to share.

If these are just partial truths at the moment, that's fine; remember the slow progress to growth of the oak.

This is our last study session with the oak. You are gradually approaching the deeps of the forest, where you will encounter the ancient wisdom of a tree that is not only even more long-lived, but can be regarded as eternal.

So this work is for you to ensure that you stand securely rooted, that your branches dance with the flow, and that you are comfortable with the inner/outer world dynamic. That delicate balance whereby you can be true both to yourself and your needs and to all your outer world duties is the pivot of your magical life. It is in the nature of living by the rules of the real world that no inner work can protect you from boring or repetitive obligations, getting wet when it rains, or periodically having a run of bad luck. When it happens, jolt yourself out of your frustration with the comment, "Welcome to the human race." Don't indulge in the trap of taking yourself too seriously. Laugh and get over it and get on with whatever it is—for the millionth time! And do it with the scent of the trees and leaf mould and the sound of the birds as your constant companions.

Remind yourself again of a most important fact: unless your work leads you to the path of a monastery or nunnery, developmental/magical work is *never a reason to withdraw from the outer world*. It's a way of *connection* that requires the opposite—an expanded awareness. And the magic of the oak in full leaf is calling to us all, demanding some time in our busy schedules, so here are some reminders to free up time to pursue the magical dynamic:

Are you getting up earlier to have some time to yourself, or have you found other solutions? Perhaps by parcelling out work in the home, cutting boring phone calls short, and combining socialising and activities, so that you have more "alone" time. Keep observing your television/film/ Internet time. Do you know yet how many hours a day you spend? You don't have to justify it to anyone, but by this stage you should know it and be happy with your choices. In the workplace, do you have clarity around your job specifications, so you're not unfairly overloaded? With modern technology, we feel we have to use every available minute. If you use public transport, use the time for yourself, for reading or just gazing out at the landscape, not on catching up with office work.

We will learn far more about boundaries on all levels in the next chapter. For now, you've read about being at home in your body, your home, your family, your society. Is checking this part of your work now? Don't dismiss the small or practical steps as unimportant: a fresh coat of paint/reorganising your bookshelves can change your attitude to your surroundings, making them a relaxing haven that feeds your new sense of yourself. It's satisfying to crumple up and throw away lists as you finish your tasks—do you then find odd bits hiding behind furniture a week later? Do you remember that clearing up is actually a part of each job? Do not neglect this simple aspect of at-home-ness. Home is your sanctuary, from where you do your most important work.

Let's recap the points of the chapter briefly:

- Check your lifestyle, your diet, your habits.

- Love your body—it's brought you this far!

- Check in with your family relationships.

- Check your physical surroundings.

That potentially is a lifetime's work, but it is also simply the background to your inner work and changes. Be as the oak: look objectively and dispassionately; lose the emotion and guilt attached to the bad eating and imperfect relationships. When it comes to making changes, start small. Keep at it regularly, being gentle and kind to yourself and others, knowing that everyone is doing the best that they can. That last one might be hard to remember when people are being difficult, so don't even indulge in thinking, worrying, and intellectualising about the truth of it. Just act as if it's true, and if you need backup, in your inner or outer world (or both) embrace the huge sustaining trunk of an oak, breathe out your angst, and trust.

Use your tree connection regularly to avoid slipping back into seeing from only our restrictive human viewpoint. Periodically look at life with the eyes of the dryad. And, like the growing oak, be firmly set on your course: your sense of feeling thoroughly at home will benefit everyone.

The Family Dynamic

If you'd like to delve into the changing nature of family relationships, first of all, beware! Unless you have severe family problems that need your attention, and professional help, looking at your family in this way can make you addicted to a pseudo-therapeutic attitude to analysing your life, sending you off on a complete tangent to this work. And it's often a cheat—a sneaky way of deflecting, seeing your own faults reflected in others, leaving you squeaky clean and *everyone else* at fault. Getting you out of that way of looking and into the place of taking responsibility is where this book started; you're growing past it, into more fruitful ways of interpreting your world. Playing at therapy and analysis is also a game to bring out the worst in others; the quickest way to make people furious is to tell them what their problems are, how they think, or why they're acting that way.

Why spend your precious time back at square one, encouraging your resentment and picking fault? How much good has that thinking done you in the past? Forget the matchbox psychology—enter your uninvolved but loving tree-space and engage with these exercises lightly, playfully, enthusiastically, and positively.

Sketch, Draw, Wonder…

Get your sketchpad and colours, take the phone off the hook, and just remove yourself from soap-opera emotion mode by connecting to the protection and nurturing of your inner oak and the serenity of the forest. Then make one, two, or more sketches of the rhythms of your family relationships. See how your children's energies reflect yours at the same age. Know that that is a part of the perfect pattern. It could go something like this:

Draw your grandparents and those of their generation as ancient trees; parents, uncles, and aunts as mature trees and so on down, with any child-relatives as seeds or fruits. Then progress the picture forward a few years; any who are deceased might be drawn as "shadow trees." Children are now saplings or seeds trying to establish their own space. (There are many different models, which can be adapted for your own circumstances. This one is to cover as many bases as possible at one swoop. The permutations are endless, dependent only on your imagination.)

Draw honestly; if you or another parent are the trees that are impeding the growth of any sapling, draw yourselves as such. Then, the magically creative part…in the same or another picture, gently rub out constricting lines or redraw completely to illustrate the relationships you would like as your ideals. Don't forget wispy energetic lines from your ancestor trees, whose influence can still be felt down your line, or from children who've moved away but whose loving energy continues.

Develop a diagram that shows your current ideal, and put it where you will see it, preferably daily. It will still be private to you, because it will just be a picture of a magical forest—if you've been discreet and not named your trees, you can display it publically, in a frame on your office desk, for example.

Wider Society

Mind-map on how the wider society impinges on you, using the headings in the chapter—your home, family, society and so on—to make sure you don't miss out any areas of your life. Does advertising affect how comfortable you feel in and with your body, for example? Again, be creative—why not draw yourself as the dryad in the tree trunk, and label your main interests as the boughs, the leaves that come from them all your interests sized in order of importance, with those that are most fertile growing as acorns? Keep it around for some days so that you can add on as more things occur. How fruitful are you being in the *outside* world? The more you spread your connections, the more lightly and joyfully you can hold them all with tree-awareness.

The Spiritual Level

Everything we do is to strengthen the connection that allows us to access the spiritual side of our lives. So make time to check in every day, entering your own private space and connecting to your authentic needs and the whispers of your soul, presented in the pictures we humans love: of forests and guardian and teacher trees. Connect to your oak tree, bringing your increased knowledge of the tree to the relationship. Rest beneath it, sit or lean against it, or meld with it ... the only guidelines are to take your time, and start and finish your meditations with the pattern you have established, removing yourself fully at the end and stating your re-emergence fully into the outer world.

And don't forget the tea and biscuits afterwards.

This spiritual element is the basis of all that we do, connecting and feeding our sense of authenticity, its whispers encouraging us to live our lives with integrity.

And, for the good of our spirit, we must get out into nature. What we see, smell, feel, taste, and hear are the firsthand experiences that make our memories. Sit on a park bench for five minutes or go hiking in the wilderness—just get out there. *The more you get out into the natural world and walk with awareness, the more natural images your memory holds, the richer the visual, auditory, and sensory vocabulary you bring into your inner space.* Bring back the birdsong, the changing colours of the leaves, the magic of the sudden sight of a deer in the distance, the smell of fox in the undergrowth, to refresh and enliven your inner world. The more you do, the more tuned in you will feel to the world that you are meant to inhabit.

As always, feel and evoke the truth of these affirmations within you.

Oak Affirmations

Every morning, during your first gaze at the day and on to tooth cleaning/general ablutions, fill yourself with these thoughts, so that they are your reality:

I dance today with the dynamic of balance.
I respect every part of my life.

When it's all a bit work-a-day:
I embrace the magical aspect of my being.

When you are resentful:
I am what I do. I respect my obligations
   and fulfil them so brilliantly that they are a joy.

When you are isolated:
There is a web of connections in the world, *and I am part of it.*
Today it is easy to shake the web and activate my connections.
(Follow this up by doing something it make it true, no matter how small. Repeat the affirmation regularly through the day, with more small actions, until smiling on the bus, holding the door, paying a compliment, become a habit.)

At night, remind yourself:
I honour my authentic self. I will sleep deeply
   and sweetly and awake to another day of dance.

For inspiration:

I am open to inspiration and can trust my instincts.

During very busy times:

**I am of service. My resources are limitless,
my inner core secure. I regenerate each night.**

Practical Work

There are so many things one can do to reinforce the easy, flowing dance from the forest to the grocery store or mall, and practical projects all help us in our work of maintaining awareness:

- Find a place to have a campfire and make a definite date to have a midsummer or midwinter fire; put it on the calendar and invite your friends.

- If this is impossible, find a group that has open community fires periodically—maybe the boy/girl scouts. You will enjoy community, will connect privately with the slow burning of at least one oak log, and can also toast marshmallows.

- Go on walks organised by rangers to see the hidden life of the forest—you will soon be using what you see to enrich your inner life as well.

- Be proactive through every level of your life: how can you help, how can you be more in touch? *Choose only projects that you delight in.* For every one you reject, you allow a space for someone else to find their niche.

- Think young: change, adapt, and develop new skills. Keep up to date with technology.

- Look around the house again—are your favourite bits of wood in evidence? Are you replacing artificial with natural fibres and wood? (This is entirely dependent on your own taste and preference. Just *be aware* of your choices.)

- Wooden light pulls and banister caps often come in the form of carved acorns, and are very cheap. Why not indulge yourself? They were originally used to protect the house from lightning.

- Varnish acorns and keep a bowl as an ornament or string them to make a necklace.

Doodling

This section naturally overlaps with those that have gone before; interactive magical change doesn't fit neatly into pigeonholes. I hope that you're now enjoying this method of opening up your mind. Do you consciously give yourself time to drift to the forest, to tree-awareness, *before* you scribble, sketch, or doodle? Can you draw an oak branch, a leaf, and an acorn so that you at least can recognise it as such? Do you now keep a small pad of paper by the phone or armchair? Are your sketches rigid and constricted, or are you also using soft shading and fluid lines where appropriate? Are you drawing energy lines, webs of connection, things that we intuitively know about but can't see with the physical eyes?

Most importantly, is this work a source of expansion and fun? If not, how can you adapt it to make it so? If you're struggling with coloured pencils, ditch them and buy wax crayons. Or throw the lot in the bin and play with magic markers and a school exercise book. Keep experimenting, keep fresh, keep enjoying.

Craft Your Own Visualisations

Visualisation 1:

To rid yourself of a too strong attachment to linear time, connect to oak

Images that might be helpful: See with the eyes of the oak dryad. Express yourself as a "tree person." Dancing through the seasons, remaining unchanged within. Acorns growing; connecting to youth within. Time as a coloured stream enveloping the forest and looping in a spiral: touching parts of the past, present, and future, all within you eternally. Serene detachment, connecting to your life at any age … or to your eternal self. Evening in the forest; acceptance; change and stillness. Eternity.

Visualisation 2:

For inspiration, connect to the lightning strike of magic

Images that might be helpful: You as the ancient tree, observing human behaviour. Lovers lingering; children running; a lone walker noticing nature: all aspects within you. The power of an impending storm; security in your strength. Thunder. Rain streaming down your trunk, dripping. Lightning searing, connecting you to all the passion of your life; brilliant with inspiration; the current flowing, grounding in the earth. Outworn ideas as branches shedding, painlessly, burning on the forest floor; a bonfire of your blinkered perceptions. Feel freer; stretch and grow once again. The rain streams; you settle back into timelessness, to ponder a new revelation.

Visualisation 3:

To grow your excitement in nature, connect with the night forest

Images that might be helpful: Great oaks, standing still as time passes. The movement of insects crawling on bark; squirrels in a treetop; a tree creeper running up the trunk. Be present with the hearing of the deer, the eyes of the fox, the nose of the badger. Glowing green eyes of nocturnal animals; follow their movements. A shadow in the hollow of a tree: a huge owl. The secrets of the night forest, full of wonder.

Inspiration

How we envy the inspiration of the great artists: how wonderful to create a masterpiece! Many of us will never reach those heights, yet we can all access inspiration to drive our lives and make them magical.

Sometimes, by a happy accident, by a synchronistic series of happenings, inspiration strikes. It's expansive and wonderful when it does, so can we actually encourage that to happen more often, or are we simply at the whim of fate? Well, we have Visualisation 2 above, to keep the possibility in the forefront of our minds.

Let's consider the idea that inspiration is constantly in the ether, in the refinement of the air we breathe. The problem then is not the length of time we have to wait for it to come along, but how to access it—if you like, how to attract the inner lightning flash. We know by now that listening and making time to hear that inner prompting is vital, as is respecting your instincts. Providing your intuitions are legal, decent, and responsible, then go with them! By being open, you will keep your life fresh and your interest in it high. Practice drawing lightning strikes to help you stay alert!

An attitude of awareness keeps us open to inspiration. And we know this delightful paradox by now: we keep our keen engagement with life by regularly withdrawing for inner refreshment.

Exercise to Keep Your Real World Fresh

After your next visualisation, come back to your everyday reality, affirm that you are back, and then really *look* at your surroundings with fresh eyes, ears, nose, skin. Reread that last sentence: it's an exercise that can surprise you. "See" with all of your senses—mentally or out loud itemise what you feel, see, hear, taste, and smell, and note what impression it makes on you. Then withdraw briefly and return to do the same thing again, appreciating everything you see.

This is a wonderful small habit to get into—try it out if you are a passenger in a car along a regular route. Close your eyes for a couple of minutes and open them to really *see*—you'll be surprised how much extra information your brain will take in as you really *notice* the surroundings flashing by.

And keep doing it, because all our senses get jaded very quickly. They need to filter experience for us, so they quickly go into the default setting—everyday reality, "waking sleep." Our noses become immune to perfume or aftershave; we filter out irritating background noise; we adjust to a bath temperature, or a new taste such as hot curry, very quickly. And this is another reason that we should go on ranger tours to view wildlife: our overworked eyes usually record what our brain expects and so we need to be shown how to look with fresh eyes.

The "in-between times" we are creating at the end of our inner work allow the freshness of the world to strike us anew every time. We actively encourage these windows of opportunity by using our whole awareness at these times. From a fresh appreciation, inspiration strikes, even if it starts as the homely but overwhelming urge to paint that wall, or the resolve never to have to look at that painting ever again when you open your eyes—no matter if it was your granny's favourite! Remember: small, simple encouragements. Our world is made up of tiny everyday acts which incrementally add up to our quality of life. So the obvious way to change it is in the same way—until we wake up one day and realise that magic has gradually become part of our everyday reality, an inspiration that will explode on our consciousness. Buy roses on that day to honour the beauty of your spirit, shining through your actions to enliven and enrich the world.

When inspiration strikes, of course, we realise that skills are necessary to bring our ideas to fruition in the world. And throughout, we are working also at developing our skills with the energy for growth and serenity of the oak. If it's true that genius is 1 percent inspiration, 99 percent perspiration, as Edison said—and circumstantial evidence seems to bear him out—our work is just to follow our true path and work hard in the world, trusting that the inner impulse we've recognised will guide us to those skills we need to learn, those contacts we need to make, as our inner authenticity is being reflected and served by what we do.

Magic of Doorways

As you prepare to leave the shelter of the oak stand, look out in the world for the chance to visit an ancient public building or tourist attraction where you can experience the solidity of a panelled oak door and engage all your senses as you step through it into the church, library, or wherever. First sketch its construction; how is the wood complemented by the clenched nails, the latch and lock? Take some time later to consider the oak's association with the door, rereading from the chapter—from this world to other realms, from inside to outside, from known to unknown, mundane to magical…

Later, you can allow the oak dryad to guide you by evoking a sense of threshold and of being on the verge, at a meeting place between present and future:

The oak dryad speaks:

Long before you were born, when I was old and full of years, I was content to be cut down, knowing that my million acorns assured my immortality. Broad planks from my trunk, tall columns of oak and a massive lintel make up the doorway. This is a way to be taken by those who wish to progress on their true path. Step through, traveller, and may your journey be blessed.

Night-Time Oak Visualisation of Belonging

Once again, help yourself to restorative sleep with an oak journey of belonging. Remember, the idea is not to stimulate but to help you drift, so gently, slowly, without emotion, tell yourself a story along the following lines:

You are drifting gently in a walk that leads slightly uphill to a circle of tall, mature trees, silhouetted in the deep gloaming that will soon be complete darkness. As you stroll, you become aware of an emanation on the breeze, a feeling that strengthens, that you are on exactly your right path. The fresh air is elusively perfumed, carrying the green scent of the oak trees. Breathe it in: you are travelling to where you truly belong, on every level… where you are completely accepted for all that you are and where the simplest acts of your life are rich and colourful and deeply rewarding. Your relaxation deepens; in this world there is no rush or confusion.

The aura of the trees invites you upwards, so you approach the summit of the small hill with no effort. As the trees tower over you, stop on the edge of their dim presence and ask that you may take your rightful place in the circle of belonging.

As an answer, you notice a couple of down-hanging branches through which you must pass: a hanging portal into the deep enclosure. You pull aside one branch, and the leaves whisper "welcome" in your ear. Once within, you pace a full circuit of ancestor trees, feeling their familiarity and acceptance, and layers of anxiety and stress which were so deep you weren't even aware of them gradually dissolve from your muscles, your tendons, your spirit.

You feel the strong desire to sleep and find a natural seat in the bole of a huge oak. You are wearing a loose, soft, warm garment, large enough to wrap you completely as you sink between the roots of the tree. Deep beneath, imagine the roots . . . a mysterious web of connection to all other like-minded beings. You too are part of a web of belonging. Snuggle down, feeling the hard trunk and roots supporting you in absolute comfort as you stretch out, as if the tree grew especially to accommodate you, into deeply affirmative and restorative sleep, in your own place of belonging.

Moving from Oak to Yew

Once again, we must be on our way. This time, we move from the regal, flowing solar energy of the King of the Woods deeper into the forest, to the mysterious groves of the yew. Take time first to look around your environment, internal and external. Gently, dispassionately, look at your head space, your heart space, your home, and your workplace.

Have you internalised the lessons from the oak? You have learnt from the trees that there is no hurry to this process; everything is working out in perfect time. Are you just reading, or are you *doing*? Are you thinking, or are you *experiencing*? You are the sum total of your experiences so far: have you learnt to evoke a magical energy for change from within yourself?

Your notebook should feel like a confidante—you have so many comments and check marks on it. Don't be worried about its neatness; it's your working document.

Are you still sceptical? You *feel*, but wonder if is it true? If so, relax and trust.

And as a sop to your logical sense, ask yourself this question: is it better to feel that life is magical and that you have a degree of control, or to feel frustrated and unconnected? Trust yourself not to lose your critical faculty. Know that you are sensible enough to give yourself reality checks, as you compare inner with outer reality. But just sometimes, give logic a bit of time off, as you drift into the timeless magic of the trees.

If we cannot alter our reality (I believe we can, and that this is the way, but you don't have to agree), we can certainly alter the way we feel about our lives. And we can relax into positive feelings, and then observe, as a tree would, what comes along in our lives.

Remember, everyone takes full responsibility for this journey; each of us crafts it perfectly to our needs.

Does the voice of the oak dryad strengthen and nurture you, reminding you of where you belong? Are you working to develop the strength and grace of the oak and developing an inner sense of yourself as sovereign? Most importantly, do you feel that you are fulfilling your obligations to society whilst still focussing on your own goals? Is your strength slow-grown, dependable in the outer world, well-rooted for nourishment, as you reach to the sky and the possibilities of your inner life?

Be aware of your inner sense of magic developing every day, every hour, every time you look out at the natural world. Go back through your diary and remind yourself of what you've done, on the physical, mental, and emotional planes, and you will find that work with the first three feeds the fourth, the spiritual. We need these reviews because we are so miraculously adaptable. Without them, we just don't realise how far we've come along the way, although the attitude of friends and family—and their complimentary comments—are pleasing reminders to us.

And don't think of moving on until you've had your party or celebration! Include family and friends, whether you choose to tell them the reason or not. Theme it to the oak, and if the season of midsummer falls right with your work, so much the better. If not, adapt.

If you have a bonfire or barbeque, try to get just a few oak chips to add to the charcoal. Make oak leaf prints with the children on a cheap paper tablecloth or surround candlesticks with acorns. Have a competition or games and crown a guest as oak king or queen—if they won't think it too odd. Have a Robin Hood party and ask everyone to wear green, or have a picnic under a huge oak tree. Feel the *strength* and *nurturing* of the oak as you prepare: you are celebrating *belonging*, finding your space, and so you might honour that by inviting your friends to help with the preparations.

Focussed plans take time and work. We must allow our new ideas to sink deep within and become part of our new way of thinking. These times of consolidation are an ideal time to dance with the joy of the trees in regular celebration. Think also of yourself standing between two strong oak pillars in a deep doorway. The door is ajar; you have only to ask, and to push, and you will continue your journey into the forest. But that is for later ... For now, enjoy your achievement—celebrate!

The Yew Tree
Surrendering to Life

Yew Qualities:

They are disinctive.
They are prodigiously generous with their gifts.
They are a bridge between the worlds.

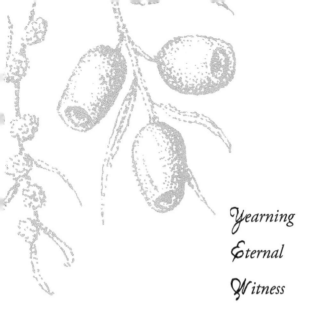

Yearning
Eternal
Witness

7

Yew and the Magic of Boundaries

Tree quality: They are distinctive.

The yew dryad speaks:

The light becomes more diffuse and dappled. Before you duck under my low boughs, pause, look, feel. My ancient arms, bending to the ground, stretch far. There is my massive trunk at the centre of a magical dim circle of green.

I invite you into this space.

Under my dim, green canopy, you walk on ruddy earth, springy with my needles, enclosed in my grove. Does it seem dark with my red-brown bark and deep glossy foliage? As you stand on the edge of our new relationship, think of all you are bringing, all you have gained so far from my cousins, the birch and the oak. Remember all the similarities there are between the trees, and between trees and humans, on every plane.

Welcome to the Grove of the Yew

The European yew has *difference* as its characteristic. And difference is immediately intriguing to our imaginations. Do not be concerned if your native yew is smaller or only accessible as an ornamental variety in a park. Yew manifests in different forms worldwide and, in spite of the tree's difference in size and longevity on different continents, has from times of antiquity been marked out as special by our ancestors.

If you have no access to huge yews, then suffuse your senses with pictures and impressions of the mighty European yew—through the Internet, books, posters, and pictures—until you can see the dim groves in your mind's eye. Then, when you visit your native yew, see if the yew impressions you have gained internally transfer to the actual tree before you. A tree does not have to be huge to carry a potent energy. Later in your studies you can look at other trees—especially old evergreens—and see if they hold part of the message and resonance of the yew for your area, and there are suggestions from other students as to substitutions in the study session.

The wind blows through the birch, which reaches out to us through its pollen and falling leaves, attracting us with the magic of its appearance.

The oak exudes a solid strength that is charismatic; it draws us.

The yew keeps its distance, physically, with ancient long branches delineating its space, creating an atmosphere that is removed from everyday life.

We have practiced politeness in our dealings with the trees, and so it is now second nature to us to ask the trees if we can connect and work with them. Now we are glad that we've learnt our manners, for here we are approaching Otherness. Yews—and all of the other longest-lived trees in the world—are our cousins but set apart by their ancientry; they are the elders of our tribes.

The yew has gathered superstitions around it like a cloak; it is shrouded in mystery, and reminds us that life is about lightness and darkness, joy and sorrow. To attain maturity, and the internal serenity of the trees, we must acknowledge the whole gamut of human experience and our human reactions to it. Being in tune with the trees does not pull us away from the natural realities of life—and darkness of all kinds is essential for balance.

With the oak we have been out in the blazing sunshine at high summer, at the height of our strength, and it is a very human wish to stay there. Yet nature teaches that the constant of life is *change*, and there is a time when outer gifts must give precedence, so that our attention can focus on our inner strength and the challenge of accessing inner wisdom.

All that is required as we move from the place of the oak is to reframe our boundaries to include and celebrate darkness. We must recognise and embrace its essential nature; for from darkness and stillness emerge wisdom and inspiration.

Three impossibilities to remind us to respect and love the darkness: sleeping in full sunlight, concentrating when exposed to flashing lights, and maintaining focus when a light is shone in your eyes. Just sleeping with the curtains open, with the morning sun striking the pillow, prompts us to burrow under the covers and embrace the last moments of darkness! Too much light in the wrong place is cruel, so walk with confidence into the dim, sacred light under the shelter of the yews. They are old teachers.

The Necessity of Boundaries

The yew aspect of our personalities will reinforce our sense of necessary boundaries, if we allow it. We might feel an instinctive aversion, thinking that such an attitude is unpleasant or off-hand, but if entered into in the right spirit, it's far from it. The need for boundaries is not something to suppress; we all have a basic need for, and right to, inner space. But boundary awareness does convey a very particular resonance that some will not respond to well, because it is not what they are used to.

We have practiced keeping our essential selves and our needs balanced against the world's demands, but the charisma of our oak-selves can act against us in our search for our own time and space. The more capable we are, the more in demand we will be. And it is a hard fact that those lovely encroaching friends of ours, for whom the concept of boundaries was invented, will be just the ones who can trample ours down without even noticing what they do.

When we develop a deeper understanding of the necessity for respecting our own boundaries, it will manifest in our behaviour. From our inner attitude will arise our own particular ways of maintaining our space, and as we become more confident and less *involved* in an ego-driven sense, it is easier to use them. Now is the time to focus on ring fencing and on keeping our own time sacrosanct.

We will still be fully active in the outer world, of course, fully engaged and fulfilling multiple contracts with others, as we should. But into this we can incorporate our new way of relating, which will be intuitively recognised by most people. It will, to a certain extent, set us apart.

We do not *look* for difference, apartness, and we do not court it; we are not affected by the glamour of it. Wanting to be different for the sake of making an impression is the spiritual equivalent of putting our energy into "dressing to impress" instead of developing the inner qualities that really would make a difference. Our energy goes into our work, and any changes are just a natural by-product.

The yew invites a turning inwards, the deepening of our thoughts, and a true sense of our self-sufficience. So, with boundaries in the back of our minds, let us start in the usual way, with the physical tree.

The Unmistakable Yew

The European yew's appearance is simply magnificent. Stop now to find large colour images of some ancient yews, in books or on your computer, then take five minutes with a yew image to connect to your breathing, to your inner forest, and jot down your immediate impressions, no matter how disconnected they might be. Single words or phrases might arise. Lastly, copy the picture; sketch a part of the yew that attracts you—bark, leaves, fruit—in your notebook before you continue.

Ideally there will be some species of yew within walking distance, and although your local variety may be much smaller than the European giant, in a park you may be lucky enough to find one that is full of years. But baby ornamental or grandmother tree, do visit one as soon as you can.

Reread the yew dryad's welcome at the beginning of the chapter. Does it reflect the state of mind in which you have visited the other trees?

Hopefully you will now visit in a thoughtful, aware mood, inwardly or out loud asking for permission, and waiting to intuit what form it takes. If a response is not forthcoming, just sit quietly where you feel comfortable. You are in the habit of taking gifts, perhaps some nuts to feed the wildlife; scatter them with grace and thanks. All of life is interconnected and gifts will be interpreted by your tree-relatives exactly in the spirit in which they are intended.

So, your first task is to search out your yew! And when you find it, or a stand of yews, even if they are relatively young or in a hedge, their "dark" quality can have a psychological effect that might be unnerving in its difference. *Respect your feelings.* Go slowly. The trees tell us that there is no destination, just a journey through life; no need to rush. The yew is a powerful teacher, and taking your connection lightly is the best way to engage with it at first.

Symbolism of the Yew

The yew shares many symbolic characteristics with the oak—they represent the ends of a spectrum. One carries within it the resonance high summer, whilst the other reverberates to the life force at the dead of winter, standing firm and strong in the dark times. The regal status of both was documented in ancient Ireland, where they are two of the seven chieftain trees.

They balance each other in almost every way, elegantly and completely. Both, compared to other trees, are incredibly long-lived and have drawn symbolism and mythic associations to themselves effortlessly, and both are huge and imposing. To read about them is to engage with myth and kingship, strength and longevity. There is often significance in their placing, indicating their sacred status and honoured place in human communities.

And when we compare their appearance, we see how they complement each other.

Oak Tree

Yew Tree

Oak: Tall, strong, stretching to the light. Leaf edges curling in a wave. Cups holding acorns of shining green/brown. Seasonal leaves, green in summer, yellowing and crisp brown in growth and decay.

Yew: Hunched, massive, stretching and curling back down to earth. Leaves needle-like, green. Red arils cupping the green fruit. Constant glossy leaf.

There is one important respect in which the yew stands alone, for it is one of the contenders for the crown of the world tree of the ancient Norse, which connects all the worlds and represents the tree of life. There is scholarly disagreement about the derivation of its name, Yggdrasil. For long it has been considered the ash tree, but now a case has been made for it meaning "yew support," and this makes sense for several reasons—for if we were choosing a tree to bear the title "tree of life," would we not choose the longest-lived tree and one that is seen to be always green?

Whatever the truth of this association, the physical tree hints at a universal connection to all others through its biological peculiarities. It crosses the boundaries of scientific tree-definition, with characteristics and growth patterns veering between those common to deciduous and evergreen trees. This is part of its connecting and overarching aspect. It is a one-off, unique, and it fulfils a very special purpose.

So let's tie all this in to the first yew lesson—that of boundaries.

The Yew as a Boundary Tree

The first boundary is appearance, which prompts a certain response. *Our appearance has the same effect.* It might seem a simplistic statement, but the effect of outward appearance is profound. Never underestimate it. As we filter the thousands of impressions we receive every moment, so do others. So our appearance prompts others to a snap evaluation of our attitudes, politics, job . . . it either attracts or repels people. And what we have hitherto done intuitively, we will now do with awareness. By clothing ourselves, we are erecting a boundary to admit only those whom we wish to. So our choices affect *and censor* our contacts and life experiences, and we make them every moment without thinking. With the attitude of witnessing which we have learnt from the trees, we will begin to be more thoughtful.

Stop now to think of some examples of dress that would immediately alienate you—even though you would be too polite and well socialised to make your feelings plain. Take a couple of minutes to write quick lists of appearances that attract or repel you, to refer to when we work on this boundary in the study session.

All trees share a common dance between the inner and outer worlds, but the yew expresses this in a more overt and robust way, removing itself into the deep forest and making its own shade by the profusion of its growth. We will call this the dance of "shielding and allowing," and the boundary function of the yew is part of that shielding.

From time immemorial—evidenced by archaeologists—yew has always been used as a boundary and marker tree. It is often found in churchyards, especially those that predate the Christian building, denoting its associations with the ancient sacred. Ancestral and folk associations with the yew and our pre-Christian heritage emphasise its nature as the guardian between this world and others, between life and death—the mysteries of life. Deep wells and springs were also set apart, mysterious portals to otherness, where our ancestors deposited gifts to the otherworld as votive offerings, and yews often grew—and continue to grow—alongside.

A magical example of such yews by an ancient water source is at the world-famous Chalice Well, in a small town at the mythic centre of England, Glastonbury. The lower gardens contain a pair of large yews, guarding the lawn and lower pools, and there is a yew with two trunks twining, resonating with folktales of the eternity of love. Glastonbury is said to be the "heart centre" of England. A large yew at the top of the gardens overhangs and shades the holy well, from which pours a constant, never-varying supply of chalybeate water, so rich in iron that it stains all red, giving rise to its old name "the blood spring." It is connected in legend with the cauldron of Celtic mythology, the Fisher King, and the chalice of the last supper, buried under the nearby Chalice Hill.

As well as having yews in abundance today, archaeology round the Chalice Well uncovered an ancient yew root dated to around 300 CE—Roman times—tying in with local knowledge of two ancient processional ways, which are documented into modern times. One was of oak, the other of yew, both marching across the landscape towards the town. Again we see the connection between these arboreal giants, this time fulfilling a traditional role of avenues: marking out space along which to approach the sacred.

Do not be disheartened if your area seems devoid of tree-myth, or if, in particular, you have no large yews and magical waters. We cannot all live in recognised mythic spots and we do not need the glamour of *specific* legend, though yews often attract them. Part of our journey into tree-ness is to discover the stories of ancient yews or other trees in our own locality. Stories arise as we connect to them: simply to imagine an ancient tree's historical associations is magic enough. It links us not only to history, it helps our brains grapple with an understanding of eternity. Being placed on sacred ground, yew shields the space, marking it as different from its mundane surroundings and calling to those who seek otherness.

Yew hedges are distinctive, dense and impregnable, and ideal for boundaries. As ancient enclosure for stately homes or surrounding the past glories of old gardens, there is much evidence for them in our landscapes. Finding an ancient yew hedge is a direct link back to our history, and an invitation to explore and discover what it once shielded.

Poison and Healing

The second boundary of the yew is a rather chilling and unique characteristic: almost every part of it is poisonous. But paradoxically, the tree feeds wildlife, which can absorb the nourishment without digesting the poisonous seed. To larger mammals, including us, it can be fatal, and this is often given as the reason for the yew growing in churchyards—a space set apart where grazing animals were not allowed.

Considering this yew aspect we enter the darker world of the mysteries.

What has poison to do with our journey? Well, a great deal, when we consider the toxicity abroad in our complex world. Take a few moments now to jot down modern materials and processes that might poison us. Looking round any modern home, list the constant noise, light, and artificial materials that make a less-than-healthy environment. Scan your fridge contents dispassionately (are you impressed with your choices?) and listen to its constant electrical buzzing. Take a quick mental trip through your day out in the noise, fumes, and emissions of your locality, and add to the list. Then do the same for your environment—landfill sites, power pylons and cables, and so on, and see how long the list becomes.

We now need to ring-fence the developments we've made in our personal strategy for health. We do it with reference to the yew, allowing our sense of its innate qualities to evoke within us a dim, shining barrier to keep us from harm. Within this barrier we can make good choices to set us in the space that can become sacred.

With the oak we considered our physical health, which is still ongoing; with the yew we set boundaries to guard our emotional and spiritual health as well. But we must now consider a serious question:

As the yew itself is poisonous, surely if we identify with it, then we are too?

Well, we all have the potential to be, and it's important to recognise this. We might say that it's our survival instinct that gives us the capacity to be poisonously destructive—an instinct that might one day save our lives. Living so securely, we constantly suppress it, as society demands we show only our acquiescence to its rules. But that instinct cannot be held down completely; if we don't acknowledge it, it will creep out in destructive habits and ways of relating.

If you just want life to be sweetness and light, then the earthiness of the forest will be problematic for you—but then so will so many wonderful aspects of our less-than-perfect lives. Let us be in the real world and admit that the most important toxicity we experience might be in relationship, and if that is so, that we contribute to it.

We try to be honest and authentic, but society's messages are so complex and sophisticated, how can we trust that our judgement is not skewed?

Experience and Popular Culture

We are all shaped in part by our culture, and if society is unhelpful to our health on all levels, we will suffer. So, as an exercise in how norms and expectations have changed, put this book down now, and think of a list of pop songs from your youth. Recall phrases from them and from those that you heard your parents and grandparents sing. Sing or hum them to remind yourself. Then switch on the radio or think of modern lyrics and music—and more importantly, the feelings they evoke.

Popular song deals almost exclusively with romantic relationships, and if through the yew tendrils of family memory you can stretch from Frank Sinatra to the present, you will see the change in the lyrics' messages you have received over the years. Think now of the differences. Back in our grandparents' day, popular songs were simple and joyful, suggesting that romance would add to an already happy life—we'd all be "picking up lots of forget-me-nots." So why has that changed? Paradoxically, the easier life becomes—and in the main we are much less self-reliant than our grandparents—the more needy and unhealthy our songs become. Many of them now glorify and wallow in permutations of teenage angst; they focus on lack and unhealthy co-dependent relationships. These are messages that sink into our beings in our most formative years: unless we have lived in a bubble, we have almost certainly been affected by them.

Fortunately, as we mature, most of us grow out of adolescent thinking: that suffering makes us interesting and deep, that jealousy is proof of someone's love, and that possession is a valid word in relationships. But deep down inside us, those early ideas and influences are still lurking. It is helpful to stay aware that there is an urge in our culture and the media to assume dysfunctional relationships are the norm—just look at any soap opera. When we go to the wisdom of the forest, being as a tree teaches us vital lessons: that only good-quality relationships are relevant to our lives and that the journey of the soul needs simplicity, honesty, and integrity to feed it.

Whilst searching for this simplicity, we will accept that, like the yew, we are nourishing to some and toxic to others. The propensity to be destructive is within everyone. And we can add to that our essential personality, which means that *we can't please all of the people all of the time*. Temperamentally, we will just not gel with some people. There's no judgement here. But it's difficult to admit to ourselves, because we all have a child's wish to be loved and appreciated by all, even though we know that's impossible. So let's just determine to grow up and learn to live with it.

The yew teaches by example that we can accept and acknowledge those we do not get on with, and just stay a mutually respectful distance from them. Trying to please will…well, you finish this conjecture. It will rarely end in a win/win situation! If this is relevant to your life in the world of work, then remember your yew boundary—there need be no overlap between friendship and professional interaction. Be gracious, get the work done, and let others be.

The Distinction of the Yew

"Nice"—what an overused adjective. It's lukewarm, describing everything in the middle spectrum of experience, and is used to damn with faint praise. In the forest, it would be a wildly inappropriate word to use for the yew. As you develop into your tree studies, *it will be a similarly inappropriate way to describe you.*

Because of the space we gain from spreading out into expressing our true selves, we will find our ability to be courteous, pleasant, and empathic enhanced. But through the trees, we develop a way of looking at things so that our opinions tend to be original, distinctive, idiosyncratic, individual—any one of a dozen descriptors—but we will no longer belong to that group whose opinions can be predicted, who can be called "nice." You will think for yourself. The tree-stance gives you clarity of thought, unencumbered by baggage. Embrace the difference that comes from an enhanced and expanded view of the world, from the congruence that you will find as your inner beliefs start to harmonise with your outer experience.

Many people will react positively to your clear thinking and strength and you will express it thoughtfully—the place of tree-ness in the back of your mind reminds you there is no need to try to impress or overwhelm anyone with your opinion. But, conversely, you will have no trouble standing up for what you believe in, when it's relevant.

Use your sense of the yew boundary to protect your beliefs and worldview from your mundane human contacts. Develop a connection to the intuitive part of yourself in the study session. Use that instinct so you recognise when people might be on your wavelength. We all have that sense, we just have to cultivate it. We are getting these messages all the time, but are usually too busy being busy to *notice*. Stepping back into the forest gives you the space for the messages your busy brain usually blanks out.

You can meet like-minded souls in your inner grove, and work there to develop those qualities that may reflectively attract others in the real world—as within, so without. Such friendships are invaluable, but until you encounter that real fellow feeling, better to keep your distance than to expose important parts of your life to people who cannot understand you.

The yew dryad speaks:

Look back over your journey so far…from the airy wonder and anticipation of the birch, through the deep-rooted connection to the world of the oak, to the distinction of my yew. There is further growth, nourishment, and fruit for you in this dim place. Use my connection to relate with simplicity and integrity. Let your true self shine through and let those who do not like you go their way with your blessing.

Enjoy the work on this in the study session.

Specialism and Timelessness

The yew just can't help being what it is and looking it!

Uncovering your true strengths and focusing on them, you will find as you specialise in what you really love, you will stop spreading yourself too thin—"Jack of all trades, master of none"—and start being *good* at things, and feeling good about them and yourself. Ring-fencing time for our passions and putting up boundaries to protect them will cut us off from peripheral experiences, but we will make in-depth connections between each of us and the spirit of our enthusiasms, and share with like-minded friends on a deeper level. So don't underestimate the *spirit* behind your enthusiasm—a relationship as valid as that between human/human or human/tree. Examine other-than-human relationships within the spirit of your passions: you and music (a very potent one!), or sailing, and craftwork, and baking, and hiking in the countryside … what's on your list?

How fast an evening goes when we are engaged in an activity that makes our creative juices flow, our hearts sing. How dull the minutes when grinding away at a mundane job.

Being as authentic as the trees, living the lives we are meant to live, is the way truly to understand the yew. Within the boundary that safeguards our essential selves, we enter timelessness in our everyday lives as we do what we love, as well as enjoying the essence of our inner periods of refreshment with the trees.

Set out the boundaries to distance yourself from all that leaches away your joy, your energy, and the minutes of your life. Learn that which delights and enchants you; study, downsize to reduce your outgoings—do anything to work towards attaining those things that are your passion. Work towards being in a position to find every day exciting and rewarding, including the time spent earning your living.

Being true to our authentic selves and protecting them, setting boundaries to acknowledge and respect them, brings awareness into all aspects of our lives. From this we will, like the yew, flourish within the sanctity of our protected space. From here we can contemplate the mystery of life, with all its darkness and the potential, and set bough and seed for the future.

Lessons from the Yew

Boundaries

The yew dryad speaks:

My trunk is the central point for a radiating circle of branches.
Wherever you are, you also are the centre of your world. Your
ambience encircles you always, flowing from your integrity
and personality, flavouring the atmosphere, your unique signature. Within your boundary there is an innermost space,
your sanctuary. From there, you can step out into the world,
welcoming all who are of good intent.

So far we've been focussed on expansion and looking out, and considering our contribution to the wider world is a useful approach in these self-
centred times. But now we have to hunker down and really concentrate on
our own needs in greater depth.

We have defined ourselves by looking at what is acceptable and desirable and what our aims are, but the salient question defining what we are
at our very core is, *what are our boundaries?*

Start now to make notes on what is anathema to you, totally unaccept-
able. We all have lines that must not be crossed, so think about where the line

is drawn which, if crossed, would change your sense of yourself irrevocably. Which of your rules are non-negotiable? This is the self-understanding that shows us what our boundaries are protecting.

Our job in part is to disentangle our genuine boundaries from superficial judgements. Those that are genuine are sacrosanct, whilst those we've inherited, we can begin gently to push to give us more leeway, freeing us to re-engage with the world with more clarity.

Your Local Yews and Yew Substitutions

Even if your local yew is a small bush in a local park or garden, every yew carries a unique "signature" which has a commonality at core with all others of the same species. Worldwide, many students mention the forceful energy of the yew, no matter how small or young the tree. There are substitutions that can be made for the yew, dependant upon your responses to your local trees and their local associations and folklore, for the art of connection is how we learn from our own natural environment. Some students have been happy to buy a specimen Irish yew for the garden, to use in conjunction with native trees, for it's essential to remember that the criteria for longevity, regeneration, and immortality in Europe does not apply worldwide.

In Australia, where all the trees have a sense of "toughness" and need to be resilient to extremes of temperature, the Huon pine excels. The Antarctic beech shares with the yew a habit of growth from the mother tree, so it never dies, and the tree fern has an impressively fast recovery from devastating fires. All these relate them to the yew qualities of longevity and regeneration, whilst other trees are hard enough to be virtually termite, drought, and fire proof. Look around to see which of your native trees have qualities of immortality—and *why*. With relationship comes understanding.

In New Zealand, the Maori associate the koru spiral, inspired by uncurling fern fronds, with new life and regeneration. They use the puriri tree as a resting place, a portal place, which certainly relates to the nature of yew. Many of the cemeteries are planted with sequoias as well as yew.

In the United States, the Florida and Pacific yews are smaller than the European, but much in evidence. There are local tree catalogues—for example, for Seattle—which make hunting down large trees possible, but again, substitutions are perfectly in order. It is the main *quality* or *essence* of the tree we relate to, whether it's an Italian cypress or a species of juniper whose branches can root and found new trees. If the very oldest and most impressive trees in your area are cedars and redwoods, then they might share a yew resonance. If all the trees in your region are evergreen, then the notes on the contrast between evergreen and deciduous trees will be irrelevant. In these study sessions particularly, be aware of crafting your own path. If you don't live on the continent of Europe, you have some fascinating exploratory work ahead of you!

Reread the guidelines from the chapter before you go to visit whichever trees are relevant to you. Remember, most people find that the atmosphere of the yew (and trees like it) encourages a slowing. So slow your breathing; enter into a slightly different time zone of perception to examine the tree closely.

Part of your gift might be to speak of its beauty: the flaking bark of russet, brown, and purple tones; the mysterious, sinuous patterns of the trunk; the springing needles of glowing green leaves, the brilliant red arils that feed wildlife all winter. Admire and celebrate it. Speak out loud or write your thoughts.

If this last one doesn't quite feel "you," tell yourself again that some boundaries are self-imposed and should be gently pushed—attempt a poem admiring a non-human and see how it feels! It is a wonderful way to communicate with the whole of the natural world. Start with simple observation of what's happening, as if speaking to a friend:

"Your dark green leaves bend and brush my forehead as I pass underneath…Trunk gleaming from the recent rain, polished skin covering your pulsing life…pools in the bole of your trunk, spilling onto twisted roots…Springing needles underfoot…" and so on. Concentrate on the physical tree whilst in its aura.

Boundaries Set by Appearance

Our first connection to others is through our outward appearance. What messages do you send out to the world? Divide a page in half and list aspects of your appearance: hair, grooming, clothes (itemise for style, age, quality, type, and so on, right down to jewellery, underclothes, and shoes). Then, on the opposite side, write down the impression you think that makes.

There may be duplications—writing "business wo/man" for most of your outer clothes for example—but what of your hairstyle, rings, nails, and personalised silk socks? It seems important that we assert our individuality even when we have to conform to a dress code—just look at the bizarre tie choices prominent men make! How do you assert your sense of self? And what aspect of your personality flashes through? This is your "secret signal" that is picked up by others in sympathy with you, *so ask a friend to take a photo of you when you're not expecting it.*

Compare the way you look when you're not posing to the impression you think you make. Is it a shock, or as you expected? What is your expression—stressed or relaxed? Try to look through eyes other than your own. What is the difference between boho chic and bag-lady? Is it just our perception? Even if your signals to the outside world are congruent with your intent, it is fascinating to examine the how and why of appearance. Do you alienate with your bling, your smartness, or your scruffiness? And the last question to be answered is: "Is your individuality of appearance genuine, or coming from arrogance or a need to be noticed?"

Think it over and jot down your feelings: be honest, this is just for you.

Then write a list of what repels or attracts you in appearance, and make a list of friends, colleagues, and acquaintances who break the "appearance rules" you've grown up with.

Have your ideas about dress changed and matured over the years? Most of us retain the prejudices from our formative years—we retain a fondness for how we dressed when we were 14 to 18! It's another thing to be aware of as we disentangle what is relevant to us now. What fills you with horror? Miniskirts, uniforms, tie-dyes, power dressing? *How prescriptive and habituated are you to only finding a certain style acceptable?* Does appearance activate your judgement button? Of course our intuition comes into play to sum up new people and goes far deeper than these superficialities, but fine-tuning our appearance can clarify to ourselves and the world what we are.

Affirmations

This chapter is so personally biased that you will devise your own affirmations. But here are some on all aspects of boundaries to start you off.

Yew Affirmations

To remind yourself each day:
I wake to a fresh approach. Trivialities no longer influence me.

For each morning:
My boundaries are valuable; they protect my sense of self.
From my strong boundaries I face the world in a relaxed and loving way.

Before stress situations:
My boundaries are set to safeguard my deepest self.
I trust them and my intuition.

When feeling insecure:
I am always safe. I view the world with the eyes of simplicity and truth.

To guard against being judgemental:
Nature abounds in glorious diversity. I respect all differences.

To acknowledge your deepest instincts:

I thank and trust all my feelings and my survival instinct.

I ask them to lie dormant until a time of need.

I accept every aspect of myself. I send gratitude to it all.

When feeling cut off:

My boundaries allow always for all loving kindness to enter.

My love flows out unimpeded and activates a return flow.

To engage with the world with confidence:

I am aware of my boundaries; they protect me whenever I need it.

I send respect to all I am not in tune with.

My boundary fence holds me safe in my integrity.

I am secure and held; I act with confidence.

Doodling

All our levels of being have to have their integrity protected. For the purposes of this exercise, we will imagine the physical, mental, and emotional levels connecting to the integrating spirit of all things. These levels are as misty shadows surrounding your physical body, reaching out further and further.

Start by slowing, breathing, and remembering that you are more than your physical body. Then draw yourself—any sort of silhouette or stick figure will do—and working out from the figure, shade in a number of larger layers around it. Colour in the layer nearest to your body; what colour do you instinctively choose? Write in the people whom you allow that close. Intimacy is not just physical, so identify core companions, even if you only see them infrequently.

Colour in successive layers going farther and farther away from your body, and label them, until you get to colleagues and nodding acquaintances. Do not enclose the last layer—let it spread out to hint at a colour that connects you to the whole world.

Look at the picture and note that the membranes or layers are not solid. Which people and things will slide through to become nearer or farther from you in the future, do you think?

An alternative sketch would be of a sacred area, surrounded with concentric circles of yew hedges, open or with broad and attractive wrought iron gates. Mark each area of territory; imagine the beautiful garden they will lead you to. Place people and situations within the right areas, and make sure any gates are easy to open. We are defining boundaries, not prison walls, and relationships are fluid and changeable. Nature shows that life is about flux and gentle change, so make sure the signals you give reflect the mature attitudes that are right for you now.

Craft Your Own Visualisations

In this set of visualisations, we are examining boundaries through our internal sacred space.

Visualisation 1:
Develop a sense of the ever-present yet fluid boundary
Images that might be helpful: A safe space ringed with yew trees.
Being rooted in the centre of a rainbow globe of light. The world is beyond; situations/people asking permission to approach. A signal allows them to come as near as is right. Communication from far away space; intuit connections or endings. Figures moving into fields of colour of the different realms, nearer and farther. Your core-self safe and strong, radiating goodwill.

Visualisation 2:
For a sense of sacred space, connect to the yew sanctuary
Images that might be helpful: A hill, the top ringed around by successive yew hedges. The opening cut in each is an organic doorway to enter. Looking back through the green fringing; connecting to the world but separate. An ancient yew in the

centre, shading a decorated tent, open on all sides. Shielded and withdrawn, a private space of clarity and timelessness. The boundaries pulse; the energy of the yew hedges maintaining sacred space. Your haven. Being at home on the physical, mental, emotional, and spiritual levels.

Visualisation 3:
Connect to the cosmic yew
Images that might be helpful: An ancient yew; it expands and fills your vision, changing character. Look deep into the earth; animal burrows and roots. Sense the inner fire of the earth feeding its deepest roots; magical water wells up. The trunk leading to the sky. Stars and planets hung from its branches; winged creatures in its crown; hoofed and furred and horned creatures round its trunk; fish in the pool fed by the stream at its roots. The world tree, in perfect balance. *So are you.* Relax and know the truth of this.

Practical Work

It's time to get out and about, and ground all our mental and emotional efforts.

- Find shards and flakes of the yew from around its trunk. Varnish or polish them to reveal the brilliant colouring. Use for craft projects, weaving into textiles, covering boxes.

- Find a flake the shape of a miniature shield; keep it by you.

- Find an arrow-shaped twig or piece of bark as a remembrance of protection and focus.

- Plant a yew on your garden or yard boundary to remind you of the strength of your protection. (Poison alert: not if it would be a danger to wildlife and children!) There are many columnar yews available for small gardens.

- Use the list you made in the chapter of toxic things around you, and start to change and minimise their effects on you. Place it to keep it in the forefront of your mind, and resolve to, for example, go to town less, buy less, and eat better and fresher; wear more natural fibres; think about energy conservation and where your energy comes from ... or any other ideas that are relevant to you and your lifestyle.

Remember, all these physical things make a foundation for the health of your subtler bodies—mental, emotional, and spiritual.

Remember the messages of popular songs? Just for fun and celebration (never neglect this aspect!), find a pop song with a positive message; sing and dance along to it regularly. You can extend this simple fun to make a sacred dance—circular, like the yew boundaries around your sacred space. Is this pushing your boundaries? Good. We go inwards to come back out in a more liberated and accepting way. So, just in the privacy of your room, even if only once, dance!

Personal Toxicity

Does this fill us with trepidation? Of course not! We are by now adept at looking at situations without blame. We no longer think, for our own security, "It's not me, it must be the other feller." We accept life as a rich mixture of interconnecting relationships, and we have learnt not to need to blame. But still our behaviour under stress can be toxic. The wrong situation with the wrong people can cause us all to be as poisonous as the yew. If we were actually trees, we would probably achieve perfect authenticity and harmony, but, being doers, not be-ers, we are imperfect.

It's salutary to confront our weaknesses, but we won't examine them in detail or become caught up in our own enthralling habits—how easy it is to frame bad boy behaviour as glamorous! And over-examination leads to rehashing old wrongs, blame, judgement, self-righteousness—leading to a soap opera alert! We're reframing in a positive, kind, and gentle way, from the sacred cathedral space of the forest. No shame, no blame; we are all doing our best in the testing circumstance of getting on with our lives.

So get your notebook and pencil, sit in your imagination under that huge ancient yew tree. Take on its witnessing aspect, and jot down answers to some very personal questions:

When the going gets tough, how do you react? Are you a shouter and screamer: explosive; open in your responses? Do you lash out immediately like a spooked animal? Or are you brooding and seething, sulky and manipulative in your responses? Storing up slights? Do you withdraw so everyone knows you feel hurt?

You might belong to one category, or you might recognise behaviours from both camps. This is just part of you, of knowing yourself. It's a matter of personality and temperament. But looking at our behaviour can take fortitude, so consider: maybe these past responses have been the only way you knew to maintain your boundaries. If so, acknowledge their value but take a few moments out to devise an affirmation, consciously choosing a better way of responding.

And whilst we are reconciling with our defence mechanisms, there are two more important questions to answer: How many times a day/week/month/year do you get frustrated or unhappy or angry with others or situations? Is your degree of response *really necessary every time?*

We have all probably developed habits that will cling. It is easy to rail against how unfair people are to us; that's the position we've always viewed the world from. As an antidote, ask yourself every day, "Whom have I upset today?" What response wells up inside as you remember your petty thoughtlessness, anger, carelessness, or unkindness? It's a sobering and very fast way of enlarging our thinking and altering our focus—and amending our habitual ways of behaving!

Successfully aligning our life's journey to the song of our soul leads to serenity and harmony, but breaking bad habits takes time and awareness in the moment. Fortunately that is just what we've been practicing, for indeed, we never "break" ourselves of habits—we don't change them by our will. Rather, they are gradually replaced with a changed emotional response that allows a better alternative.

Our Shadow Personality and Toxicity

Just acknowledging this side of ourselves will go a fair way to ensuring that the outbursts be kept to a minimum. We all shout loudest when we feel we're not valued or respected. And we can minimise the problem by being straight-forward.

Without thinking too hard, make a mental list—no need to jot everything down, and take only a few moments. List situations that you would find toxic. Do they have a theme? Do they all provoke a similar emotional response? Is that your main weakness? Look back over relationships that have been toxic. Are there similarities?

You might muse on the deeper levels of these questions at your leisure. Just do it *lightly*, for a light touch is the essence of tree work. Remember, you are the dispassionate witness.

When you have finished, thank yourself for doing your best. Do it formally; do it out loud. Drink a toast to your boundary and survival mechanisms, and wish them a peaceful slumber. They've been vastly overworked up until now—especially when you think that a lot of our toxic responses come from when we perceive a threat.

As we expand our awareness, and engage with life from the witnessing perception of the trees, we find less of our sense of self-worth is dependent on external circumstances and opinions. Therefore we are less inclined to perceive threat; our defence mechanisms become less likely to cry "wolf" unnecessarily, and our inappropriate responses will subside. We can ask our intuition to reactivate them if it should become necessary.

With the oak, we first began to look at physical health. When we connect to the eternal nature of the yew, we safeguard and encourage the robustness of our mental, emotional, and spiritual health.

If you haven't yet devised your affirmation from the previous section, play with the ideas below to form one that is just right for you:

I honour my defence mechanisms, which act to keep me safe. Thank you. Please rest sweetly, ready to spring into action whenever I truly need you.

And some more phrases to pop into the cauldron: Disagreement is not threat; it does not reflect on anyone's worth. Conflict is inevitable; I can see all points of view. I save my energy for worthwhile endeavours. I trust myself to resolve issues kindly … And so on.

The Value of Toxins

Let us remember now that all things have their value and their place. Having done the work, we can reframe the toxic aspects with one key fact about the yew:

The fatal poison of the yew is now harvested to synthesise into anti-cancer drugs.

The potent and potentially dangerous nature of many plants gives us our most useful medicines. Within ourselves, our defence mechanisms protect and shield, as the yew does. We aim for serene lives, following our true path with fluidity and grace. But there is a potent core within us: our defensive tools that are always only sleeping.

Who's to say how we will use them when it is necessary? We, our families, and our communities do periodically need protecting, so imagine the value of these mechanisms by quickly concocting a little story for each of the following statements:

- Your extraordinary temper saves a life.

- Your intolerance sees through lies.

- Your righteous indignation brings down corruption in high places.

- Your overwhelming indignation gives you a burst of strength to rescue someone or save the day.

By doing this you will have imagined yourself as hero/ine for four stories—and stranger things have happened in many "ordinary" lives.

As a weed is simply a flower in the wrong place, so our deepest instincts and traits are simply negative if used inappropriately. With the exercises, and the witnessing skills we have learnt from the trees, hopefully those extreme parts will be satisfied to lie dormant until needed in a just cause, just as the active yew ingredient lies in the tree until used to give fresh hope to cancer sufferers.

Distinction and Specialism

If you had to choose just three things from every area of your life, wouldn't you choose very carefully? Wouldn't you choose the best examples, and choose things that you truly love?

We humans are irresistibly attracted to variety. In search of it, we can spread ourselves too thin, squandering our time, effort, and talents—having four okay coats instead of one we love, playing four instruments badly instead of practicing and excelling at one. We owe it to ourselves to specialise a bit. Think in terms of capsule wardrobes, kitchen equipment, hobbies, and groups of friends. These are the concerns of the oak work, which it would be good to revisit. How far have you got in slimming your life down to aspire to excellence?

Are you still using the exercises to help you? Are you setting your alarm to do affirmations regularly; doing the tree meditation; placing wood where it will remind you of your intentions? Is cleaning and clearing your space and your mind an ongoing exercise? *Are you simplifying?*

The yew has beauty, resilience, and longevity. Trust that *so do you.* Do not disguise your own distinction from yourself with frippery and add-ons.

The yew always puts its energy into developing a good root system; *so can we.* As we set up systems to support our lives, then we draw nourishment from those roots that sustain and transform us. The ambience of the yew, the sense of distinction, of boundaries, is within us when we need it, freeing us to relax into serenity and show our distinctive, magical side to the world.

The Yew Sanctuary

Consider now social boundaries that pertain in other cultures. Many ethnic societies have strict rules on periods of withdrawal from society—after childbirth and bereavement particularly. Are they restrictive and unfair? Or do they allow the individual space just when they need it most? You decide.

What are the times in your life to withdraw, in order to come back refreshed? On the first day of your holiday from work? After a family landmark? After a personal major achievement? For your un-birthday—just because you want to? Or once a month for twelve hours because you know it would be good for you? Instead of celebrating with a night out, why not treat yourself to a night *in*? Use it in a spiritually and physically refreshing way—staying up watching the stars, or bed before eight; reading inspiring literature, or watching a film that appeals to your highest self.

Factor in this time, mark it in your diary and ring-fence it. The yew is not at everyone's beck and call the whole time. It is available to us, but on its own terms. *So will you be.*

Ponder that, rewrite it for yourself; use affirmations to internalise it; allow it to relax you, and know that it is part of the secret of how you can live your life in the most positive and magical way.

Night-Time Visualisation: The Yew and the Pool

Follow all the usual guidelines for visualisation, and allow yourself to settle down into regular breathing that brings you in touch with your physical self. Take your time; allow space for the images to rise, and the evocation of your feelings...

Allow yourself to gradually withdraw to your inner imaginal space, without any expectation... you are entering timelessness. Breathe gently, and savour it.

When you are ready, find yourself walking through an avenue of young yews at twilight. Their solid shapes are a sacred pathway, and you feel cloaked and protected by the dim light. Protection and love are emanating from the trees... The processional is a boundary way separating you from all your mundane worries, and draws you deeper into relaxation.

At the end of the avenue, there is a vast ancestor yew, shining silvery and magical in the light of the new-risen moon. As you approach, you see that the silver is reflected in a circular, moon-shaped pool at the base of its gnarled, twisted roots. The still water is like a mirror, and the yew casts deep shadows. Occasionally a yew berry falls and ruffles the surface and you sit on a comfortable root, totally absorbed and captivated by the ripples. Follow the course of one seed with your inner sight: fruit of your achievements sinking into the depths of your being, nourishing your sense of self... Fish hang, fins moving infinitesimally, far down in the limpid water which is a gateway to a deep otherworld. They are denizens of an enchanted realm, keepers of a treasure store of hidden wisdom... As you imagine receiving that wisdom, see a stream of bubbles of inspiration rising up from the depths, bursting on the surface, filling you with possibilities.

Be here quietly within the magical boundary of the yew. The deep connection of water follows underground springs and feeds the roots of the yew. Know that you are receiving the quiet blessings of protective tree and deep water, bringing you peace.

When you feel the time is right, come back to the everyday world, bringing those blessings with you.

8

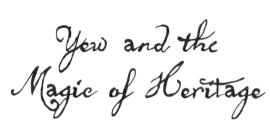

Tree quality: They are prodigiously generous with their gifts.

The yew's simple sense of presence as we enter its atmosphere thoughtfully can provoke an evocation of heritage—of all that we gain from the past, and all that stretches forward into the future. Yew and other long-lived survivor trees are a bridge to help us reach through time.

The Family Line

We all have a personal and cultural heritage, which can both sustain and sometimes hinder us. So far, we have been untangling some of its effects to ensure we develop to the best of our potential. If our work is taking effect, then the effects of our earlier environment, having been examined, might be beginning to lose their stranglehold on us. We are already more accepting of being *who,* and *what*, and *where, we are now*: just that. And we cultivate the dispassionate tree view, a witnessing stance that tells us that all is as it should be.

Looking Back

Take a few moments now to think back on *positive* things from your past, but, to help to maintain our dispassionate tree perspective, don't do it in colour. This is the past. Try rerunning it in sepia tones or black and white (a commonly used trick to distance ourselves and prevent us getting over-emotionally involved). With an old and jolly piano accompaniment, imagine *positive* images of your earlier life as a film. Allow the frames to flit before your eyes. There you are at the school sports event, at your first camp, on your first date ... And there in the shadowy background are those who supported you—if not relatives, then friends and extended family. Where did they all go? No need for guilt if an aunt or distant cousin did the job of nurturing you better than a close relative. Believe that they were all doing the best they could at the time. Let those whom you've lost track of go with grace, and with thanks for their kindly influence upon you. Smile at your young self, still present in your older body. Think about heritage ...

Recognising our place in the middle of a long line of forebears and descendants, the continuity of heritage, can inspire us to be the best that we can be. For if our line goes back into the mists of time—the time of myths, legends, and hero/ines—then our forebears, ordinary folk, lived lives that will seem amazingly strange and wonderful to us. Adventurers, puritans, scholars, artists, alchemists, scientists, warriors ... they dance down the years in an exotic carnival procession from antiquity to the present day. We can imagine the type of people they might have been, and, as their stories are lost in the mists of time, we can visualise them as the very best—the bravest, most skilful, strongest, most fine and noble—they could be.

What tenacity and strength of spirit they must have had to get through hard and primitive times. Pondering their example, it will eventually occur to us, no matter what age we might be:

We are the ancestors about whom tales will be told!

What a responsibility! What an adventure! What a challenge to be the best we possibly can be, to live up to our true potential.

As with us, so with the yew; it is an ancestor tree, which is why its folkloric associations are legion. If it seems difficult to compare yourself to a tree whose lifespan is longer than ours by several thousand years, try making an affirmation to help connect you through ancestry and heritage. The yew has profound messages, which we can view as its gifts:

- By example, it links us to long life.

- It roots us firmly in the here and now.

- It invites us to compare how we act now with our ideal, leading to us modifying our behaviour.

In this way, by acting as we wish others to remember us, we gain congruence, balancing our inner and outer worlds.

In a larger context, the yew reminds us of our responsibility to the future; it allows us to see our actions in mythic terms and it gives us a wakeup call, reminding us of the brevity of this life.

You'll notice the paradox here—the association both with long life and mortality at the same time. We have all the time we need, yet none to squander. The work is here to do now, today. And the responsibility now is to our heritage.

Embracing this, instinctively we turn outwards once again—to our family, community, work, and neighbourhood—and really question what we can do to make a difference. But, remembering our distinctiveness, we consider what we can do *on our terms*. We walk through the ornate wrought-iron gate in our yew boundary hedge, to connect with the world from a new and long-lived perspective: that being true to ourselves is the only way to manifest our gifts and make our unique contribution. And we don't have to be in our middle years to do it. It is an indication of our development, not our chronological age, to address the gifts of our heritage. When we are ready, the work is there—and we've all heard of "an old head on young shoulders."

The yew has the quality of being generous with its gifts, *and so do we*. The only question is how we express them in the world.

The Expression of Our Gifts

The gifts we add to the treasure chest of heritage will spring into being from our uniqueness. Some people will have a great impact on the wider world, others just on their immediate friends or family. That is down to factors such as temperament and circumstances. Yet, like the ripples in a pond, when our berries fall on to the surface of the water—when we express our gifts in the world—we have no idea of the far-reaching effects they might have.

Here are three examples of the gifts of heritage:

Firstly, consider a person unknown to the wider world—it could be anyone's grandmother who, through her life and influence, has added immeasurably to a family's heritage. Her descendants may bond for generations over stories about her eccentricities and triumph over adversity.

Our next example is a specific person who never married or had children: John Chapman. Yet he added to his national heritage, roaming widely and transforming parts of America by establishing extensive stands of apple trees in many states. He has gone down in history as Johnny Appleseed.

And our third person might have been "invisible," yet posthumously became a national icon. One of America's foremost poets, Emily Dickinson, was unknown in her lifetime, even to her neighbours. True to her own nature, she lived the life of a recluse in one room of the family home. The vast majority of her poems were not found until after her death and form a wonderful heritage for the nation and the world, totally undreamed of at the time.

So, three very different people: one who added to their family store, one who deliberately set out to change the face of his country and succeeded, and one whose genius just had to be expressed, although she was psychologically averse to social contact.

Think of others whose gifts were only recognised after their deaths; they also carry an important lesson for us. Van Gogh sold only one painting in his lifetime, but what a legacy! Great talent is often unrecognised at the time. So the questions are: How many well-meaning people try to pull others whom they can't understand from their chosen course? Looking back over your life, has this ever happened to you? How far should we allow others to steer us into more pragmatic, sensible life choices?

The social media is full of examples of people who have made good, and almost every person who's "made it" seems to have received appalling school reports and bad career advice! We cannot all be geniuses, and we shouldn't think that "making it" (usually referring to celebrity or self-made millionaires) is relevant to our own journey. But we can all follow our own path and shine with our own authenticity; we owe it to ourselves. Looking at others' stories reminds us that many of our gifts and qualities do not fit into society's boxes, or tick lists of criteria for achievement. This indicates the limitations of society's expectations; it is no reflection on our individual talents but reminds us that we are far too complex and wonderful to categorise.

The outward expression of a person's drive and deep impulses is the heritage they leave. Act from your true instincts and your legacy is bound to manifest—as loving kindness, as creative output, as achievement, as contentment that people can warm themselves around. It doesn't have to be a national contribution, and we probably can't see it now—how many times do we only see a pattern to our behaviour and achievements with hindsight? But we *will* be ancestors, and our contribution will be there, either in the world or in the hearts and minds of others. Let's act with respect for that thought.

Late Bloomers

We all need role models, so for those who are older and feel that it's a bit late to start to create a heritage, consider just one role model of excellence and achievement later in life who's already been mentioned. Amongst the thousands of late bloomers round the world, Grandma Moses achieved fame with stunning naïve paintings documenting American rural scenes. She was described as a cultural icon, an inspiration for all older women, and was still being cited as a role model when in her nineties. A rural upbringing in a large family and a life of hard work makes her story a triumph of the creative spirit. She became a farmer and the mother of ten, and turned from embroidery to painting late in life. She produced over 1,600 paintings over thirty years and had her first solo exhibition at eighty. Her timeless subjects are a present-day link to our history: they are inspirational to us all, and they are echoed worldwide by ancient artists and craftspeople quietly and creatively working today.

Our work with the aged yew reminds us that we can all express ourselves late in life; we will see its relationship to creativity later in the chapter.

The Yew in Antiquity

Heritage is defined as "valued possessions and qualities such as cultural traditions that are handed down." So let us look at the yew in this light.

Long, long ago, the yew may have been the only evergreen tree in the British Isles. If so, it is no wonder that, with its shining green and red in the depths of winter, and its unique regenerative habit—of which more later— it has always been associated with rebirth and the eternal endurance of the spirit. As a huge living symbol of our intuitive understanding of the mysteries of life and death, regardless of religion or creed, it is of inestimable value.

The yew has lived alongside humankind since our earliest times, being imported as a status wood even in places where the tree did not flourish, for it has the distinction of extreme beauty. If someone gave you a gift today, you wouldn't want it to be tatty or to fall to pieces immediately. If it looked beautiful and timeless, you would treasure it and hand it on. Enter the yew, whose prime attributes are the strength and quality of its wood, used in a multiplicity of ways. Regardless of its beauty, let's look first at the uses prompted by the practical, measurable qualities of its wood.

Weaponry

Some of the earliest artefacts found are of yew. The very earliest, found in interglacial deposits in Essex, England, in 1911, is a yew spear traced back possibly as far as 450,000 years—a period usually associated with tools of bone and stone. Fire-hardened and then ground to a point, it is still a formidable object, and an impressive testament to the endurance of the yew and to its usefulness to the hunter-gatherers as far back as the Lower Palaeolithic.

Fast-forward thousands of years to between 4040 and 3640 BCE and we have the oldest yew bow found in the British Isles, in Scotland—the "Rotten Bottom bow." Preserved in peat and found by a hill walker in 1990, it is on display in the Museum of Scotland, Edinburgh. Yew was the favourite wood for bows right into the medieval period, and the yew longbows of the English archers are justly famed.

The reason for this is in the very special qualities of the wood of the yew: firstly, it is the hardest of the softwoods and so relatively easy to work. Now, bow makers have their own mysteries, but they will disclose that yew must be carved so that the heartwood—the inside core of the branch, resisting compression—is on the inside, or belly (facing the archer), whilst the sapwood, just below the bark, will be outside, as it resists stretching. Taking advantage of these two characteristics results in a uniquely strong, resilient, and springy longbow. Their effect on the battlefields of medieval Europe goes a long way to explain why archers are iconic figures.

By the sixteenth century, the large yews of Europe had been decimated by the demand for bows, and the story is a fascinating history of one species' usefulness to man. Demands for yew wood became so great that they were actually endangered, resulting in a plea to the Holy Roman Emperor to halt a practice that had wiped out the majority of the most ancient trees all over Europe. Two of the yew's properties are *shielding* and *protecting*, remember, and the document pleading for the trees' preservation so many hundreds of years ago stressed the damage caused to other forest trees by the wind after the removal of the yew. The forest as a whole needs its sheltering defence.

The yew dryad speaks:

Imagine my protective grove … and this time, through the dim light, a figure seems to grow from the side of my trunk. With joy you recognise the oak hero, Robin Hood, dressed in his traditional Lincoln green. He looks like a king, but of the forest, not of a court, and you realise that a crown would not be right for this protector of the poor. Instead, he holds his symbol of freedom from tyranny. His status is held in his trusty yew longbow and the quiver of arrows strapped to his back. In a blink he is gone in a swirl of leaves—undulating oak and needle-sharp yew—strength of the summer and winter combined, to keep safe all through the year.

Yew Artefacts

For those of us who are not warriors—and remember that that does not necessarily imply actual fighting in the present day—yew has many other practical uses from antiquity. "Domestic goddesses" from the Bronze Age onwards have used the yew in domestic tools: spoons, handles, and bowls, wheels, cogs, wine barrels, and parquet floors. Yew also had its part to play in the wider life of emerging Bronze Age trading cultures: the fibrous yew tied together the planks of the earliest cargo-carrying boats, and modern reconstructions have proved the efficiency and seaworthiness of these craft.

There is also evidence that yew was used medicinally. We touched on this in the boundaries chapter, *but we will never explore that aspect*. Learning from the trees, we must always respect nature's power—and the incontrovertible fact is that all parts of the yew are poisonous and have a deadly effect. Respect for nature tells us to keep away from any and all natural poisons.

That forbidden aspect notwithstanding, the yew is a practical benefactor in myriad ways.

Heritage, Creativity, and the Arts

Heritage evokes the idea of *gifts* handed down, and the yew's gifts are still relevant, for we can use them to nourish our essential selves. What inspires us into anticipation, focus, joy, and our work in this world is our creative impulse, channelled through the skills we develop. Making connection to our true selves opens the channels for these impulses. The yew, through folklore and practice, has associations with creativity from the earliest whispers of our ancestors.

You might inherit a parent's hair colour or distinguishing features—shape of nose, curve of the cheek, your stance, weight-distribution, and skeletal structure. Maybe you feel that heredity's actually been over-generous with your family shape? Yet that is who you are meant to be.

Even more amazing are the non-physical family gifts enshrined in our genes: a talent for woodwork, mechanics, music, art, gardening, or an inbuilt understanding of an abstract subject such as math, running from generation to generation. We don't need to get into the "nature versus nurture" argument, for both undoubtedly contribute; we simply *observe* that skills run in families.

So sketch your family characteristics—what has been physically handed down from your forebears? How tall, short, stocky, strong, athletic, or bent are you compared to your parents and grandparents? Sketch your relatives beside you—stick figures will do—emphasising the characteristics you share. There will be time to ponder the skills that you have received in the study session.

Music

Heritage cannot be separated from mystery, and they meet perfectly in the contemplation of music, that elusive, potent force by which we time travel back down the track of memory. Traditionally, the harp music of ancient bards was able to provoke tears, laughter, or restorative sleep. When Merlin raised Stonehenge, he did it with magic and with music, which can be a bridge to other ways of perceiving.

So, unsurprisingly, the oldest wooden musical instruments we have are of the oldest wood, the yew: three drone pipes from the early Bronze Age, found in Ireland. The drone can be said to symbolise the harmony of the spheres, maintaining the cosmic dance, which may be why bees, with their buzzing drone and their gift of honey, were venerated in ancient religions. Stepping forward into recent history, the beauty of yew wood and its tonal qualities made it a wood of choice for the curved backs of lutes, and today, instrument makers choose it for the back and sides of guitars and lap dulcimers. From the heritage of the ancient harp, yew is still being used for plucked-string instruments to transport listeners to another realm.

If your creativity takes the form of music making, or if music enriches your life, know that the resonance of the yew has been music's companion throughout human history.

Writing

Magic and the shielding and protective strand of the yew is shown in a very arcane form—the ancient Irish writing symbols called Ogham (pronounced *Oh-um*). Poets and magicians both used yew staves to inscribe the Ogham and as a way of remembering. In the Ogham tree alphabet, the yew tree is the last tree/letter/name and has its own sigil—five short straight lines across a central vertical line—in an alphabet that has birch (one line to the right of the central vertical line) at its beginning and oak (two lines to the left of the vertical line) as number seven, significantly next to another evergreen, the holly.

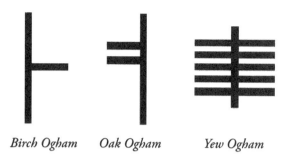

Birch Ogham   *Oak Ogham*   *Yew Ogham*

For now, it is enough to know that the yew, through its historical association, supports our writing. And although we no longer cut rods on which to carve our writings, from the earliest Christian writings to the poetry of today, the symbolism of the yew has always been a vibrant image. If you are a writer, think of the ancient status of the yew and the heritage of writers through the ages. Tune into the yew and your own deep understanding as you start your next creative piece of writing.

Visual Art

Potters have used yew leaves as a decorative motif back into antiquity; the short parallel needles invite us to arrange them in simple geometric patterns. You've already sketched a leaf: now scribble a line of them along a margin and realise what a satisfying repetitive device it is. Draw it as a border, overlap the parallel needles to cross-hatch; the possibilities are endless, and require no artistic skill to produce a satisfying result. Imagine your border on the lip and the belly of a clay pot, round, generously shaped and recently excavated from the ground. As we do this, our scribbles link us back to the earliest art and the forgotten artists who created it, on the far sides of the mists of old time.

The yew's heritage to the woodcarver is the sheer beauty of the wood, veering from satin-pale blond to its characteristic rich reds and russets, and a knotty habit that produces unique effects. It has always been an inspiration to carvers and visual artists, and remember, wherever a lute appears in a still life or musical scene, the yew has a covert presence.

Continuity, Status, and Adaptability

Our study will help the heritage associations of the yew to sink deep within us. It represents the continuity of life and the deep-rooted nature of our true connection to the earth, and it brings understanding from the past to be used in our present.

Over millennia, the yew has witnessed the unfolding of our human story and the natural world. Communities, groups, and couples met, planned, preached, and made declarations of war and of love under the yew of the village. Tradition states that Robin Hood and Maid Marian plighted their troth under a yew, which is still to be seen: the massive Doveridge yew in Derbyshire, England. Its huge canopy is supported by strong wooden scaffolding, so you walk under a tunnel of leaves towards the huge trunk. What a link with history!

Memory and tradition, time travelling and permanence are all ideas enshrined by the yew. Take a moment to celebrate its heritage and status.

The yew dryad speaks:

See a landscape in your own country. From above, the roads and highways are mapped out, the tracks and trails of commerce across the land, and the hilltops and ridges, burial mounds and sacred springs. All are marked by my yew tree, the symbol of the ancestors, planted by the wise ones of the land. I doze in my tree, a silent witness to the modern daily race, to the sacred paths, to the passing of those warriors and leaders who sleep now in the earth, but whose spirit is still present to inform and guide through the living. I am used by each generation according to its needs, and I endure, to make connections and pathways on every level.

The spirit of those long-ago times can still be accessed, for a gift of the yew is its *endurance*. Our ancestors have proved that yew fence posts can outlast those of iron—and remember the resilience of the yew-string ties of those ancient seagoing boats.

The yew, living as near eternally as any being on the planet, also speaks of *adaptability*. Its uses have changed over centuries, and its symbolic nature is not limited to just one religion. During the spread of Christianity through Europe, the missionaries' instructions were not to destroy existing sacred places or sacred trees but to adapt and use them. And they followed these guidelines to convert pagan sites to Christian use. So it is generally accepted by yew specialists that ancient yews now in churchyards were already growing on—and adding to the sanctity of—those sites long before Christianity. And in the UK, from past times when coffins would rest at the edge of a churchyard before burial, yews were planted to provide a natural roof, fulfilling their sheltering and protective role.

The Fortingall yew, in Perthshire, Scotland, was 56 feet in girth when intact and reckoned to be over 5,000 years old—a notable example. Its status as a sacred tree is supported by the accepted tradition that it marks the very heart, the *axis mundi*, of Scotland. Simply by visualising this magnificent ancestor, we can link to our earliest history and beliefs every time we wish to remember our deepest connections to the past. And any living tree can point us in this direction.

The tree simply witnesses as its symbolism is adapted to new ideas, to fulfil new needs, and so maintain an eternally relevant relationship to humankind in both practical and esoteric significance. *So do we maintain our value and relevance to the tide of life*, as we incorporate the best gifts from our heritage into our own lives, transmute them for a new age, and pass them on with love and no judgement to the future.

The Gift of Eternal Growth

The yew becomes bent and twisted as it becomes older, but remains strong. Eventually it grows in girth until the crown, which has become large as the tree can support, is inadequate. This is where the wonderful symbiosis of the lives of the forest comes into play, as fungus eats the heartwood away, leaving an outer structure that can continue into the future. But this is a part of the yew's mystery, which we will visit in the next chapter.

For now, we know that our strength can continue in differing forms until the end of life. The yew is a constant reminder of the continuity of our lives and our line, from father to son, mother to daughter. In imagination we use the witnessing yew as a catalyst to view a past far distant—and envision a future yet to come.

Pause for a moment to review the relationships between our three trees.

Whether early or late in life we can evoke the inspiration and anticipation of the birch, transmuting it through the maturity of the oak and engaging with the ultimate timelessness of the yew to manifest new things appropriate to our maturity of thought.

All it takes is our awareness: we evoke, develop the witnessing aspects of the trees, step back from over-involvement into forest-serenity, and the trees will always be there, as teachers and guides.

Lessons from the Yew

Heritage

The yew dryad speaks:

Within my circle, past, present, and future weave together as their influences do in your life… As you pause beneath my boughs, you are walking the spiral of life, poised between ancestors and descendants, of blood and of spirit. From your centre, you can journey both forward and back in the imaginal realms, harvesting gifts from the past and building on your heritage to hand on a legacy to the future.

We are the ancestors about whom the tales will be told!

Now we will focus on our position poised between past and future, and how it might inform our lives. I hope the thought provoked a frisson of excitement in you, for understanding and interpreting elements of life in a symbolic, mythic, or folkloric sense enriches us immensely. It can inspire us to be the best we can be. It has resonances that carry us back to childhood, when the world was bright and all things were possible. It brings us into simplicity of thought. And as well as speaking to our deepest aspects, it is fun!

Every day, we are both reaping the harvest of our lives and actively engaged with setting the legacy we will leave. Since you started this book, has the way you have been setting your legacy—behaving, acting, and reacting—had any effect on the daily harvest? Has your witnessing approach, your increasing patience and kindness, resulted in increased energy or more positive responses from others? Do you need a shorter recovery time to get back on course each time you fall into the old traps? Are you developing an ability sometimes to *stop* yourself from falling in the first place?

Take your notebook and jot down notes on this. Remember, we're so adaptable that we need frequent reviews to show us just how far we have come.

We've looked extensively at outward appearance; now just consider and write down the answer to the question: "What is your style in this life?"

Your style, flavour, individuality determine exactly how you can and will act, and how you *just can't* act, in spite of any advice you might be given. The most kind and useless sentences begin, "If I were you…" Your actions, expressed through your whole persona, constitute your "style." And this essential signature is informed by a series of archetypal images, shadowy and huge, existing in the realm of the imagination.

Starting from the list of twelve common archetypes below, supply examples for each that are relevant to you. Some will doubtless come from pop culture or fiction, and you'll notice how the media regularly rifle mythic stories to engage their audience on a deep level.

The innocent/inspired fool	The lover
The orphan	The artist
The mother/father	The jester
The hero/ine	The magician
The explorer	The sage/expert
The rebel	The ruler

This is not a definitive list, but a starting point for your thoughts, and you are bound to think of others. Think of a story/film/mythic example of each from your own main influences. My personal favourite as the most perfect example of father/sage is Gregory Peck as the wise lawyer Atticus Finch in the film *To Kill a Mockingbird*. A folk example of the innocent/inspired fool archetype would be Jack the Giant Killer. A cultural example would be any individual who cuts through obstructions that defeat clever thinkers to gain results, such as Bob Geldof setting up Live Aid.

How would you match the following personas with the archetypes?

King Arthur	Merlin
Buffy the Vampire Slayer	Stephen Hawking
Romeo	Snow White
Coyote	The Madonna
The Fonz	Captain Jack Sparrow

Now, if you are a clearly defined entrepreneur, academic, boss, or home-maker, you might recognise your predominant mythic influence which supports your best endeavours. But bear in mind the fluidity of life and the myriad demands made upon your range of skills, all in the course of one day. Becoming attached to the idea of our predominant archetype is not healthy! These are liminal connections, and we should not identify with them as if they will manifest in the real world. Becoming unhealthily attached to a grandiose influence—seeing ourselves as Merlin or Morgan le Fay, for example—

indicates an insecurity that compensates with self-aggrandisement, and those feelings aren't relevant to our new thinking; they are simply a distraction.

So hold the ideas lightly, respectfully, and don't over-identify, but examine how many different expressions of the self come to the fore in any one day.

Archetype examples throughout the day

Morning
Tidy house—Cinderella drudge
Prepare family for day—mother/father
Work presentation—sage
Taking training session—mentor

Afternoon
Planning meeting—artist/fool/creator

Evening
Collect kids—homemaker/sage/peacemaker
Special evening with partner—queen/princess/
    king/prince/knight
Later—lover...

How many people we have inside ourselves! Truly, human beings are amazing. We can, and must, retain a firm sense of ourselves *as we actually are*, but that doesn't run contrary to also having an awareness of the archetypes in the imaginal world. So if we feel we're not fulfilling one of our necessary roles well, if we feel less comfortable in a particular role, we can look in visualisation at the archetype that can support us. What archetypal presence would we give to the three trees? Some possible answers have been given in the chapters. Think of them now. Which is an enchantress or wizard? A prince/princess, a king or queen? What other archetypes do they key into?

Just for fun: a snap decision for you. Which hero/ine from myth or story appeals to you beyond all others? Write it down now: Sir Lancelot, Sleeping Beauty, the Little Mermaid? The disguised Cap o' Rushes, Maeve of Ireland, or Friar Tuck? Which film star? Which pop singer?

What does that say about your yearnings? What part of you is longing to be expressed?

Family Heritage: Gifts and Skills

Start with a fun drawing. Sketch your family characteristics: what has been physically handed down to you? Your strength, height, weak chest, strong bones, fuzzy hair, big feet ... Then draw your ancestors beside you, emphasising the characteristics you share. Remember, these bodily limitations and resources are the physical chalice which holds your potential.

Find (thank you, Internet!) and read the poem "Heredity" by Thomas Hardy: "I am the family face ... " Now think of the non-tangible gifts—your inherited skills of math, woodwork, cooking, nature, the arts or the sciences—things you just have a natural facility for. Everyone is born with their individual seeds for achievement.

List now all the aptitudes inherited from your family and culture. At the same time check with each one that, although you may have *developed* them because of family expectations, *using* them is your authentic choice—your enthusiasm will tell you the truth of that.

Next to the list add those skills particularly your own, developed with no expectations from your family, and draw connecting lines as you cross-reference the two lists. Do they interact in a positive way? Could they? How have they manifested so far? How can they in the future?

Put your thoughts and conclusions on one of your tree-diagrams to see which are roots, which are fruits, and how you get from one to the other via strong focus and direction, doing what you love and are good at.

In order to achieve, we use our yew-boundary awareness to allow us to *keep* making time, *keep* our awareness so we act productively. What shields and protects us? Are you allowed non-negotiable quiet time, and if not, shouldn't you work on that? We all know people who should have written a book, recorded an album, entered and won that competition ... but they didn't. Make time, and ring-fence it!

If others' memories of you are to be of someone in love with life, bursting with enthusiasm, taking every opportunity, then you must keep up the appointments with your inner work, making regular time for enjoyable practice. So what protects you? Is there anything that tells others that you are on your own mission and not to be disturbed? Jo in *Little Women* had a cap she wore when "genius was burning"; fathers operating tools wear a "danger" hat to warn their children. Remember that the yew shields and protects and set up systems that make your intentions—to claim your own time—clear. It's far fairer than shouting in frustration when you get overloaded.

Affirmations

The following affirmations are to keep you keyed into a strong sense of pulling from the past and seeing yourself as a conduit for the future.

Yew Affirmations

For recognising your heritage gifts:
I have unique gifts for the world.
My life is an expression of my authentic self.
Within me is a treasure store of gifts. I allow them to manifest.

To make the most of each day:
I have all the time I need, yet none to squander.
I am relaxed and active.

To protect space to develop your talents:
I balance my inner and outer life with grace and ease.

My unique gifts are relevant to my life.
> I adapt to the changes of my life.

To protect your secret dreams:
I keep my treasure safe and work towards my dreams.

On timelessness and relevance:
Time and age are irrelevant; I use my gifts
> to the full in the here and now.

Engage Your Senses

Connections to the past can take us by surprise: activated by our senses, by-passing our rational mind, and taking us straight as an arrow into the past. Scents and smells are evocative; the smell of the yew is that of the primeval forest, and the decomposing needles on the forest floor smell dark and fertile.

Hearing is said to be the last sense to linger. Think again of songs that evoke a positive response in you, and ask yourself the question: how will you use them?

- Think now of a song to represent feelings of joy, empowerment, youth, love. Start playing or singing it regularly.

- If you haven't already, sing a song from a previous generation, from your youth, from significant parts of your life.

- Treat yourself to a CD that resonates from the past, or find the radio station catering to your tastes, to regularly surprise and delight you.

Most of us loved music in our youth and idolised our musical heroes, following them obsessively. Music represented something very profound to our young selves. It encapsulated the spirit of excitement of growing up and the promise of our potential, soon to be realised, making things seem possible.

That attitude is too extreme to maintain as we mature, but look back and note that, as our senses become dulled with age, music seems to lose its hold on us. Yet it is still there, as potent as ever it was, and it is still a conduit to potential and change.

The yew dryad speaks:

How dim are the echoes from the past, yet they reverberate through life, informing the present, as the layers of bark are laid down to form the shape of my tree. Listen to the song of the birds, and the rhythmic creak of the branches as the wind increases; this is the song of my life, the forest's natural symphony. The never-ending melody is compounded of every aspect of sentient life ... the hooting owl in my branches, the bark of a fox, scratching of the tree creeper, snuffle of the badger trundling down to its sett amongst my roots. Listen ... imagine the gentle sound as a fungus cap pops through the cover of the forest floor ... As the wind rises, the gale screams through the crown of the trees, swaying them violently and clattering their branches. The spirit of the forest conducts the score written by the weather ... and then all becomes calm once again.

As we exercise our imaginal muscles and embrace evocation as a real way to alter our lives, we will rediscover that music is a potent resource to support us. Pop gives us joy, spontaneity, and an immediate emotional connection; orchestral and inspirational music connect us to a profound sense of beauty, timelessness, an earthly hint of the music of the spheres themselves. So some research is now needed.

Find some good background music to complement your next visualisations. What is there about it that makes it suitable? Note the effects, and continue if you find it helpful. Consider the different instruments and begin to explore the quality of response you have to strings, wind instruments, and drums. Which type of instrument or style of music attaches to the yew, to the oak, to the birch, in your mind?

This is a tiny section of work with immense potential. Do not be dismayed if classical music leaves you cold, but you yearn for natural sounds of wind, water, and birdsong: all are now readily available on CD. The sounds of nature and of music are expressed simultaneously in the spheres of the material and the spirit; like the yew itself, they are a bridge to the higher planes.

Craft Your Own Visualisations

Visualisation 1:

To meet your archetypes—a reminder of your resources
Images that might be helpful: The heart of a very ancient wood, resonant with the past. Boar and stag and the quiet life of the forest over the centuries. Oak facing a circle of yew, shielding, eternal, vigilant. Green figures, noble-looking men and women. An invisible connection to their archetypal qualities evoking an echo; pledging their support. A cloak of green; the leader of the group salutes you—Robin Hood, of the longbow of yew wood; an image of strength and integrity. This is the third time that you may have visited these permutations of these figures in your inner world. Are they now familiar? Do you see them as a resource to interact with, and do they all represent different archetypes? Can you see your relationship developing?

Visualisation 2:

Connect to the yew gifts of quality and beauty
Images that might be helpful: A woodland centre; a wooden primitive roof stretching over the forest floor; shelves of wooden artefacts. Piles near the edge of the roofing: bowls with fungus growing, platters shiny with damp; children's practice crafts being returned to nature, including yours. A magnificent central stand

of yew sculptures to handle, suffusing your senses with lines and colours. Symbolic meaning lies within their shapes. A small shelf holding an ancient artefact: a polished wooden spear, straight like a unicorn's horn; a relic from nearly half a million years ago. Quality, longevity, purity of form. Your gifts are also of the best quality you can make; the practice pieces have disintegrated back into the forest. Their legacy is in the skills
you carry into the future.

Visualisation 3:
Connect to the yew promise of eternity
Images that might be helpful: Warm, cloaking clothes and boots. Evoke deep winter; invigorating cold; the snow-clad forest. Bare deciduous trees; flurried snow; dead leaves beneath. The sun as a white disc. A monochrome world. Total stillness, awaiting the year's turn. Footmarks of small mammals in the snow. A time to observe. A mammoth old yew, shining leaves and vermilion seeds blazing life and colour. Winter birds feasting on the nourishment; promise of life in seeming deadness. Your spirit fed and warmed by this promise. All is love and security.

Visualisation 4:
Referring back to your personal past
If you wish, you can craft this visualisation from scratch, for only you know the gifts and restrictions gained from your past. But don't do this if you are in any doubt. Trust your intuitive response: as always, these are just suggestions and you make the decisions. If your past was unhappy and continues to intrude upon your life, remember that help is available from qualified practitioners. Use the internal template of the forest to support you as you think back on your childhood dreams, hopes, and aspirations. Here's an example:

Under a huge ancient yew, listen to the yew dryad recounting his/her history:

The yew dryad speaks:

When I was young, and rooted from my parent, the weather bent me. Through the grove which my brothers and I made, the movement of large animals pushed their way through the forest. Wild boar scratched against my bark and broke and trampled young saplings and twigs. Now microscopic fungi eat at my heartwood. Sit in my gentle shade and think back on your childhood dreams, hopes, aspirations—have they got lost along the journey, broken off as my branch is broken by the antlers of the great stag in its passing? Has their shape changed and matured, so that their essence is still intact within you? What can you do to reclaim your dreams in a new and mature form?

Now bring your optimism and your ideas back with you to the present.

Other approaches might be to visit happy highlights of your life as if walking among them or riffling through an internal photo album, or to craft a visualisation of yourself as an ancestor. Imagine yourself dressed symbolically to help you identify with this status role. Look down the tunnel of the future and see what gifts you send. Imagine writing to a descendant, or simply breathing blessings, love, and all your best qualities down the years to the unfolding future, with all its myriad possibilities.

Doodling and Crafting

Don't resist—it really does help! Reread the section on the yew and crafts—has it any relevance to your life? Should it have? If the answer is an immediate "No, can't do it!" or if you are severely challenged on the craft front, just start with something basic:

- Make a potato print. Cut a potato in half and carve a simple yew leaf—a few straight lines around a central stick—using a potato peeler. Blot excess moisture, apply paint, and print. Amaze your children! Make paper for Christmas! Not important enough? Yet the noble yew was once a sapling— and this journey is partly about losing our self-importance.

- Experiment with non-firing clay to make unique buttons. Form the clay into the shape of flattened yew berries; make two holes with a thin knitting needle. Let the buttons dry, paint them green and red, varnish, and sew on as a decorative embellishment to your knitting or textile projects.

- Use the same clay to make, paint, and varnish personalised counters for board games and decorate with yew-leaf designs.

- Make a unique monogram based on yew shapes. Include the initials of your loved ones. You can use your yew monogram on anything of beauty and quality you produce; it needn't be prominent. Quality and durability are gifts from the yew; do something beautifully!

And when you've experimented with the craft aspect, you can go back to the drawing board, drawing an ancestor yew at very centre of your life, with all the strands coming from it, or sketching a traditional family tree and marking every one in your family as one of the three trees. Is your wise child a yew? Was your mother a birch?

Then draw the future: sketch yourself as how you want to be in ten years, then as a vigorous, healthy old person. Explore how you intend to look, act, and manifest your gifts.

Practical Work

- Have you marked all your birches, oaks, and yews on a local map yet? Do it now, and imagine lines of force between them, as their energies interact and inform each other.

- Observe the yew in all seasons. When is it of most use to the life of the forest? When and how are you of most use in the lives of others?

- Robin Hood and Maid Marian plighted their troth under a yew. Why not visit one at significant times so it can witness your important life events? Or resolve to do significant things in the right way at any place that's worthy of your intent.

- Buy a yew box to keep precious things in.

The yew was significant in folkloric mysteries, being used for writing that could be both protective and magical. So tune in to its essence before your next piece of writing. Ask that you be inspired by that ancient wisdom. Evaluate the effect afterwards. Did it help get you into the writing zone?

When we understand our place in the ages-old song of life we realise that each of us adds a uniquely wonderful thread of melody. Considering our history, both personal and cultural, allows us to connect deeply to that which will be most enriching and put aside any past associations we no longer need. Free of any negative notes of our past, and able to draw on strengths that are our heritage from family and community, our melody becomes light and rich and strong, allowing us to sing out our individual gifts to the future.

Night-Time Visualisation: The Fortingall Yew

Drift away into a perception of the incredible age of the yew and what it has witnessed.

You find yourself in the heart of Scotland, in the cold, clear, refreshing light... the grey and green of a churchyard, serene and peaceful. A protective wall has "windows" of wrought iron through which you see a spreading crown of green... the Fortingall yew.

Pause and consider that this might be the oldest living thing on the planet... You take the grey stone path to the tree; determine to walk slowly and with due thought. You see that there are carved words inscribed on each alternate slab.

Take time to breathe in your understanding of the words as you go... Pause on every blank slab and read the message on the next. Each engraved message is illustrated with a simple symbol... the first is a carving of the shape of the tree itself.

As you read each message, imagine what each illustrative design might be in turn before you progress further. Each message and picture remembers our common ancestry, of lineage and spirit.

Read the first slab: "Up ahead stands Fortingall's oldest resident, a 5000 year old yew tree"...

Consider the concept of time, and then walk on to stand on the next stone.

"Imagine those who have passed this way before"...

Pause and consider at each slab, then continue.

"Stone Age Man"...

"Bronze Age Man"...

Remember, imagine each illustration before you proceed further.

"Reindeer, Boar and Wolf"...

"Picts"...

"Scots"...

The path turns 90 degrees to the left...

"Roman Legions"...

"Christians"...

"Warriors"...

"Explorers"…

"Scholars"…

"Kings and Queens"…

"Worshippers through the Ages"…

"… and YOU."

Step off the end of the path and turn right to walk along the wall. Here is the gate of wrought iron railings, which swings to allow you in.

There are two relict trunks left of the mighty ancestor, still glowing with red-brown bark, and with deep green leaves around and above you. They are enclosed in a circle of markers delineating its original girth of 56 feet (17 metres) in circumference. Red berries glow and burst their sweetness on the carpet of dead brown leaves under your feet.

In your imagination, all those chapters of history can unfold in whatever way you wish: tattooed Picts, kilted Scots, and the Roman legions who never conquered north of Hadrian's Wall… Scholars and explorers who visited this yew before their travels in this sacred place, purported to be the heart of Scotland. You are still beneath the yew as you allow the image to fade from your consciousness and the outside world to claim your attention.

Somewhere deep inside, you are always in the centre of your world. Within you is a vast ancient tree connecting you to the deep past, which enriches and informs you. Come back filled with resources, with certainty, with completeness.

9

Yew and the Magic of Mystery

Tree quality: They are a bridge between the worlds.

At last, after a gradual process of reviewing our relationship with our three teacher trees, we arrive at the contemplation of absolute mystery.

What an inexplicable wonder is this life—and how unexpected are we and our fellow humans! The intoxicating, intangible sense of mystery, otherness, the magic of the more-than-human world, is the impetus that has led us through the book. The rational mind has no equipment to understand or define mystery: to attempt that is as doomed as taking a spade expecting to dig up the actual Holy Grail. Some things belong in other realms than the physical, yet they impinge constantly on our everyday consciousness as yearnings, urgings, and intuition, reminding us that we should always reach for the unattainable, attempt to come to terms with the magical inexplicable. This is what makes us not merely travellers but *questers*.

Mystery and Ancient Symbolism

Mystery is best related to through sideways and oblique connections, through which we gain an inkling of an invisible current of life that pervades the universe. After consideration and practice, we can embrace that stance with ease and confidence.

The most helpful tool for this is a thorough understanding of symbolism. We've worked with it extensively, but as we've come to realise how vital it is, we will just clarify here: a symbol is an object that represents more than itself, something standing for something larger and more abstract—a pink heart on a valentine's card; a skull on a poet's desk. If you started the book as a very literal-minded person, our examination of the trees as symbols—of new beginnings or kingship, as bridges between earth and sky, as portals to expand our consciousness—will have gently stretched you. We've been developing our symbolism muscles, so we can view the whole world in an expanded way—not all the time, maybe, but regularly, through visualisations and in flashes and moments of insight.

The yew's symbology resonates back into far history: the darkness, the brightness, the colours, its shape and habit all serve to draw us deeper into mystery. And what was relevant to our ancestors remains valuable to us today.

Colour Symbolism

Close your eyes now and quickly imagine then hold in your mind a screen of Brilliant Red. What impressions do you have? Then repeat the exercise for Dark Green and Rich Brown. You will find that each colour has immediate impact. Jot down your impressions quickly.

The larger and more intense the swathe of colour, the greater the effect—and yews can be huge, surrounding and flooding us with the impression of their rich tones. Next time you visit your yew, view it with soft eyes, blurring the outlines, and saturate your senses with its colours, which have been used in art from Palaeolithic times. You might feel yourself dwarfed by an intensity of hues that open out as if to reveal their nature to you.

A rich legacy of cave art from our earliest ancestors has been found worldwide. All ancient cultures utilised earth pigments such as umber and sienna, shades that replicate the yew's red-brown bark. Most importantly, red ochre, colour of the yew berries in midwinter, was a vital symbol of life and rebirth, blood, fire, life-sustaining warmth, and protection. We know this by the way it was used by our ancestors to paint bones that were then buried in the foetal position, as if in the womb. The earliest example of this is the famous "Red Lady of Paviland," discovered in a cave in South Wales, a ritual burial we know now to have been a young man, and the oldest ritual burial of a modern human found so far in Western Europe. Red ochre was also used to coat weapons and in cave paintings, notably from Spain, France, and Patagonia, through to Australia. In the present time it is still used for body painting by some tribal societies.

Put the book down for a moment, and just surrender to the mystery of the imaginal realm, which is as real as the world of the five senses.

The yew dryad speaks:

See on the screen of your closed eyelids a cave wall, lit by a flickering torch. You are back in far history, at the time when my tree was the only evergreen, when it symbolised the eternal life of nature.

In the dim light you discern shapes that do not look random, and you move closer... The rock has striations and cracks, gleaming and of a deep green, where seams and veins of copper have oxidised. Like graffiti making the shapes of underground tree roots and branches, they stretch across the cave wall. Move closer, to see the smaller blobs of colour... You peer to see that red ochre pigment has been spattered over human hands, leaving a reverse imprint on the wall—each hand surrounded by a brilliant circular red berry of colour, between the branch-like veins of minerals in the cave wall. One hand has four fingers and a stump, and you feel an immediate connection to history, to the hunter who lost his finger in an accident millennia ago. You find the imprint of a perfect hand, and place yours by it... The flickering torch lights your hand with fire-red and as you feel your life within, you are drawn effortlessly back to the present...

Brown for the stability and nurture of the earth; red for life and blood and vitality; green for eternal growth cycle: these things are our concern in this chapter, and we can use colour along with our other techniques to lead us to the heart of the qualities we wish to evoke.

Mystery of Time and Longevity

Ancient, Venerable, Notable, Extraordinary—yews are the only trees so very old that in 2010, these new classifications were devised for them, based on age, girth, and significance.

Deep knowledge is the gift of any aged thing, linking us to the far past. Every European yew has the potential to become a mighty ancestor with a lifespan of thousands of years. Its method is part of a mystery for it regenerates in a marvellous way, shared with few other trees around the world.

The yew you visit or see on the Internet may have boughs large enough to bend down under their own weight: that is the tree's habit. And when yew boughs touch the ground, magically they can root and grow new trunks in their own right. Sometimes you will come across a huge tree stump in the centre of a circle of yews—the remains of an ancestor tree that has "birthed" a circular grove by this method. No wonder the yew symbolises regeneration. You may find yards of sinuous roots, reminiscent of skin-shedding snakes, which are also ancient symbols of regeneration.

There is something ultimately reassuring in this lesson from nature of continuing renewal. No matter what the truth of our own continuing existence *vis-à-vis* physical life and death, the yew hints to us: if this rebirthing quality is evidenced in one species, why not in ours, albeit in a form that we will never know?

These thoughts provoke ideas that can help free us from time's yoke.

We tend not to understand time. Although we pin it down to minutes and hours, we are constantly surprised by its nature, as in the phrases, "I've lost track of time," "Time just raced away," "Isn't the time dragging?" and "Where did the time go?" Maybe our very surprise around a linear view of time is proof that, while it works for all practical purposes, it is not natural to us.

So let us just suppose that time is *not* linear, but has more complex patterns that actually allow us to live a long and satisfying life no matter how few years we have left. Consider our lives as a spiral, not a line. As the earth goes round the sun we experience the same seasons, but each with its own new freshness. So it is with our life situations; we spiral round throughout our lives, revisiting themes and types of events, but from a different perspective. This would explain why we periodically find ourselves "back here again"—visiting similar situations, liable to make the same old mistakes. We should regard that not as cause for despair, but for interest and examination. Every time we revisit we will view from a different place along the spiral and a different perspective, so we consider two things:

- Looking below the surface of a problem that is new but familiar to us, how are we informed by past experience of this type of situation?

- How does our enlarged, experienced vision help us to deal with things this time around?

From a forest perspective, we can see imaginatively into the past and project into the future. In that inner space, we can connect to our personal longevity as a reality, for a day can stretch to a hundred years if we choose. We curve round the spiral of life, sometimes speeding, sometimes pacing ourselves, often alternating between a stroll and a frantic dash, but always moving forward, along a tree-lined spiral path up a hill. If the path dips down, we might briefly touch a part of the track we've already walked, and plunge into associations of the past journey and our younger selves. When the path soars, we can gain intimations of the greater patterns of life. But always we are spiralling along our appointed route. In the glorious reality of paradox, we have complete free will, so it is of course a route appointed by ourselves, as all our actions today help to form the path of our future.

And every moment can be used to the maximum as, like the trees, we simply live our lives in the moment. Being embodied. Remaining aware and connected to our current reality. This attitude, with its space for quietness and internal reflection, slows the illusion of linear time and suddenly, as we've discovered before, we have time for everything.

Step back under the yew or another long-lived tree in your area. Ask for knowledge of longevity and for the ability to understand it—not rationally, remember. It may be through a feeling, a quality, a realisation that can be as relieving as removing a too-tight shoe. Just suspend rational judgement and surrender to the idea that such an exercise may allow you into the mystery of deep time ... for you also are a holder of history.

Mysterious Ways of Connection

The yew is woven into the stories of our European forebears, of saints and families who have made alliances with the tree; and the evidence of their connection is there on our maps. Scotland and Ireland particularly abound with place names referencing the yew—often indicated by "Io" and "Eo." Of the many examples, the Gaulish tribal name Eburones means "yew," and in England, the ancient name for York, Eboracum, means "place of the Yew." Youghall in County Cork, Ireland, means "yew wood," and there are dozens of such references in Scotland. Evidence is also in personal names: the Irish name Eógan means "born of the yew," and the Irish Eóganachta dynasty who ruled in the Middle Ages were "people of the yew." There are a wealth of Celtic personal names that mean "of the yew" still in use, the most common being Yves, Ivor, Evan, and Owen for boys, and, for girls, Yvette, Yvonne, and Lavonne, as well as a Scottish clan grouping, the clan McIver. The connection of the yew and the clan Frazer is an anecdote from history: after the Jacobite rebellion the clan were no longer permitted their tartan, and so used the yew as an emblem, a means of identification and for clan solidarity. The tradition continues to this day in the wearing of a slip of yew in the bonnet.

We may be enthralled by the possibility of an expanding sense of mystery in our lives; we may be scared. But the yew is the tree that can help us, *gently* inducting us into our first explorations. As with our other trees, we can ally ourselves to the yew by name or emblem to strengthen our natural affinity to its qualities. And we can connect to it to encourage this sense of affinity if we feel a lack of yew qualities within us.

There is a mystery as to how we can exchange and gain in this way. Simply, once again, start with the process of staying awake to possibility; carry out the yew exercises in the study session with an attitude of awareness and allowing, without being wedded to consequences. And we can use folklore and myth—an area we will explore later.

Mystery of Sacredness

The mention of saints brings us to the mystery of the sacred—which might be another way of interpreting the "otherness" that we seek, the heart of life's purpose, which has been our preoccupation.

We know that the yew has always had an association with hallowed land and churches, and we've looked at its connection with water. Now add to this the fact that islands also were regarded as sacred to the Celts. In the most practical way, islands are the easiest places to keep separate from the mundane world; their integrity as dedicated places is safeguarded by the force of the ocean itself. For this reason many islands, like the yew tree, have associations with the dead; the graveyards of particular Scottish islands abound with rulers and notable clerics too many to be named here, brought together to a final resting place that emphasises their status. Avalon, the legendary enchanted isle of apples where King Arthur goes to be healed of his wounds, is a paradisiacal isle equating to Avallach, the Celtic isle of the dead.

Set-apart-ness is important to our sense of the sacred and essential to our exploration of mystery; that's why we've spent so much time on making space for it. Removed from the mundane world, we might have experienced it during our regular visualisations, or when we have honoured our instinct and withdrawn to the forest, nature's cathedral.

All of these elements come together in the holy isle of Iona off the western coast of Scotland, so formative in the story of Celtic Christianity; it will come as no surprise to find that the name derives from "yew." Whether in ancient sacred places, over holy wells and streams, or on islands, the yew will add to the aura inherent in the place. From the beginning, we have noticed the yew's invitation to approach in a considered and appropriate way, different to our normal mode of being: it has a psychological effect. The very silhouette of a venerable yew invites us to step from the mundane to the sacred, for its boughs bending to the ground form a doorway. Like its cousin the oak, it is a portal and can be used in a thoughtful moment in a park by stepping through with awareness, or in our visualisations to lead us to totally new territory.

Mystery of Layeredness

Guided by the yew, this new territory might lead us nearer the heart of mystery, which we approach by considering the word "surrender."

Underlying what we have been practicing daily, a constant motif is the need to surrender our expectations and open ourselves to possibilities. Only by shedding past ways of thinking can we free ourselves to lead a creative, magical, and joyous life.

So let us at last return to that first quotation that started our journey:

No problem can be solved from the same level of consciousness that created it.

Rereading this reminds us of how far we've come in accessing a new level of understanding; and how we've learnt that there are a thousand ways of getting there—layers linking us to mystery and wonder—and a thousand perspectives—human, tree, animal, and planetary—and ways of approaching life. I hope you've found it an exciting journey so far, but to what extent have you succeeded, do you think? As you approach the end of this particular journey, review your progress once again. Are you still charting your course? Still keeping a diary? These are wonderful tools, but whether you have been diligent in note taking or have followed a more intuitive route, think of how far you have come, and be happy.

The layered scales of the yew bark form long, sinuous lines along the trunk, reminiscent of horses' or unicorns' heads, snakes and stag's horns: strange zoomorphic impressions that hint that there is so much more within, if we could just access it. *The same is true of us.*

We can shed, and shed, and shed our outmoded and limited thought patterns, as a tree its leaves; the resultant fresh-springing growth of our more authentic selves is both joyous and liberating. Books on physical decluttering may seem mundane, but appropriate physical acts ground our aspirations and help us to realise our dreams. And they hold a rich nugget of wisdom within their pages: that, as we are born and die with no possessions, then one of our jobs in life may be to keep sloughing off those things that we accrue and that stick to us. This applies especially to *perceptions* formed by past experience, so that if we can approach each new experience with a freshness, inquisitiveness, and anticipation, it appears to lengthen our experience, for we are absorbed fully in each moment.

Within ourselves we have a myriad of characters and viewpoints. We can look to the archetypal levels and act "as if" we were the hero, the scholar, the wise person, the child. We can turn to the natural world for the vitality of the horse, the magic of the unicorn, the nobility of the stag, all in the imaginal realms. And we can feel the armour of our preconceptions flaking from us naturally, like bark, without effort, revealing more and still more of our shining self. This leads us to the most magical aspect of the yew, as it, and we, surrender to the...

A Hollow Yew Tree

Mystery of Hollowness

Hollowness is the wonder of the yew.

Human physiology dictates that our core functions are kept safe and deep within our bodies; with the heart as our symbol of life force, our growth should provoke the expansion of our spiritual heart. All trees, on the other hand, have their active pulse just beneath the bark, so that with age, the heartwood—the dead wood at the tree's core—gets compacted and dies. The yew lives long enough for us to see how that contributes to its near immortality.

Walking round any truly ancient yew can be a shocking experience, as the whole perfection of the trunk suddenly reveals a yawning chasm of hollowness, half of the trunk eaten away. It could seem like an allegory of decay, yet if we understand the process of the tree's longevity, it is an exquisite example of symbiosis that is a fundamental lesson for our own lives.

Elderly trees are often brought down by their own size and age. We see the results regularly after storms. But if the yew splits, it resists disease, and its rooting habit means that new growth can spring from it. And more importantly, by the time its bulk becomes too big, fungi has already started eroding its heartwood, making the structure lighter, more flexible and resilient to the elements. So what might seem evidence of decrepitude is exactly what allows it to continue growing healthily, having adapted late in life to its circumstances.

The yew dryad speaks:

Walk around my ancient trunk: step forward and explore... Within is decay and flaking matter feeding microscopic organisms. But see the thickness of my trunk still remaining, the sturdiness of the living tissue. Look outside at my aged bark; from the lowest parts of it are growing tiny new sprigs of yew, each with its own leaf. Hollowness leading to eternal life is part of my natural mystery. In old age, my inspiration to grow and expand still springs from the depths of my being. All my old, compacted wood has gone. My boughs have rooted; soon I will be surrounded by my offspring. My contribution to the natural world perpetuates.

The yew is hollow; *so are we.*

This is a surreal concept for most of us to comprehend, but scientists know that matter is empty. The atoms that make up our bodies are mostly space, and without this, like a deflated balloon, our volume would be unimaginably tiny. The fact is that we are empty space.

Allow that fact to sink in for a moment.

It is less challenging to look at our physical bodies, to see the same truth on a grosser level... Think now of our bodies as being a series of tubes, making up the continuous space that is our digestive system, constantly processing our nourishment—an indication of our hollowness. Food enters the tube, is processed, and exits as waste. The bowels and bladder fill and empty, expand

and contract—what a brilliant system. Think of the chest, a protective cage around the vast emptiness of our two lungs, inhaling the precise mix of gas we need to sustain life, processing it to oxygenate the blood, and exhaling waste gas through the same hollow tunnels, in and out, every second of our life. Think of our reproductive organs, designed in women to expand into internal space to gestate new life: miraculous.

As in the body, so too the spirit. If we can perceive our essential selves as being largely hollow, then we can imagine the job of that space is to be open to a larger spiritual influence. By allowing that understanding, we give permission to connect to the beneficent currents of the universe, which can imbue us with creativity and achievement, each according to our gifts and inclinations.

We will work with these images in the study section very soon.

Openness is also a mental attitude, and it bestows freedom. It is said that "knowledge is power," but it is also true that "the dissemination of knowledge is freedom." No, we don't give away our business secrets, but we have been refining our relationships so that we are in position to express ourselves authentically, in our natural state of being "openhearted." Our heart has a simple function, yet our culture attaches to it a huge symbolic importance as the seat of our emotions—those emotions we engage when we evoke.

Mystery and Liminality

Liminality applied to humans indicates a state of being in not quite one state or another—between waking and sleeping, for example. It also applies to physical space that is ambivalent—the seashore, is it water or land? Similar questions apply to the edge of woodland, marshland and estuaries, the meeting of wild and cultivated land, or the top of a mountain or a cave. And then consider liminal times of day—dawn, dusk, midnight, midday—or the changeover of the seasons.

All of these places and times we can visit in imagination or actuality; all have an ambience that encourages the exploration of the mystery of life. A group of yews, or one large one, can change the atmosphere of a small space, giving us a sense of liminality.

It is this sense that we acknowledge when we approach the tree with respect. It is this sense that we pursue when we *think like a tree*, to keep ourselves fluid and open to the best we can be, for liminality describes our state of expanded awareness. Within it, we can engage fully with the world of the five senses and all our responsibilities, and *yet* maintain the witnessing brief of the trees. We hold two or more worldviews in awareness at the same time, having an understanding of the wider physical world, the realms of the unseen and the imagination, our place as a physical and more-than-physical entity, and a non-rational understanding of the patterns of our lives. What a lot of perspectives to hold at once! The only way is to cultivate an urge to trust and surrender, to act with grace as well as we are able.

If we tried to keep all this constantly in the forefront of our minds, we couldn't cope with the everyday world. Yet because we visit our tree-perception regularly, this wider context becomes the larger background that colours life and is a never-failing resource.

We might conclude that, as well as being more space than matter, life is more mystery than matter. And all the work we have done has been in the mysterious uncharted realms of the imaginal world, encouraged gently by our work on the ground, as we integrate our inner and outer lives and gain congruence.

This all starts with an intuition that all of nature is inspirited; and therefore we can make connection and draw benefit from the entire sentient world. We do this with the three keys to transforming our lives:

- Expansive, limitless inner reflection

- Symbolic and mythic connections

- Evocation

Through these, the paths of the forest become clear tracks leading to the wisdom of our mentor-trees—the birch, oak, and yew—which silently witness our lives and those of our forebears and descendants. Through gently disengaging with the sensation-led, rushing urge with which the modern world tries to programme us, through sitting quietly and imbibing the lessons from the trees, we can step through a magical portal.

This will lead us simultaneously into two realities: the first a fulfilled, loving, creative, and productive life in the physical world; the second, an expanded life of grace, beauty, understanding, and acceptance—an awareness of blessedness.

We started with a quotation; let us end this section of the book with one:

Trees are sanctuaries. Whoever knows how to speak to them, whoever knows how to listen to them, can learn the truth. They do not preach learning and precepts, they preach, undeterred by particulars, the ancient law of life . . . Whoever has learned how to listen to trees no longer wants to be a tree. He wants to be nothing except what he is. That is home. That is happiness.[3]

With the last study session on the yew that follows, you will have completed the formal part of your journey.

Linger long in the forest, whenever you wish to. Learn how to want to be nothing but yourself, for you are wonderful. Take the wisdom of the trees, and know that you are welcome.

---

3   Hermann Hesse, *Bäume. Betrachtungen und Gedichte* (Frankfurt, Germany: Insel Verlag, 1984), English translation available at www.goodreads.com/work/quotes/2225608-b-ume-betrachtungen-und-gedichte (accessed September 2014).

Lessons from the Yew

Mystery

The yew dryad speaks:

Within my boundary, there is space for mystery, not to be interpreted by the mind but simply accepted. Gain an intimation of the strange deep truths of flowing life force in the seen and unseen worlds, as you observe the interplay of light on dark leaves, the inscrutability of the shadows, the enigmatic shapes shimmering on my bark… Here is liminal space, liminal time; here is a meeting place between the worlds. Here is a place to be open to otherness.

This is a study session about *not* understanding, and about giving up the need to.

So this session could just consist of blank pages—but that is more the way of the mystic, to simply *be* and allow the mystery of life to unfold within. As magical people, we are embracing life as *doers,* so here follow the suggestions.

Make a point of allowing time: contemplation of mystery demands it. Ideally, each idea in this section would be surrounded by pauses … to … indicate … time … for … thought … Or there might have been one suggestion per page, in the centre, with space for your thoughts around it, or any other visual aid to help you to just slow down. So you must make the gaps for thought in your style of reading. Settle down in your favourite chair, with a cup of tea. What better use of your time is there? If you can think of one, then go and do it, and return to this with a clear mind.

A good understanding is essential in most areas of life. But the liminal X percent of our lives will always be shrouded in mystery, and that fertile, magical space informs the way we grow and the shapes we make.

The trouble is that, as "needing to understand" is our default position, we can tear ourselves apart applying those criteria to the larger mysterious patterns of our life. Most of us don't achieve adulthood without being touched by one of the following questions: Why the divorce? Why the injustice? Why rich and poor? Why inhumanity, pain, and suffering? Why don't the good prevail? Why do the evil prosper?

To all of life's imponderable questions, we can simply choose to answer, "Not my problem." That sounds crude and callous, but it need not mean we're uncaring or that we shouldn't actively work to right the ills of society. It does mean that on a deep level we *accept* that "fairness" is too simplistic a concept when viewing the bigger patterns of life, so there will never be a satisfactory resolution to these questions. One thin thread of tapestry wool cannot understand the beautiful pattern it helps to make in the fabric.

Fortunately, there is also space for optimism. With hindsight we often detect vague hints of our pattern—time makes many things plain, allowing us to view life and its consequences differently. A typical example might be: "The marriage wasn't good, but I wouldn't be without the great kids." So going forward as if all is right seems simply the most sensible option, trusting our deeper senses and instincts.

How far we are able to surrender, to allow mystery, will depend on two main factors: how adept we have become through practicing the past exercises and how temperamentally suited we are to allowing uncertainty as a good thing.

If you know you will find difficulty in being "allowing" in your attitude to life, then practicing trust affirmations regularly, not just occasionally, will be useful. We are acting "as if" as a magical position in the world; therefore, as there is no way to safeguard ourselves from the vicissitudes of life, it does seem sensible to act "as if" life is beneficent and to be trusted.

I know that life is good. I am fortunate and trust the process of life.
Life is beneficent and things will work out for my ultimate good.
It is my joy to live my pattern, even though I don't understand it.

Ideas and Ideals

We can now consider abstract ideas: truth, honour, integrity, justice. In order to relax and have trust, we must act as if the universe is predicated upon the highest ideals. No one would relax in a basically unsafe situation—and we are dealing not only with day-to-day events, but with the understanding that the entirety of our lives will be for the best and that the universe will support that. To be magical we get in tune with the flow of life, which we are accessing through those qualities mirrored in the integrity of tree-life.

An underpinning theme through the book has been to attune ourselves to our highest ideals, and now we are making the choice to do that more consciously. Engaging with mystery, we expand our awareness of universal harmony, leading to the highest way of being that we can attain … and the next sections should help in achieving that.

Colour Symbolism

First for some fun! Colour linked us to the Stone Age in the last chapter, and fun with colour can take us back to our childhood selves, playing and learning in a way that most of us have nearly forgotten. Try this:

- Buy pastels, a paint box, crayons—any medium that allows for shading and mixing of colours, rather than restricting you to harsh lines.

- Experiment with colours in this order: blue, yellow, red.

- Load up your brush with your first primary colour: now play!

Spend some time just filling a few pages—first with washes of single colour, then gradually painting in shapes with variants of intensity to deepen, lighten, and brighten parts of the page, and to focus the eye.

When you have done this with blue, yellow, and red, study your pages and notice the qualities inherent in each. There is a whole theory attached, but for our purposes, it is enough to notice your responses to the three colours—dependant on the shades you choose, of course. But as a rule, blue seems to retreat from you and your eye is drawn into the picture; it calms. Yellow is expansive, glowing outwards from the page; it is energising. Red is strong—it can be powerful, dignified, energetic, or oppressive.

When you are ready, repeat for green, violet, purple, and orange. Then consider ... what effect might washes of colour have in the inner space of your mind and on your visualisations? You probably already use green extensively in your inner landscape; think of how other colours can enhance your inner world, and jot down your thoughts.

Now consider, how would your mood would be affected if your being was flooded with a colour? What colour are your walls at work and home, and what feeling do they evoke from you? What colour are your lampshades? Do they give the effect you wish? What splashes of colour give you delight in your house and garden? Which colours energise you and do you often wear them?

What has this to do with mystery?

Use your knowledge of the *personal* responses you have to colour to aid your evocations. No matter what traditional association a colour has, it is what it evokes in *you* that is important.

Abstract Qualities and Colour

Now, in a meditative state, we will return to the contemplation of our highest ideals, and paint a symbol for these qualities, in an appropriate colour. Sit with your art tools around you as you wonder:

- What colour and pattern or shape is mystery?

- What colours symbolise liminality? Truth? Justice? Honour? Love?

You might choose a mix of commonly held symbols—scales for justice, for example—and some that are completely personal. Few would think of pink in relation to justice, but if you do, then so be it. You could complete a painting simply of form, shapes, and colour(s) for all five qualities, and put them around where you can consider them.

Mystery of Our Own Insignificance

We are each the centre of our universe, and through our lives our reactions tend to come from our constant swinging between two opposing poles of thought:

- We are the centre of life, and everything we do is of immense importance.

- We are insignificant, and nothing we do will make any difference, so why bother?

In our personal lives, we are kingpin and go with statement one. Then, when a job gets too big—from disciplining the kids to stopping global warming—we quickly switch to statement two!

Casting ourselves in the role of star player in our own drama is inevitable, but if it also casts everyone else in a subservient role, that is pretty disrespectful, and the practical disadvantage to us is that it takes too much effort and is not sustainable. So losing the self-importance is a good idea. The converse, truly believing that we are unimportant in our own lives, is as bad for us; belittling our intrinsic worth and our value to the world is damaging, and not the sign of a healthy mind.

Let us allow ourselves the ultimate relaxation of acting from a new state of mind, and living with the delight of paradox, instead of switching stances ineffectually depending on circumstances.

So here is statement three:

- I am simultaneously vital and unimportant. I dance with the dynamic of seeing my true place in the universe and keeping my sense of perspective.

How Can We Know What We Can't Imagine?

We can find many inspirational quotes telling us that freedom is gained when we stop jockeying for position and withdraw into a greater understanding. And from that stance, we can allow our worries to dissipate into acceptance and gratitude. If we don't, then the blinkers we've grown will continue to restrict our worldview. Blinkers can be useful, but are very limiting, armour, protecting us from all we don't understand—and restricting one's understanding can happen individually or to whole cultures.

An example: *The person next door is inferior to me—in spite of their qualifications, intelligence, and circumstances—because of their race or gender.* Not many of us make such crude assumptions; yet we know that there will be some form of armour restricting us, and, regardless of the morality of prejudice, that it's just not helpful to us to carry that rusty old stuff around forever.

A particular worldview can affect whole civilisations—the lack of perspective in ancient Egyptian pictures must make us wonder how they actually saw their world. In ancient Greece, Homer's repeated phrase "the wine-dark sea" asks just how the Greeks saw the colour blue, and the Tahitians were blind to Captain Cook's ship approaching, as such a huge structure was not in their paradigm.

We are trying to get into harmony so that we can co-create our lives. But things not in our current paradigm will be invisible to us or distorted to make them congruent with our worldview. So how can we know what we can't see or comprehend? The antidote is to first recognise the possibility that there are some things we are blind to; to stretch and expand; to show a willingness to engage with mystery. Having connected with the trees, now we expand to recognise a whole gamut of life forms with which we can connect. And this thought, from German philosopher Friedrich von Schelling, is the perfect reminder of that:

> *Mind sleeps in stone, dreams in the plant, awakes in the animal and becomes conscious in man.*

Write it out, decorate it, and place it where you can see it frequently.

Affirmations

There is more in the world than we can imagine, but our deep selves can know and connect to it in an intuitive and non-rational way, if we can just stay open to the possibility. And if we give these ideas *space and time* to grow.

So let us encourage this expansion with our affirmations.

YEW AFFIRMATIONS

To relax and just allow:
I am allowed to be unimportant.
I release myself from over-care.
I allow life to flow through me,
 bringing its change and blessings.

To connect with hollowness:
I breathe through my being; I am a clear expression of spirit.
My body is a mystery; life flows through the spaces.

From my hollowness, I allow new aspects
    and understandings to emerge.

Whilst visualising colours:
I suffuse myself in the relaxing, enlivening green of life.
I breathe in the calming, peaceful blue of the sky.
The vibrant pulse of nature's colours feeds my spirit.
By my awareness of beauty, my spirit is nurtured.

To expand your vision:
Liminality, new ways of living, are always open to me.
I relax and allow the space for inspiration.

Expanding Our Vision: States of Consciousness

The occult writer Colin Wilson devised a scale for charting levels of consciousness, which might help with such questions as "How do we know if we're in 'expanded consciousness'?" and "What does such an imprecise term *mean*?" The definitions that follow are necessarily subjective, as is our own judgement of our state at any given time. But here are the states below the ecstatic visionary state, to start us off.

The base level is that of deep sleep, followed by dream sleeping, or that state immediately preceding sleep.

When waking, we might be in any of the following states: unresponding; not engaging; in a passive and reactive state where we find life a struggle; active, with a spontaneous happy engagement. And the last of the "normal" states is transcendent awareness, where time is irrelevant.

Where are you on the scale this moment? Have you experienced all of these states at different times? Ask yourself, and jot down the answers to, these questions:

Which state are you in after a trauma? When falling in love? Recovering from an illness? At your paid employment? With your personal and extended family? Doing this reading work? When visualising and evoking?

Part of mystery is that non-physical aspects—feelings and attitude—can colour our lives far more than, say, our health problems. And regardless of what we might have assumed up until now, our mental and emotional states are *not* dependant upon our physical circumstances. This is great news, for while our life circumstances—such as finances and health—can take considerable time to alter (if that is even possible in some cases), we can still begin to view and respond to our lives completely differently. Access the forest perspective; respect your feelings; notice your state of consciousness and determine to maintain a state of being engaged, spontaneous, and joyful.

The Tree Connection to the Greater Whole

We have been working on the premise that the tree connection far exceeds its physical being, and the tree of life is the ultimate expression of the greater connective qualities of tree-ness. It is a wonderful template, connecting the lower, middle, and upper regions of the world and giving nourishment to all the living creatures of the earth. The concept of a world tree has been used into antiquity as a way of understanding spiritual connection. You can explore the Internet to find traditional views of the world tree, or you can just get out your sketch book now.

Draw or sketch your favourite yew as the world tree, massive and stable. Continue your drawing deep in the earth, with the roots fed by an underground spring and aerated by tunnels from worms and underground mammals. Draw every variety of fish you can think of in the pool gathering near the roots. Draw every animal, reptile, insect, bird you can think of in its branches. Place the planets and stars in its upper branches, shining bright.

And you can suggest other life forms in the tree itself—roots turning into snakes; a flurry of leaves as a bird's wings; bark shapes as the faces of mammals—and the yew dryad resting at the junction of the trunk and a large bough. Use this picture as an aid to contemplation and a remembrance of connectivity.

Crafting Your Own Visualisations

Take plenty of time; how better to deal with mystery than in the liminal space of your inner imaginal world?

Visualisation 1:
Welcome mystery

Images that might be helpful: Liminal time—dusk, dawn, midday, or midnight. Liminal season—summer/winter solstice or spring/autumn equinox. Liminal space—forest clearing, seashore, mountain, marshland. The perfect time arriving. A yew wand held upright, to connect and anchor you securely; the essence of mystery of time and place and space flowing through the wand, beneficent and loving. Confident and happy, lying back and simply allowing time for images and colours of time and space to fill you. Releasing the need to understand rationally. Being part of the greater life; a sense of wonder, fulfilment, and joy.

Visualisation 2:
Connect to layeredness

Images that might be helpful: Trees in high summer. Layers of clothes separating you from your surroundings. Making a fire in a clearing; discarding and burning the clothing layers. Name the layers as they burn: residual bigotry or prejudice, personal insecurity, entrenched opinions, fears from childhood, a need to be confrontational, adolescent responses, whatever seems relevant. The garments transforming into pure, living energy of fire, dissolving into the sunlight. Donning light garments of love and gratitude. Soaking up the sunlight; the green energy of the trees, allowing life to flow through you.

Visualisation 3:

For a clan connection with the three trees

Images that might be helpful: The edge of a wood; grass and wild plants, fragrant and colourful. The pull of the trees; a narrow path. Allowing instinct to take over. Stroking the leaves and bark to greet the trees, your green cousins. Birch leaves blowing; catching one, tingling with anticipation of wonderful work still to be achieved. Going deep, holding images lightly. A huge guardian oak; threading a spray of leaves and early acorns through your belt, the leaves covering your abdomen. Security, control, and ownership of every aspect of life. A clump of evergreens, dominated by an old yew. A low-hanging branch; leaves and berries droop, clumping over your heart, opening and expanding into a larger appreciation of life, spilling through your body. Three very different energies; birch, oak and yew; see how their qualities interact, swirling in your other-than-physical being. Affirm a clan connection to one or all the trees. Give and/or receive a symbol or gift; the wonder of completeness.

Visualisation 4:

To understand your hollowness

Images that might be helpful: Viewing your body artistically, not with physiological exactness. A beautiful internal form appearing gradually: smooth tube of the throat; branching lungs with alveoli-like tree branches; a perfectly formed heart; the tube of the gut; a deep red tunnel snaking its way through your body. Blue, healing air in your balloon-like lungs. Hold these background images lightly around your heart as a golden, healthy, pulsing organ. Open space around it, allowing for expansion; filled and brightened with loving kindness with every breath. The wind blowing through a hollow yew becomes the cleansing wind of spirit constantly blowing through you, sweeping the old away. Every day a fresh new start, continuing throughout life. Developing your capacity for expansive, harmonious life.

The Future: Colour It

As in the last chapter, as you craft your own visualisations imagine the words of the dryad helping and guiding you. Your age and where you are in your life will suggest subjects relevant to the higher qualities and mystery; these are your starting points.

Try viewing an ideal future, and then colouring it. See yourself as a tree with new shoots growing, branching out in new and unexpected directions. See yourself on a coloured spiral of life, reaching down to the past and up to the future. Have a light-magnet to attract all you need ... take a colour bath to cleanse you of the residue of the day ... let your mind run free.

After your inner work, ask yourself what physical activity will reinforce what you've done. One example might be Visualisation 2 on layeredness, which you could follow by sorting old photos and disposing of now-irrelevant items from your past. Connecting inner and outer work is one of the secrets of change, so keep connecting up your two ways of being by combining these exercises.

Mystery of Magic and Vision

Love is the greatest and most potent aspect of mystery. And in Irish legend, the yew figures frequently in stories of love—and loss, reminding us once again of the contrasting elements of the tree. Deidre and Naoise, Tristram and Iseault, Cucullain and Fand, Etain and Midir ... the yew in each of these stories indicates the transcendence of love. Although many are suffused with Celtic sadness, the message is of death not as an end but a transmuting into a mysterious other, symbolised by the yew.

Myth and legend are important in our work, and one particular Irish tale—a love story with a happy ending—hints at what is essential for our spiritual health. So, as story is another path into mystery, enjoy this one; read slowly and see the action in your mind's eye, and draw scenes from it if you wish to. Clothe the body of the story with the embroidery of your own pictures.

Aengus Og, the Irish God of youth and love, was visited in his dreams by a lover who played and sang to him in his sleep. So profound was his love that he pined and wasted away without her, so his mother the queen Boann (for whom the river Boyne is named) sent search parties out for a year with a description of the vision's otherworldly beauty. Then his father the Dagda did the same but also with no luck. At last, in the third year of searching, she was found. And this was at the lake of the Dragon's Mouth. Her father was Ethal, the sidhe (fairy) king of the locality, and she was with one hundred and fifty other girls chained, all of whom could transform into birds.

Her name was Caer Ibormeith, or Yew Berry, and when Aengus saw her and asked to marry her, he learnt from her father that she was fated to change annually between the form of a beautiful maiden and a white swan. The time of her transformation from woman to swan came at the summer's end, at the lake of the Dragon's Mouth, and there Aengus waited patiently.

Yew Berry and her maidens appeared, and, on Samhain Eve (Hallowe'en), the magical time of transformation, he undertook the challenge of identifying her from her maidens, calling to her as she rode the waves in the flock, and so he won her, on the understanding that she would continue to change shape. So she transformed him into a swan and they flew away together ... and the song of their joy and delight as they flew towards his palace of New Grange brought slumber to the people of Ireland for three days and nights. And together they could live as swans or transform back into their human forms.

Take a moment after reading to evoke strongly the sense of rightness and harmony in the image of the two swans, their wings creaking, flying higher into the sky, white against blue, with the green earth beneath them ... and enchanted music lulling us all to a magical sleep as they pass.

As with all myths, there is a deeper meaning hidden within the story-line, so what messages has it for us? Who was this otherworldly lover called Yew Berry who came to a young god in a vision? Here are some points, going through the story, to start us disentangling the threads that make it such a potent tale:

- Yew Berry, like the tree itself, stands for liminality, mystery, and our deepest connection to the things that feed our spirit, personified.

- Without this/her we will not thrive and be fulfilled, but will simply exist.

- When something is missing, our subconscious will try to let us know.

- We, like Aengus, connect to our needs through dreams, inner faculties, and yearnings.

- When we get a message, we must enlist every help to pursue what we need.

- We must *know* it to identify it accurately; it will respond to our call.

- When we find it, we can have it, *but not in our present state.* The things of the spirit cannot exist in the world of the five senses, so *we must be the ones to transform* to reach a new understanding of how to be in the world of matter and of the spirit simultaneously.

These messages—and you may find others hidden—are embellished with symbols. The swan is traditionally a messenger between the worlds, of spirit and matter, of life and death. The lake is healing: we are healed and transformed by love and connection, the greatest mysteries, for water traditionally symbolises love, connection, and the deep currents of our lives. And there is mystery in the story—why are the women chained? Some versions say they are chained in pairs. This might indicate reciprocity—loving as a two-way flow that frees both or all; we both receive and give blessings by following the call of our spirit. But there might be any number of other interpretations.

Caer's fairy heritage represents a hidden and inner component we need for good spiritual health, which connects to Aengus's home of New Grange, a Neolithic chambered tomb, indicating the necessity of being out of the world regularly. New Grange as a place of burial shows that, when "out of the world," we are in the nurturing ambience of heritage and ancestors. The message is that, as for Aengus, when connecting to our soul's calling, we enter mysterious realms to receive rest, refreshment, and completion. The place of our greatest wholeness is in a sacred place deep within, to which we need to surrender and retreat regularly.

The Last Night-Time Yew Visualisation

For sweet sleep, imagine picking a yew berry from an ancient tree.

This is your passport, your key, to connect you to any story that will relax you into an appreciation of your wider life. You find a door in the trunk of the yew: it opens easily and you step through it to find yourself in a hollow trunk, open to the air...

As you allow the wind of spirit to blow through you, imagining the energy flowing up from the roots to the top of the branches, set your intent to drift into a sweet, restorative sleep. Lean against the inside of the trunk, and look up into the dark, star-filled night sky. The light of the stars is pouring down, and earth energy pours up, whilst you are safely held in an ancient liminal space.

From this awareness and connection, you can journey to wherever you wish, to whichever myth, legend, or fairy tale will be most pleasing to you at this time ... perhaps finding yourself by the lake, witnessing Aengus and Yew Berry's meeting and evoking the sublime realisation of the connection of love throughout the universe, of which human love is a reflection. Or you can just let your imagination fly through the firmament and under the earth, and understand the web of life that connects the smallest insect to the cosmic patterns of the stars, each in their appointed place.

Set the scene so that you can see, hear, touch, and smell your surroundings of natural beauty—a perfect backdrop for whatever will be enacted. You are in charge: this is your journey into a place of joining of two realities of your life—the focussed imaginal of waking and the wild virgin territory of dream. Drift and adventure until morning finds you refreshed and alert and ready for the wonder that is your life ...

A Life-Plan

Once we get the balance right, between focussing and letting be, between being in the world and retreating for sustenance, we understand the opposing forces within the trees and can draw upon them as resources to support us at any time—and especially when we are in danger of being overwhelmed by the need to understand. As Humphrey Bogart famously said in *Casablanca*, "It doesn't take much to see that the problems of three little people don't amount to a hill of beans in this crazy world." And it's easy to accept that—until times of trauma, when our sense of perspective goes, and our own personal "hill of beans" turns into a mountain of despair that overwhelms us. Then we need answers, fairness, to understand our circumstances—and yet we know that we never can.

No work we can ever do will protect us from anguish, sorrow, wretchedness, and fear: experiencing these is part of the human condition.

That is when the value of our work will be tested: when the overview of the trees allows us to keep our equilibrium and to know, "This too will pass," and we gather our resources around us as a way of working through our challenges.

For, in spite of present fears and wretchedness, our larger, witnessing self understands that our resilient spirit will maintain, like the dormant tree in deep midwinter. Impossible as it may seem in any negative situation, as stressed with worry and pain as the rational mind may be, deep within us the lessons of nature tell us that the spring will return. Our perception of it may be irrevocably changed and different from the past, as every spring of our lives must be to some extent, but still it will be a time of growth and movement once more, with fresh blessings and challenges. And life will be good again.

I know that this enlarged worldview can be of inestimable value at times of trial, and I hope that all your testing times will be few and that the expanded life-view of the trees will support you safely and benevolently through them.

May our lives be blessed by the grace of the dryads,
The majesty of the trees,
The nurturing of the forest:

And through their connection may we explore a life suffused with magic, wonder, and love.

Last Leaves

Bile, the Sacred Tree

There is a wonderful tradition from Ireland of *bile*, the sacred tree. Each tribe would originally have had a totem tree, a link between our world and the otherworld, and in legend, this sacred tree would produce a variety of fruits.

What a wonderful, nurturing, generous image to integrate the lessons of all our teacher trees. From one liminal connection to all the worlds, we can visualise a sacred tree-of-the-worlds, which can grow the gifts of the whole forest. The foremost of these will be the pollen-light inspiration and straight-growing focus from the birch, the steadfastness and nourishment of acorn, and the connection to spirit and ancestry from the bright glimmerings of yew berries.

Everything we have learnt from our trees insists on their use to us in the real world, as mentors who lead us into expansion. For what is sensible about living our lives just from a material viewpoint, when the whole of the natural world hints that there is so much more? When the mysteries of life so far outweigh the certainties?

The ultimate gift of the trees is that they simply *allow*. Without the capacity to continually try to find justice, make patterns, and make sense of all of life's imponderables, they use their energy to express and maintain their essential selves.

So can we.

Their physical existence causes an effect on their immediate environment, which then changes in response. With enough of them, with care and monitoring, *and time*, the desert could become fertile land again. *So can the desert regions of our hearts and spirits regenerate into the green lushness of the forest.*

There is a saying, "Look deep into nature, and you will understand everything better." If you have been following the exercises, you will have proved the truth of this saying. So...

Dance with the birch...

Stand firm with the oak...

Sink deep into an understanding of the yew.

Let's embrace a life lived from a wider, greener perspective, where the forest mentors are always there to remind us of the bigger picture, to give us perspective, and to remind us of our human state—just human animals, just spiritual beings, just simple people reconciling all the facets of our personalities. What better work in life than to fulfil our potential as humane, responsible, glorious, loving people?

If you will, now that you have finished the book, go to the trees as often as you can, and enumerate all their qualities, as a gift to them. Talk, recite, and thank them. Think of all you share with them, and all that is wonderfully different: all the opportunities we have just by virtue of being human. What a mystery, that we are so complex and wonderful. What a gift, to learn, to grow, to travel through the forest.

Let us finish with a quote from philosopher and physician Albert Schweitzer:

The deeper we look into nature, the more we recognize that it is full of life, and the more profoundly we know that all life is a secret and that we are united with all life that is in nature. Man can no longer live his life for himself alone. We realize that all life is valuable and that we are united to all this life. From this knowledge comes our spiritual relationship with the universe.[4]

Aided by our connection to the trees, to the natural world, to the beneficent and unfathomable patterns of the universe, may we each grow to our full potential.

Through the seasons of our lives and our growth, may we be blessed with tree wisdom.

---

4   Albert Schweitzer, *The Spiritual Life: Selected Writings of Albert Schweitzer* (New York: The Ecco Press, 1999).

ACKNOWLEDGMENTS

Thanks...

To the trees; and to all who first effected my deeper introduction to them. For the opportunity to explore these ideas through talks and workshops over the years.
And to the team at Llewellyn for their support.

Especial thanks to Philip Carr Gomm for generously allowing the use of his tree meditation; and to students and friends for sharing their invaluable knowledge of working with trees on three continents: Art, Barbara, Brenda, Cathryn, Cyd, Dean, Elkie, G. Sam, Jacki, James, James and Janet, Jon, Judith, Kathleen, Kevin, Lorraine, Michael, Penny, Renu, Richard, Ruth, Sally, Sara, Sarah, Stefanie, Steve, Tiki, Todd, and Trudy: your commitment to living spirituality and your wise comments were inspirational, and could have made the nucleus of another book.

And lastly, to the organisers and co-facilitators of an enchanted camp on the River Severn, where, through the magic of time, place, and ceremony, more than a hundred people transformed into a Celtic forest before our eyes.

BIBLIOGRAPHY

Bach, Edward, and E. J. Wheeler. *The Bach Flower Remedies.* New York: McGraw-Hill Contemporary, 1998.

Frazer, Sir James. *The Golden Bough.* Ware, UK: Wordsworth Editions Ltd., 1993.

Gifford, Jane. *The Celtic Wisdom of Trees.* Hampshire, UK: Godsfield Press Ltd., 2000.

Hageneder, Fred. *The Living Wisdom of Trees.* London: Duncan Baird Publishers Ltd., 2005.

____. *Yew.* Gloucestershire, UK: Sutton Publishing, 2007.

Harvey, Graham. *Animism.* London: C. Hurst & Co., 2005.

____. *Listening People, Speaking Earth.* London: C. Hurst & Co., 1997.

Hole, Christina. *British Folk Customs.* London: Hutchinson & Co., 1996.

Hopman, Ellen Evert. *Tree Medicine, Tree Magic.* Washington: Phoenix Publishing Inc., 1991.

Hutton, Ronald. *The Stations of the Sun*. Oxford, UK: Oxford University Press, 1996.

Kindred, Glennie. *The Sacred Tree*. Derbyshire, UK: Self-published, 1995.

MacLellan, Gordon. *Talking to the Earth*. Somerset, UK: Capall Bann Publishing, 1995.

Mountfort, Paul Rhys. *Ogam*. London: Ebury-Rider Books, 2001.

Murray, Liz and Colin. *The Celtic Tree Oracle*. London: Rider & Co., 1988.

Paine, Angela. *The Healing Power of Celtic Plants*. Hampshire, UK: O Books, 2006.

Paterson, Jacqueline Memory. *Tree Wisdom: The Definitive Guidebook*. London: Thorsons, 1996.

Patterson, Barry. *The Art of Conversation with the Genius Loci*. Somerset, UK: Capall Bann Publishing, 2005.

Pepper, Elizabeth. *Celtic Tree Magic*. Newport, RI: The Witches' Almanac, 1996.

Phillips, Roger. *Trees in Britain, Europe and North America*. London: Pan Books, 1978.

Radford, E. and M. A., ed. C. Hole. *Encyclopaedia of Superstitions*. London: Hutchinson & Co. Ltd., 1961.

Singh, Satya, and Fred Hageneder. *Tree Yoga: A Workbook*. Baden-Baden, Germany: Earthdancer, 2007.

INDEX